Organumics

An Epigenetic Re-Framing of Consciousness, Life, and Evolution

Ben L. Callif

First Edition

S. **Woodhouse** Books

Chicago • Milwaukee

Organumics: An Epigenetic Re-Framing of Consciousness, Life, and Evolution

By Ben L. Callif

Published August 2019 by:

S. **Woodhouse** Books

S. Woodhouse Books
An imprint of Everything Goes Media, LLC
www.everythinggoesmedia.com

Publisher's Cataloging-in-Publication Data

Names: Callif, Ben L., author.
Title: Organumics : an epigenetic re-framing of consciousness , life , and evolution / Ben L. Callif.
Description: Includes bibliographical references and index. | Milwaukee, WI: S. Woodhouse Books, an imprint of Everything Goes Media, LLC, 2019
Identifiers: LCCN 2018912736 | ISBN 978-1-893121-75-1
Subjects: LCSH Epigenetics. | Genetics. | Heredity. | Heredity, Human. | Human genetics. | Genomes. | Gene expression. | Consciousness. | Evolution--Philosophy. | BISAC SCIENCE / Life Sciences / Genetics & Genomics | SCIENCE / Life Sciences / Evolution | PHILOSOPHY / Mind & Body
Classification: LCC QH431 .C35 2019 | DDC 572.8/65--dc23

23 22 21 20 19   10 9 8 7 6 5 4 3 2 1

Cover and interior design by Mike Wykowski.

Printed in the United States of America.

I have so much gratitude,
but this book is dedicated to my mentors.

Murray Blackmore—You are an excellent mentor and a brilliant scientist.
Thank you so much for all your encouragement. I look forward to someday
reciprocating your support.

Marieke Gilmartin—Thank you for showing me what intelligence,
perseverance, and passion can achieve. Your success always reminds me
of who I can be if I put in the effort.

Patti Zeimentz—Your impact on my life is evidence that belief exerts
a powerful influence over reality. Please accept these words in exchange
for the notebooks you once gave me.

Finally, this book was particularly inspired by you, dear reader.
I hope you find it inspiring in return.

Table of Contents

"Each living creature must be looked at as a microcosm—a little universe, formed of a host of self-propagating organisms, inconceivably minute and as numerous as the stars in heaven."

—CHARLES DARWIN, *The Variation of Animals and Plants Under Domestication*

Introduction

"So, naturalists observe, a flea
Has smaller fleas that on him prey;
And these have smaller still to bite 'em,
And so proceed ad infinitum."

—JONATHAN SWIFT

The Revolution of Evolution

In contemporary society, there are many valuable ideas percolating and developing in laboratories and the halls of academia that remain unknown to the general public. Epigenetics is one of these—one of the most revolutionary ideas to arise in biology in the last century—but far too few people seem aware of it, much less understand it. One important aspect of epigenetics is the notion that personal experience and the experiences of our ancestors affect our biology. These changes can be expressed variably in our lifetime and can also be passed on to future generations. Epigenetics is only now becoming a hot topic in scientific research, even though the idea arose in the early 1940s,[1] approximately ten years before the helical structure of DNA (deoxyribonucleic acid) was discovered. Although the field is relatively new, epigenetic researchers have already made an array of stunning discoveries. Some of the most interesting and novel findings that are emerging from the field include the idea that our environments and experiences profoundly alter our genetic expression and that biological inheritance extends far beyond

---

1   Conrad H. Waddington, "The Epigenotype," *International Journal of Epidemiology* 1, no. 1 (February 2012): 10–13, https://doi.org/10.1093/ije/dyr184.

the transfer of DNA from parents to children—a concept broadly known as epigenetic heritability.

As controversial as evolution still remains in some segments of the population, epigenetics is equally as debated in scientific circles. It is well substantiated that epigenetic phenomena occur, but many experts in the fields of development, biology, and evolution debase the concept as the unscientific conclusions of poorly designed experiments. Even those who accept the results of recent epigenetic experiments tend to treat them with trepidation. In the minds of some scientists, the biological changes observed in these studies are too small to affect the process of evolution.[2] While a healthy skepticism is necessary for the proper practice of science, it is worth noting that evolution by natural selection was also met with staunch criticism by the old guard.

The theory of evolution by natural selection and the field of epigenetics both seem to induce similar kinds of cognitive dissonance in people. This could be because it is difficult for humans to notice the constant changes our perspectives, memories, and bodies go through. Similarly, but perhaps more understandably, we cannot directly observe the extremely slow and consistent process of natural selection. This inability to recognize gradual change is partly because of a perceptual bias known as change blindness. Change blindness is the psychological term for how difficult it is to notice changes on the timescale of seconds, let alone years or millennia.

The resistance to these macro-level changes, however, can also be connected to the limitations of the modern-day human perspective. In the past, religious mythologies contained pantheons of gods or hierarchies of angels that represented the way in which humans are embedded within much larger *organized* systems.

The objective mindset brought about by the scientific enterprise seems to conflict with the mythologically-based *subjective* framework that is passed on through religious tradition. The newfound objective infrastructure of perceptual reality (grounded in the impersonal, at-arm's-length scientific paradigm) has yet to replace these religious hierarchies with a comparable concept to unify

---

2   David Haig, "Weismann Rules! OK? Epigenetics and the Lamarckian Temptation," *Biology and Philosophy* 22, no. 3 (June 2007): 415–28, https://doi.org/10.1007/s10539-006-9033-y.

the various Levels of Description (LoDs)[3] that are imperceptible to individual human consciousness, like the unconscious emotions that motivate and guide all of our behavior or the psychic forces that synchronize human thought, purpose, and action into organizations of all sizes—like interpersonal relationships, families, companies, governments, societies, and beyond. Until such an all-encompassing framework can be reconciled with mythological thought, science and religion will continue to contradict each other.

It is always possible that science will reverse entirely and proclaim the research on heritable epigenetics as unexplainable nonsense, or as the overinterpretation of experiments with poor controls and confounding variables. But, as the evidence continues to grow, it seems highly likely that an epigenetic concept of heritability which is not solely dependent on random genetic mutation will revolutionize our way of thinking about not just evolution, but the human experience in general. For example, it has been shown that rats can inherit specific memories from their parents and grandparents, and there are preliminary studies which suggest that such heritability can happen in humans as well. In some creatures this epigenetic heritability can be maintained for hundreds of generations. These results hint at a hidden influence on our thoughts and behaviors—the thoughts and behaviors of our ancestors.

Since the field of epigenetics is so young and full of disagreement, professional researchers are wary to disseminate specific findings or even the general theory to the public. The fear of stepping from experimentally validated facts into pseudoscience is understandable, as many scientific laity have already been hijacking epigenetics to support their own non-scientific beliefs[4] (and yet,

---

3   Levels of Description (LoDs) refer to the different levels or dimensions with which we conceptualize our reality. Things in one LoD are nested within things in another LoD— for example, the way that galaxies are made of solar systems and solar systems are made of planets. This embedded pattern seems to extend infinitely in all directions (up and out as things get bigger, down and in as things get smaller). See Chapter 11 for more about Levels of Description.

4   David Gorski, "Epigenetics: It Doesn't Mean What Quacks Think It Means," *Science-Based Medicine*, February 4, 2013, https://sciencebasedmedicine.org/epigenetics-it-doesnt-mean-what-quacks-think-it-means; Adam Rutherford, "Beware the Pseudo Gene Genies," *The Guardian*, July 19, 2015, www.theguardian.com/science/2015/jul/19/epigenetics-dna--darwin-adam-rutherford.

these pseudoscientists may be on to something when they claim that epigenetics has the capacity to revolutionize not just evolution, but the understanding of human nature). This book alone will certainly not clear up all the confusion and disagreement. Rather, this work is intended to be an empirically-based extrapolation of what the future may hold for heritable, epigenetic expression patterns, which ostensibly allow experiences to pass from generation to generation. If such epigenetic theories turn out to be even remotely true, they have deep implications for philosophical topics like the origins of life, the progression of biological evolution, and what it means to be a conscious organism.

THIS BOOK

To simplify and compartmentalize, this book is split into two parts. The first part is my best attempt at a light, easily understandable, and meaningful overview of the basic biological concepts that lead up to epigenetics for a general audience. The idea is to give non-scientists a grasp of the mechanisms constantly operating within our bodies while simultaneously providing enough interesting factoids and trivia to entertain those with some background in biology. Part one will compile evidence that a view of evolution solely focused on genes is wholly incapable of explaining heredity and natural selection.

Part two will build on the scientific knowledge from part one to both explain epigenetics and to explore the implications of epigenetics that are more philosophical and speculative rather than scientific and realistic.

Part two will continue the pattern of part one, with a mix of interesting science and important facts related to epigenetics and evolution. This includes discussions of how memory and behavior seem to be heritable across generations (Chapters 8 and 9) and the idea that identity itself is likely inherited to some degree as well (Chapter 10). The concept of *Levels of Description* (LoDs) will be introduced to describe the embedded and seemingly infinite dimensions of reality that we use to describe the perceptually inaccessible layers of the universe, which will lead into a discussion of consciousness and its relation to biological evolution (Chapter 11). Finally, my term *organum*

(Chapter 12) will be introduced as a self-directed, self-contained unit of replication subject to natural selection.

ORGANUMICS, LIFE, AND CONSCIOUSNESS

This book is in part a response to the current tension between molecular biology and our human Level of Description (LoD). Neo-Darwinian theorists proclaim that the gene is the main substrate and primary unit of natural selection. However, from the human perspective, *we* play this role. As this book will discuss, NASA defines a living organism as a self-contained system that undergoes natural selection. And yet, according to the modern synthesis, we do not directly undergo natural selection, the genes that compose us do. Organumics attempts to resolve this tension by expanding the definition of life from organism to organum—an extension that takes into account the collective and stratified nature of life. Individualism is still a vital component of this theory, but only within the context of an infinitely connected and inseparable universe of collaboration—a single organum always exists within a group that composes a larger organum, and all organa are themselves composed of groups of smaller organa.

The seemingly infinite number of organa in the universe occupy overlapping and hierarchically embedded LoDs. Indeed, the word "organum" literally means a medieval polyphonic plainsong made up of multiple voices chanting harmoniously, and this is exactly the idea that organumics intends to portray about biology—that all life is a harmonic composition of interdependent units occupying the same space and time, but on different levels. The course of this book will describe how this framework implies that there is an arbitrary, but explanatory line to be drawn between the first living things and the first conscious things. Epigenetics creates a path to see that life (organa) arose when consciousness began the process of self-replication. But before all of that, we need to start at the beginning with the history of evolutionary theory, molecular biology, and the genetic revolution. We can't see where we're going until we know where we are and how we got here. Let's begin.

CHAPTER 1

A Brief History of Evolution

"Today the theory of evolution is about as much open to doubt
as the theory that the earth goes round the sun."

—RICHARD DAWKINS, *The Selfish Gene*

We start chapter one with a very brief overview of evolution, from Lamarck to Darwin to the modern synthesis of biology. The course of this book will show that epigenetics not only brings back Lamarck's ideas, but also uncovers a deeply held resistance to anything resembling "Lamarckism." Despite this, Lamarck is just as much to thank (or blame) as Darwin for the current views on evolution. There is so much unnecessary resistance to Lamarckism, especially considering that his ideas weren't all that different from Darwin's. In this chapter we will see that Lamarck is remembered for ideas that could easily be ascribed to many other theorists, including Darwin. Instead of the shortcomings of his theories, Lamarck would have wanted to be remembered for the emphasis he placed on behavior in the process of evolution. Even Darwin understood that behavior had to play some role in natural selection, as he described through the concept of artificial selection, otherwise known as domestication. The current view of evolution (including genetic, memetic, and epigenetic inheritance, concepts that will be discussed in future chapters) supports a combination of Lamarckian and Darwinian theories. The way scientific education frames evolutionary thought as a fight between Darwin and Lamarck is disturbing, unnecessary, and ultimately false. In the education of evolutionary history, Lamarck is framed as a failure but this is a distraction from the implications of a novel field of study: epigenetics.

Organa and Evolution

"I am a creationist and an evolutionist. Evolution is God's,
or Nature's method of creation. Creation is not an event
that happened in 4004 BC; it is a process that began some
10 [sic] billion years ago and is still under way."

—THEODOSIUS DOBZHANSKY, geneticist and evolutionary biologist

Where did we all come from? Where are we all going? What is life? These are the massive questions that the theory of evolution seeks to answer, which makes it a formidable and unifying idea in biology. Human evolution is so contentious and attention grabbing that it has been banned as a subject in several countries.[5] Even in the U.S., many school districts, parents, and religious and political leaders push for an approach to the subject based in religion rather than science. Charles Darwin's idea of natural selection has been called "universal acid"—an explanatory framework so powerful that it dissolves any other conceptual structure it encounters.[6] While this book is not solely about evolution, it is a vitally important part of its thesis and, arguably, science as a whole. As Theodosius Dobzhansky titled his seminal 1973 essay, "Nothing in Biology Makes Sense Except in the Light of Evolution."[7]

Evolution is an endlessly fascinating concept. You don't have to be a scientist or understand the theory of natural selection to marvel at the complete lack of stillness within life. From the tiniest creatures (cells, bacteria) to the much larger multicellular organisms (animals, trees), everything is constantly moving, changing, and growing. A near unanimity of scientists believe the theory that species have evolved over time, though many without scientific

---

5   Rasmus Nielsen, "Teaching Evolution in the Middle East," *Nielsen Lab*, February 25, 2016, www.nielsenlab.org/2016/02/teaching-evolution-in-the-middle-east; Kareem Shaheen and Gözde Hatunoğlu, "Turkish schools to stop teaching evolution, official says," *The Guardian*, June 23, 2017, www.theguardian.com/world/2017/jun/23/turkish-schools-to-stop-teaching-evolution-official-says/.

6   Daniel C. Dennett, *Darwin's Dangerous Idea: Evolution and the Meanings of Life* (London: Penguin Books, 1995), 63.

7   Theodosius Dobzhansky, "Nothing in Biology Makes Sense Except in the Light of Evolution," *The American Biology Teacher* 35, no. 3 (March 1973): 125–29.

expertise are not so sure. According to the Pew Research Center's website, as of July 9, 2009, only two percent of scientists agreed with the claim that "humans and other living things have existed in their current form[s] since the beginning of time." In contrast, 31% of the general population agreed with this demonstrably false belief known as creationism. That being said, 61% of the general public agree that evolutionary change does occur, even if it may be guided by a divine force. This is more reasonable than it sounds, since evolution itself is often derogatorily referred to as a "secular religion" due its nearly universal acceptance by scientists and the wide-reaching and miraculous implications of natural selection.[8]

Even the staunchest evolution-denier cannot ignore the fact that each generation of life is slightly different than its predecessor. Many creationists try to reconcile this sequential progress with evolutionary denial by making a distinction between "micro-" and "macro-" evolution. This is an attempt to separate small, observable changes, like the process of bacteria acquiring antibiotic resistance, from much larger-scale changes, like the process of becoming human from our distant ancestors. While many biologists find the demarcation between micro- and macro- evolution useful, creationists often use this distinction to argue that macro-evolution is wholly unsupported by scientific evidence. When evolution is considered, it becomes very hard to ignore the similarities between humans and animals. When viewed from the perspective of natural selection, our entire human perspective undergoes a "strange inversion of reasoning."[9] Many people are averse to this inversion because it dethrones humanity from our privileged position at the apex of the hierarchy of creation.

Evolution by natural selection is *the* definitive feature of life. It is so vital that this book proposes a new term, *organum*, to describe a living thing as *any discrete unit that undergoes natural selection*. Organum is a medieval word that

---

8   Michael Ruse, "Is Evolution a Secular Religion?" *Science* 299, no. 5612 (March 2003): 1523–24.

9   A strange inversion of reasoning is a "deeply counterintuitive idea" that often unifies two sides of a long-standing debate by challenging some of the most basic assumptions shared by both sides. Daniel C. Dennett, "Darwin's 'Strange Inversion of Reasoning,'" *Proceedings of the National Academy of Sciences* 106, suppl. 1 (June 2009): 10061–65, https://doi.org/10.1073/pnas.0904433106.

describes a polyphonic musical arrangement—a song that consists of several different voices chanting harmoniously. Consider how the original definition still applies: a universal feature of *organa* (the plural of organum, meaning many evolving life forms) is the way in which living things are embedded within each other at different spatiotemporal scales. Life can quite literally be described as infinite variations of polyphonic *organic* arrangement. The concept of organum will not directly return until Chapter 12 as there is a lot of background on biology and evolution to go through before that point.

Although epigenetics is a relatively newer field that requires less context, it still will not be directly addressed until Chapter 7. Epigenetics may not entirely revolutionize biology in the way that natural selection did, but it certainly has the capacity to change the way humans think about our own evolution. Even with its most rigorous definition, epigenetics also causes a "strange inversion of reasoning" in which the gene loses its privileged place as the sole container of heredity. Epigenetics hints at something even deeper—the inverted perspective that *consciousness* is a driving factor in natural selection and the evolution of life. Some 200 years before the word epigenetics was first used, there was an evolutionary theorist who held a similar view: Jean-Baptiste Pierre Antoine de Monet, Chevalier de Lamarck, otherwise known as Lamarck.

LAMARCK AND DARWIN

> "Epigenetics…challenges the reductionist ideas of Darwinism, Neo-Darwinism, and classical genetics by recognizing the fact that under particular situations certain acquired traits could be heritable in organisms in line with Lamarck's theory of evolution."[10]

When the subject of evolution is approached in a classroom it's nearly impossible to avoid the evolutionary theory of Jean-Baptiste Lamarck.

---

10 Andrea N. Villota-Salazar, Artemio Mendoza-Mendoza, and Juan M. González-Prieto, "Epigenetics: From the Past to the Present." *Frontiers in Life Science* 9, no. 4 (July 2016): 347–70, https://doi.org/10.1080/21553769.2016.1249033.

As one prominent evolutionary biologist noted of high school textbooks: "...every single one—no exceptions—begins its chapter on evolution by first discussing Lamarck's theory of the inheritance of acquired characters, and then by presenting Darwin's theory of natural selection as a preferable alternative."[11] And so, that is how this chapter on evolution will also begin. Lamarck's theory, also known as Lamarckism, stated that features *acquired* during the lifetime of an animal are passed on to its offspring. Textbooks invariably illustrate this concept with the unusual length of giraffe necks. They explain that, per Lamarckism, giraffes reach into the branches to eat, which stretches their necks and increases the strength of their muscles. As these muscles strengthen, the length of the giraffe's neck will increase, and its children will inherit this change. Ironically, Lamarck never claimed this idea as his own, and he had many other ideas that could be more accurately labeled Lamarckism.[12] The juxtaposition in textbooks between Lamarckism and Darwin's account of evolution is even more ironic, since Darwin himself was as much a proponent of the inheritance of acquired characteristics as Lamarck.[13]

If Lamarckism refers to a belief that Darwin also held, what ideas did Lamarck actually claim as his own? According to a scholar of Lamarck, Richard Burkhardt, the infamous evolutionary theorist would have wanted his name to be associated with "his broad view of the successive production of all living forms from the simplest to the most complex."[14] To put this in simpler terms, Lamarck believed that the astounding variety of observable life forms, from bugs to birds to mammals, had all been created through a gradual process of evolutionary change. He thought that over extremely long timespans the generational lineage of a single creature would change so much that its ancestors would become a totally different species.

Lamarck would also have wanted to be remembered for the idea that,

---

11 Stephen J. Gould, *Leonardo's Mountain of Clams and the Diet of Worms: Essays on Natural History* (New York: Harmony Books, 1998), 302.

12 Richard W. Burkhardt, "Lamarck, Evolution, and the Inheritance of Acquired Characters," *Genetics* 194, no. 4 (August 2013): 793–805, https://doi.org/10.1534/genetics.113.151852.

13 Burkhardt, "Lamarck," 802.

14 Burkhardt, "Lamarck," 804.

"behavioral change was a leading factor in organismal change."[15] In other words, Lamarck did indeed believe that giraffes would be born with longer necks if their ancestors had to stretch into tall trees for their food. However, as stated before, this idea was not original to Lamarck. Rather, Lamarck's most memorable original theory states that "advantageous changes of habit could spread in a population via imitation or learning, i.e., non-genetically, and pave the way for the selection of any genetic changes that happened to make the new habits more effective."[16] This is one of the concepts that epigenetics can refer to, and it is not exactly accepted in mainstream evolutionary thinking. It makes sense that anything Lamarckian would be controversial, since the social narrative around the history of science strongly suggests that evolutionary theory is a fight between Darwinism and Lamarckism—a fight that Lamarck has sorely lost.

Lamarck did not provide sufficient evidence to convince the world of evolutionary change, but he did give the movement momentum. After Lamarck died, one of his critics wrote: "Ah! If there existed the feeblest proof...of the possibility of the transformation of one species into another species, how would it be possible for an anatomist, a physiologist, or a naturalist to be able to direct his attention thereafter to any other sort of phenomena." In hindsight, these words seem eerily prophetic. Even though Lamarck's theories essentially supported the same conclusions, Darwin's theory of evolution by natural selection would absolutely revolutionize the entire field of biology; it reframed everything we know about anatomy, physiology, and nature. While Darwin causes controversy and resistance, Lamarck's theories are relegated to a side note in high school textbooks. Let's quickly examine what makes Darwin's ideas so much more revolutionary, aversive, and powerful.

In 1831, shortly after Lamarck's death, Darwin began his famous five-year voyage on the *HMS Beagle*. He took detailed notes of his journey that would later be published in three volumes, collectively referred to as *The Voyage of the Beagle*. These notes span an impressive range of subjects, from geology to biology to anthropology. Although today we associate Darwin's name with his work on evolution, specifically his *On the Origin of Species*, he

---

15 *Ibid.*

16 *Ibid.*

personally thought of *The Voyage of the Beagle* as the crowning achievement of his scientific career.[17] While on the ship Darwin sent excerpts of his notes to a friend and mentor, who read them at a Cambridge Philosophical Society meeting without Darwin's knowledge.[18] When Darwin returned home from his travels, he was somewhat dismayed to find that he had become famous thanks to his mentor's promotion of his work. In his own words, "I do not mean to say that a favourable review or a large sale of my books did not please me greatly, but the pleasure was a fleeting one, and I am sure that I have never turned one inch out of my course to gain fame."[19]

Darwin did not care about his popularity, so he did not hesitate to turn the insights from his extensive travels into a detailed theory of evolution, even though he knew it would be highly controversial. Darwin generally agreed with many of Lamarck's theories, particularly his suppositions about the successive generation of all life and the inheritance of acquired characteristics.[20] However, Darwin's ideas stand out when compared to Lamarck's because of his rigorous, scientific attention to detail and his multidisciplinary approach to field work. Scientists before Darwin had shown that geological history—and by association, the fossil record—extend much farther into the past than the biblical account suggests.[21] But Darwin was the first to combine the extensive fossil record into an unbroken chain through his claim that every single variety of organism—no matter how old, new, simple, or complex—had all

---

17 Later in Darwin's life, he said of *The Voyage of the Beagle*, "The success of this my first literary child always tickles my vanity more than that of any of my other books." John Van Wyhe, "Journal of Researches," *The Complete Work of Charles Darwin Online*, accessed September 2018, http://darwin-online.org.uk/EditorialIntroductions/Freeman_JournalofResearches.html.

18 John Van Wyhe, "Extracts from Letters Addressed to Professor Henslow," in footnote 1, *The Complete Work of Charles Darwin Online*, accessed September 2018, http://darwin-online.org.uk/content/frameset?itemID=F1&viewtype=text&pageseq=1.

19 Francis Darwin and John van Wyhe, "The Life and Letters of Charles Darwin, Including an Autobiographical Chapter. London: John Murray. Volume 1," *The Complete Work of Charles Darwin Online*, accessed September 2018, http://darwin-online.org.uk/content/frameset?itemID=F1452.1&viewtype=text&pageseq=1."

20 Burkhardt, "Lamarck," 803–4.

21 John van Wyhe, "Darwin vs God: Did the 'Origin of Species' Cause a Clash Between Church and Science?" *History Extra*, November 24, 2016, www.historyextra.com/period/victorian/darwin-vs-god-did-the-origin-of-species-cause-a-clash-between-church-and-science/.

arisen by the same process of gradual change. He went much further than simply claiming that one form of life evolves into another; he provided ample observational evidence to support his well-researched and logically consistent account of how these changes in species occur. He compiled his research into an evolutionary theory known as natural selection in what we today consider his defining work, *The Origin of Species*.

ON THE ORIGIN OF SPECIES

The original title of *The Origin of Species* was actually *On the Origin of Species by Means of Natural Selection, or the Preservation of Favoured Races in the Struggle for Life*.[22] This may be a mouthful, but the longer title is a fantastic summary of the specifics of his theory, so let's break it down piece by piece. As the shortened title suggests, this work was mainly about the origin of species, or how the wide variety of existing organisms could have populated the planet. Darwin argued that the lineage of one organism branches into multiple, distinct species "by means of natural selection." But what exactly is natural selection? Natural selection assumes that life is a competition, since all life requires access to a limited supply of resources (i.e., food, water, shelter, etc.). You may not survive if your immediate neighbor eats all your available food. In other words, "favoured races" are "preserved in the struggle for life."

You may be thinking *favoured races! … Was Darwin a racist?* No. Darwin was appalled at the slavery he witnessed on his travels across the globe. He described in his autobiography the arguments he had with the captain of the *HMS Beagle* about the wrongs of colonization and slavery.[23] In Darwin's own words: "The destruction of Slavery would be well worth a dozen years war."[24]

---

22 Charles Darwin, *On the Origin of Species by Means of Natural Selection, or the Preservation of Favoured Races in the Struggle for Life* (London: John Murray, 1859), title.

23 Charles Darwin and Nora Barlow, *The Autobiography of Charles Darwin: 1809–1882* (New York: W.W. Norton & Company, 1993), 74.

24 Luba Ostashevsky, "Top 10 Anti-Slavery Quotes from Charles Darwin," *The Evolution Institute*, February 9, 2015, https://evolution-institute.org/top-10-anti-slavery-quotes-from-charles-darwin/.

Even in modern biological circles *race* is still used to describe a hierarchical taxonomic rank contained within the category of *species*. (Remember this from middle school biology...Kingdom, Phylum, Class, Order, Family, Genus, Species?)

Oftentimes this concept of favoured races is described as *survival of the fittest*. While this is a catchy phrase, it does not do full justice to the nuance of natural selection and the power of Darwin's logic. The underlying confusion is that there are many types of fitness. A scrawny, puny animal—let's call him Unmuscular Michael—may have a much better chance of survival despite being much less brawny and athletic than his counterpart, Muscular Manny. Even though Muscular Manny is much more physically fit, Unmuscular Michael may better thrive in an environment where smarts are needed to find food. Similarly, if there is no shelter big enough for Muscular Manny, Unmuscular Michael may have a better chance of survival, even if he is dimmer and weaker than Muscular Manny. In terms of biology, fitness has only one meaning: any trait that enhances the survival and reproduction of an organism *in a particular environment*. When fitness is defined this way, it clarifies the logic that underlies natural selection. If you are more likely to survive and reproduce than your neighbors, you will probably survive longer and have more kids than they will.

This seems like a tautology, which is a statement that proves its own truthfulness such as "increased height makes you taller," or "1=1." With hindsight, this interpretation of fitness appears obvious, but remember it was less than 200 years ago that natural selection was formally accepted by mainstream scientific thinkers. When you consider the implications of the theory, it begins to make sense why people would be resistant to its conclusions. Arguably, the most controversial and important aspect of Darwin's theory is that human beings are subject to natural selection and species change in the same way as any other organism. In other words, evolution describes a metaphorical process of branching that connects all of us to each other and to every living thing that has ever existed in an unbroken, indeterminately vast tree of life.

This idea garners a wide variety of reactions, from a total rejection of evolution on one side to a total rejection of God on the other. But, as reported on the Pew Research Center website on July 9, 2009, most U.S. citizens take the middle-ground with the compromise that God created evolutionary change. Compatibility between certain religious and scientific viewpoints is very important to maintain societal harmony, but that is the subject for a whole other book. For now, let us leave it at this: Evolution by natural selection is so undeniable that even when its staunchest critics refute the *origin of species* component they cannot deny the truth of *the preservation of favoured races in the struggle for life*. To put this another way, even if you have trouble accepting the concept of a common ancestor, you will likely still believe that an organism will fare better if it is more prepared for the constant changes that happen in nature. It is easy to directly observe these natural changes, like the changing of the seasons, outbreaks of diseases, or the differential growth of bacteria in agar as the concentrations of antibiotics increase.[25] Although we can't mourn the loss of an individual bacterium, countless species have become extinct in our lifetime—a clear reminder that imminent death awaits any and all species that fail to adapt to the future. Throughout the history of life, a sobering 99% of all the species that have ever existed are now extinct.[26] Any organism is more likely to survive and reproduce if it is prepared for whatever change may occur—for bacteria the change could be an antimicrobial agent that will lead to death without antibiotic resistance; for humans this change could be a cold winter that requires building shelters and fires to avoid freezing.

---

25 Angus Chen, "Watch: Bacteria Invade Antibiotics and Transform into Superbugs," *Shots: Health News From NPR*, September 8, 2016, www.npr.org/sections/health-shots/2016/09/08/492965889/watch-bacteria-invade-antibiotics-and-transform-into-superbugs/.

26 Beverly P. Stearns and Stephen C. Stearns say in [*Watching, From the Edge of Extinction* (New Haven: Yale University Press, 2000), preface page X], "More than 99 percent of all the species that have ever lived on Earth are now extinct... If there were ten million species on the planet, a natural rate of extinction might be from one to ten species per year. This can be considered the natural or 'background' rate. Today, the most conservative estimates suggest that the global extinction rate is ten to a hundred times the 'background rate.'"

The Substrate Independence of Evolution

In addition to competition, another key aspect of the theory of natural selection is heredity—the way that features of an organism are passed on to its offspring. Although Darwin tried unsuccessfully to explain the mechanisms of heredity, a monk named Gregor Mendel precisely detailed the patterns of heredity in an unrelated and simultaneous endeavor. All of this occurred well before the discovery that DNA is the physical substrate for hereditary information. After the discovery of DNA, Mendel's theory was combined with Darwin's theory to create what is known as *the modern synthesis* or *Neo-Darwinism*. This is the mainstream view of evolution that is currently accepted by the scientific community. Neo-Darwinism has become fixated on DNA as the sole substrate of heredity in natural selection, but this book will argue that the modern synthesis is an unreasonably narrow view of a process that is substrate independent.

Although natural selection is obvious at some level, its apparentness is not the source of its power. Instead, Darwin's ideas are so amazingly explanatory because they are substrate independent,[27] which is a feature of many so-called natural laws. Substrate independence means that a description of a phenomenon can be explanatory in any setting or system. Waves are an excellent and simple example of a substrate independent process. You've likely seen a wave in a body of water and you may be aware that every sound we hear is a wave traveling through the air. Each different kind of stuff that waves can travel through is known as a medium or a *substrate*. For instance, water is the medium for a wave in the ocean while air is the medium for a sound wave. The description of wave phenomena as *substrate independent* simply means that a wave can occur in any medium—whether it be the ground in the form of earthquakes, in groups of physically associated objects like cars in traffic,[28]

---

27 Richard C. Lewontin, "The Units of Selection," *Annual Review of Ecology and Systematics* 1, no. 1 (November 1970): 1–2, https://doi.org/10.1146/annurev.es.01.110170.000245.

28 Paul I. Richards, "Shock Waves on the Highway." *Operations Research* 4, no. 1 (February 1956): 1–137, https://doi.org/10.1287/opre.4.1.42.

or in the human brain in the form of neural impulses.[29] Some theorists have even suggested that everything in existence, including solid matter, is more effectively described as substrate independent wave phenomenon.[30]

Another easily understandable type of substrate independence arises from mathematics. Imagine the mathematical expression 1+1. Those ones don't care what they represent—they could be apples or people or planets. No matter what the number one stands for in that expression, you know just from seeing the arrangement that there are two of those things, whatever they may be. This substrate independence is one of the reasons that mathematics is an extraordinarily powerful tool. It lets humans build massive structures like the pyramids of Giza and our modern-day cities. With it, our societies can create ships to carry us over water, on land, through the air, and even into outer space. Complex mathematics allow us to model and understand ourselves, our environments, and the very reality of our existence. The raw power of numbers is easily observable—this book, for example, was typed into a computer that converted the keystrokes into math and then into a visual representation of the intended letters. These cases are meant to illustrate the power of a substrate independent process like natural selection, but they are by no means the only instances of substrate independence in action.

This brief overview shows that the ideas of Darwin and Lamarck have much more in common than the history of biology explains. Both scientists were major proponents of the concepts of species change and the inheritance of acquired characteristics. Despite this, biological education portrays Lamarck as the owner of the theory of acquired characteristics and Darwin as the owner of the theory of species change (also known as *speciation*). Just like Darwin's theories have been amended by discoveries that occurred after his death, modern biologists have expanded upon Lamarck's theories as well to create a Neo-Lamarckian treatment of his ideas. There have been several

29 Ahmed el Hady and Benjamin B. Machta, "Mechanical Surface Waves Accompany Action Potential Propagation," *Nature Communications* 6, no 6697 (October 2014): 1–7, https://doi.org/10.1038/ncomms7697.

30 Gabriel LaFreniere, "Matter is Made of Waves," *Rhythmodynamics*. Last modified, June 19, 2011, http://www.rhythmodynamics.com/Gabriel_LaFreniere/matter.htm. See also the study of "Cymatics" for more on wave phenomenon.

recent attempts to integrate Neo-Lamarckian theories into Neo-Darwinism.[31]

These novel fusion theories hinge upon a concept that has recently gained renewed attention: epigenetics. In Greek, "epi-" means "on," "above," or "in addition to," and, as this book will show, epigenetics is aptly named. But some basic biology is required to explain the details of epigenetics. Epigenetics won't be back until Chapter 7, and neo-Lamarckism won't directly return until Chapter 11. The rest of Part One (Chapters 2–6) will review the necessary background to properly explain the concept of epigenetics and how it relates to evolution and heredity. If you're already amply versed in biology, I hope the following chapters will provide you with a fresh perspective on the details you may already know. If you don't know much about biology, or even science, I've attempted to make this as understandable and easy to read as possible. Let's start by asking a simple question: Do you know where your genome is?

31 Michael K. Skinner, "Environmental Epigenetics and a Unified Theory of the Molecular Aspects of Evolution: A Neo-Lamarckian Concept that Facilitates Neo-Darwinian Evolution," *Genome Biology and Evolution* 7, no. 5 (April 2015): 1296–1302, https://doi.org/10.1093/gbe/evv073/; Kevin V. Morris, "Lamarck and the Missing Lnc," The Scientist, October 1, 2012, https://www.the-scientist.com/features/lamarck-and-the-missing-lnc-40429/.

CHAPTER 2

Your Genome and You

After the brief discussion of evolution in Chapter 1, I introduce below the concepts of genes and the genome. Genetics has become an immensely popular topic, but the average person cannot define what a gene is with any real detail. Even scientists have a hard time coming up with a specific definition of a gene. And this is unfortunate, because genes and genetics are vitally important for medicine and health—they are relevant to every living thing on the planet (or so it seems). A gene is an ambiguous stretch of nucleotides, which is a type of molecule that composes DNA; DNA is a nearly ubiquitous aspect of cellular physiology that is the "brain" of the cell; the totality of genes within an individual is known as a genome, which is essentially, but not entirely, a set of instructions for how to create all the RNA and proteins within that individual. Each cell in your body stores a copy of your genome within an organelle called the nucleus. There are two exceptions: red blood cells, which have no nucleus—a physiology that allows them to carry more oxygen—and mitochondria, which are technically tiny bacteria that live within your cells and have their own DNA and genomes. Genomes are very powerful and effective means of storing hereditary information that can be passed on to offspring—a type of cellular memory. While DNA is a universal feature of life, it was almost certainly not an aspect of the original type of life.

THE DIFFICULTY OF GENETICS

"...[T]he American public commonly uses related terminology, such as 'genes' and 'genetics.' However, many adults who may use these terms in their everyday conversations likely lack a formal science education that explored basic concepts in human genetics..."[32]

Biology, science, business, society—all have been abuzz with genetics over the last several decades. Although the scientific understanding of genetics has evolved rapidly over the last 75 years, the public has struggled to keep up. In 2004, one out of every four people surveyed thought that genes are located solely in the brain.[33] Maybe you don't know exactly where genes are located either (see Chapter 3 to learn what a gene is). Don't feel bad. Nowadays, even experts have difficulty keeping up with the staggering pace of genetic research. Most people may not have a solid grasp of exactly what genetics entails, but no matter who you are, you are likely aware of the concept of genetics—whether it be from GMOs (genetically modified organisms), genetic editing, or genetically heritable diseases. The details of genetics can be intimidating, but a solid framework of understanding is necessary to reach the fascinating level of regulation above genetics: epigenetics.

Everyone is more motivated to learn about a topic when they feel the information is relevant to their lives, which makes this task easier, because genetics is a field of great relevance to every life. Still, it can be hard to focus on the particulars of genetics because we humans tend to ignore the inner workings of our bodies until they demand our attention.

While our bodies may seem like one continuous unit, every human body is actually a cooperative collection of more than 40 trillion "human" cells[34]

---

32 Angela D. Lanie et al., "Exploring the Public Understanding of Basic Genetic Concepts," *Journal of Genetic Counseling* 13, no. 4 (August 2004): 306, https://doi.org/10.1023/B:JOGC.0000035524.66944.6d."

33 Lanie et al., "Basic Genetic Concepts," 311.

34 Eva Bianconi et al., "An Estimation of the Number of Cells in the Human Body," *Annals of Human Biology* 40, no. 6 (November 2013): 468, https://doi.org/10.3109/03014460.2013.807878.

and an equal number of bacteria.[35] If you include other human microbial symbionts, it is estimated that you are composed of 10-times as many non-human cells as you are human[36]—that's a *quadrillion* (that's 15 zeros) other organisms living in or on your body.[37] It turns out that human bodies are more like ant colonies or cities than discrete lumps of *me*-ness or *you*-ness. Every part of your body and literally every food that sustains you are made of cellular material. And, if everything is made of cells, this raises some interesting questions. For example, why do humans look so different than the things we eat? And, why are the parts of our bodies so different from each other? Let's take a detour through our anatomy to answer these questions and to contextualize the role of the genome, the complete set of DNA needed to build and maintain a body.

HUMAN ANATOMY

Even if humans don't pay too much attention to it, everyone is somewhat familiar with their own body. That fundamental acquaintance with our physical forms shows up in idiomatic phrases like "I know it like the back of my hand," which means you are familiar with something, and "it's over my head," which means you don't understand. You will spend literally your entire lifetime with your body, so you inevitably have some relationship with your physiology, whether it is good, bad, or somewhere in between. Despite

---

35 Ron Sender, Shai Fuchs, and Ron Milo, "Revised Estimates for the Number of Human and Bacteria Cells in the Body," *PLoS Biology* 14, no. 8 (August 2016): 3, https://doi.org/10.1371/journal.pbio.1002533.

36 Yasmine Belkaid, and Timothy W. Hand, "Role of the Microbiota in Immunity and Inflammation," *Cell* 157, no. 1 (March 2014): 121, https://doi.org/10.1016/j.cell.2014.03.011; Megan S. Thoemmes et al., "Ubiquity and Diversity of Human-Associated Demodex Mites," *PLoS ONE* 9, no. 8 (August 2014): 1, https://doi.org/10.1371/journal.pone.0106265.

37 There are widely varying estimates on the actual number, but one quadrillion is conservative. Some publications, like [Josef Neu, and Jona Rushing, "Cesarean Versus Vaginal Delivery: Long Term Infant Outcomes and the Hygiene Hypothesis," *Clinical Perinatology* 38, no. 2 (June 2011): 322, https://doi.org/10.1016/j.clp.2011.03.008. Cesarean] suggest that there are quadrillions of microorganisms *in the human intestine alone*.

its immediate pertinence to every one of us, human anatomy can be a tedious subject. The human body contains over 200 bones and upwards of 600 skeletal muscles. Conveniently, it is not necessary to know all the specific muscles and bones to be aware of the functional significance of our individual parts. For example, you don't have to say, "I flexed my triceps, extensor digitorum, and flexor carpi radialis while extending my bicep and brachioradialis to wrap my fingers around the cup," you can just say "I reached out my arm to grab the cup."

It is nearly impossible to avoid the major, observable bodily divisions like our limbs, pelvis, torso, and head. Similarly, we are all somewhat aware of our internal organs. The heart sits in our chest and pumps blood throughout our bodies; the brain sits in our head and processes sensory information to induce a behavioral response; the stomach sits in our gut and breaks down food for nutrients and sustenance; and the list goes on. These examples make it clear that each of these organs has a very particular function and a specific location that is stable and constant between bodies.

Creatures as far removed from us as plants and flatworms also have bodily structures that can be called organs. Clearly the organs in plants and flatworms differ from the ones in our bodies, which makes the term *organ* very tricky to define. This trickiness can be seen in recent news reports that claim the mesentery has been branded the "79th" organ of the human body.[38] The mesentery is a very important organ that sits in between the intestines and abdominal walls and may play a role in obesity, diabetes, and Crohn's disease,[39] but because the official definition of an organ is pretty fluid, there is absolutely no reason to think that the human body has exactly 79 organs. Here are two examples of ways that an organ can be defined: "an organ is any solid thing in the body that does something,"[40] or alternatively, "an organ

38 Carolyn Gregoire, "Scientists Have Discovered A New Organ in The Digestive System," *Huffington Post*, January 4, 2017, https://www.huffingtonpost.com/entry/scientists-discover-new-organ-mesentery_us_586cfb55e4b0eb58648b3f76/.

39 J. Calvin Coffey and D. Peter O'Leary, "The Mesentery: Structure, Function, and Role in Disease," *The Lancet Gastroenterology and Hepatology* 1, no. 3 (November 2016): 238–47, https://doi.org/10.1016/S2468-1253(16)30026–7.

40 Carl Engelking, "The Mesentary Isn't the Organ You Think It Is," *Discover: The Crux*, January 6, 2017, http://blogs.discovermagazine.com/crux/2017/01/06/got-mesentery-news-wrong/#.W6Q-J3tKi6J/.

is composed of at least two tissues, is self-contained, and performs a specific function."[41]

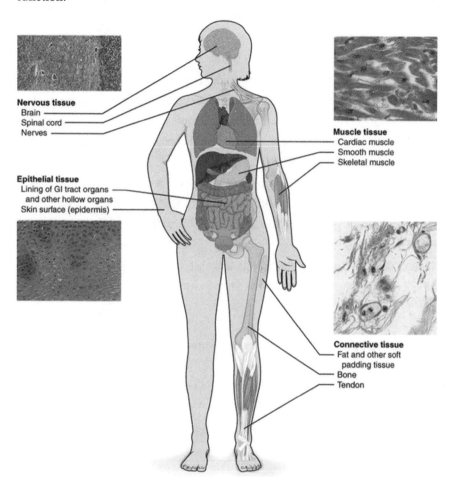

FIGURE 2.1 There are four types of tissues found in the body—nervous tissue, muscle tissue, epithelial tissue, and connective tissue. Together these four kinds of tissue compose all the structures and organs in our bodies.

Tissues are the next functional level of description down from organs. Tissue is loosely divided into four classes: connective, muscle, nervous, and epithelial (see figure 2.1). Connective tissues compose the frame of your body and serve as the scaffold to hold all your organs together. Examples of

41 *Ibid.*

connective tissue are things like bones, ligaments, and the fascia that surrounds all of our visceral organs and muscles. Muscle tissue creates and controls mechanical forces in your body. Much of our movement, both conscious and unconscious, arises from muscles. The most well-known muscles are the heart, tongue, and skeletal muscles (think biceps, calves, and abs). But there are also muscles that move food through your stomach and gut and muscles that wrap tightly around your blood vessels. Nervous tissue coordinates communication between all the different parts of your body. Notable instances of nervous tissue include the brain, the spinal cord, nerves, and some of your sensory systems. Finally, epithelia (or epithelium if there is only one) line the outsides and insides of the cavities and surfaces in your body. Epithelial tissue primarily does three things: protects, like skin; absorbs, like the linings of the lungs and blood vessels; and secretes, like our various glands (some of the major ones include pineal, pituitary, thyroid, sweat, saliva, and tear glands). Tissues perform amazing and diverse tasks which are accomplished by groups of cells doing the same thing in the same place.

Cellular Anatomy

"One key to understanding living organisms […] is the definition of
their boundary, the separation between what is in and what is out."

—ANTONIO DAMASIO, *The Feeling of What Happens*

Every cell is a microscopic *organ*ism, and, as the description suggests, they are quite a bit like little organs. These tiny units compose nearly every aspect of our being, from organs to muscles, to bones and even our blood. Although our bodies feel like whole, complete units, many of the cells in our bodies can survive as independent life forms in petri dishes (at least for a short while). The variety of structures and functions of our different cells types is reflected in the unique characteristics of the organs that they compose.

Despite their differences, all cells share certain requisite features that define them as cells. Every single cell has a membrane that separates its insides from the gas or liquid surrounding it. The internal space of the cell is filled with a gel-like fluid called cytoplasm, which is constantly maintained from the water in its environment. Cytoplasm is partially transferred from mother cell to daughter cell during cellular replication and, before the discovery of DNA, it was theorized to be the physical substrate for heredity. The specific and reliable hereditary information held by DNA is easier to decode than the information within cytoplasm. However, it is not far-fetched to suggest that the basis of life itself may be related to the maintenance and separation of an internal milieu of cytoplasmic solution from a less controlled external environment. This unbroken chain of cytoplasmic transfer from generation to generation "has remained in perpetual continuity from the first origin of life."[42] In very basic terms, it is possible that life evolved to separate a special solution of water from all the other stuff in the world.

There is not yet a very thorough understanding of these *protoplasm* theories, theories that suggest the cytoplasm is the fundamental unit of life.[43] However, cells do require an intricate organization of regulatory processes to maintain balanced concentrations of chemicals like ions and metals. For example, you may have heard that calcium keeps your bones healthy, and that a delicate localization of calcium actually keeps all of your cells functioning properly. This vital calcium homeostasis occurs in nearly every single animal cell. Strict timing and coordination of calcium movement allows your muscles to contract, your heart to pump blood through your veins, and your brain cells to communicate through electrical signals and neurotransmitters.

Like the health benefits of calcium, it is also common knowledge that lead can be deadly when ingested. Lead "looks" very similar to calcium at an ionic level, since both elements have a 2+ positive charge ($Ca2+$ vs. $Pb2+$). Scientists have theorized that lead is toxic because it can mimic many of the important effects of calcium in a cell.[44] This is a deadly problem, because the complex regulatory mechanisms that cells use to control the concentration of calcium are too specific to interact with lead. For example, if you ingest lead,

---

42 August Weismann, *Essays Upon Heredity and Kindred Biological Problems: Authorised Translation* (Oxford: Clarendon Press, 1889), 104.

43 Gilbert Ling, "Nano-Protoplasm: The Ultimate Unit of Life," *Physiological Chemistry and Physics and Medical NMR* 39, no. 2 (2007): 111–234.

44 Gary W. Goldstein, "Lead Poisoning and Brain Cell Function," *Environmental Health Perspectives* 89 (November 1990): 91–94, https://doi.org/10.1289/ehp.908991.

it can cause muscular tremors and weakness because it disrupts the important calcium signaling mechanisms involved with muscular contraction.

How do each of these cell types control the movement and concentration of calcium so precisely? Much like larger organisms, all cells contain *organ*ized structures that have evolved to perform a specific job. In cells, these compartmentalized structures are called *organ*elles—the tiny, cellular versions of organs. Most of the cells in your body have a specialized organelle called the SR (sarcoplasmic reticulum), which performs the vitally important job of calcium regulation. Similarly, the mitochondria, often called the "powerhouses" of the cell, also help to store calcium and control the concentration of this quintessential ion. If you recall the beginning of this chapter, nearly half the cells in and on our bodies are bacteria rather than "human" cells.[45] Fascinatingly, mitochondria are thought to be descendants of ancient bacteria. But mitochondria don't live on our bodies like the S. *aureus* bacteria do on our skin,[46] and they don't live *in* our bodies, like the microbiome within our guts.[47] Mitochondria are bacteria that live *within* nearly every one of our "human" cells! The rise of all multicellular life (living things with more than one cell) is thought to have occurred when an ancient, single-celled creature called an *archaeon* swallowed, but didn't digest, a bacterium.[48] Instead, the bacteria survived and comfortably lived inside the lineage of the archaeon, reproducing alongside the larger cell. This arrangement made cooperative partners of the two. After billions of years, these symbiotic "double-cells" have evolved into every type of animal, plant, and fungi—and mitochondria are now vital and numerous pieces of our multicellular makeup.

Mitochondria may live within our cells, but they are more closely related to bacteria than they are to us. While mitochondria and bacteria do have their own genomes, they lack an important organelle, a *nucleus*, which is Latin for

---

45 Sender, "Bacteria Cells in the Body," 3.

46 Elizabeth A. Grice et al., "Topographical and Temporal Diversity of the Human Skin Microbiome." *Science* 324, no. 5931 (May 2009): 1190–92, https://doi.org/10.1126/science.1171700.

47 Manimozhiyan Arumugam et al., "Enterotypes of the Human Gut Microbiome," *Nature* 473, no. 7346 (May 2011): 174–80, https://doi.org/10.1038/nature09944.Enterotypes.

48 Eugene V. Koonin, "Archaeal Ancestors of Eukaryotes: Not so Elusive Any More," *BMC Biology* 13, no. 1 (2015): 1–7, https://doi.org/10.1186/s12915-015-0194-5.

kernel, nut, or inner part. Most of your genetic material is found within this nuclear organelle and, with a few exceptions, there is a nucleus in every cell of your body that contains a complete copy of your genome. One such exception are your red blood cells, which don't have a nucleus, and therefore, don't have a copy of your genome. The word nucleus is aptly named; just like a kernel or a nut can be planted to grow a brand-new tree, the nucleus contains all the information necessary to grow a new cell. The nucleus has also been called "the brain" of the cell, since this very important and prominent organelle within our cells has intricate control over cellular behavior. Let's explore how the nucleus achieves this level of control.

The Genome

"The genome that we decipher in this generation is but a snapshot of an ever-changing document. There is no definitive edition."

—MATT RIDLEY, *Genome: The Autobiography of a Species in 23 Chapters*

Most of your cells have a nucleus, and in each of these nuclei is an entire copy of your genome. This gives the nucleus powerful control over the form, function, and behavior of its surrounding cell. But what is a genome? As of September 20, 2018, the U.S. government's website "All About The Human Genome Project" describes the genome as "nature's complete … blueprint for building a human being." As we know, a blueprint is a plan or a model for something—it indicates what something is made of and how it functions. This is a useful metaphor, but the genome is so much more and so much less than that.

Humans share 99% of our genome with chimpanzees, so most of our genome is also technically a blueprint for building a chimp.[49] On the flip side of the blueprint comparison, the genome by itself provides very little information about how an organism functions. It is more like a list of

---

49 Elizabeth Culotta, and Elizabeth Pennisi, "Breakthrough of the Year: Evolution in Action," *Science* 310, no. 5756 (December 2005): 1878–79, https://doi.org/10.1126/science.310.5756.1878.

instructions for building the many complex tools that cells use to behave and survive. As we will see, these tools are the unique identifiers that differentiate one type of cell from another. This is why you may have heard that humans share half of our genome with bananas, because our bodies share a portion of our parts list with every living thing on Earth, even if our cells don't all use those parts in quite the same ways as the cells in bananas or chimpanzees.

A genome is a concept that refers to a specific sequence of interlocking molecules called *nucleotides*. Four different nucleotides make up the genome, denoted by the letters A, T, C, and G (the letters come from the first letters of the molecules that give each nucleotide its specific structure: adenine, thymine, cytosine, and guanine). These nucleotides physically stack on top of each other to form extremely long chains, which are called *single-stranded DNA*. Not only do nucleotides stack on top of each other, they also horizontally match with one other specific nucleotide, like a puzzle piece. The rule is As stick to Ts and Cs stick to Gs. When two strands match in this way they create a strong bond and extra stability, much like a zipped-up zipper. This is *double-stranded DNA*, the DNA that is referred to in colloquial uses like "it runs in my DNA" and "his DNA was at the crime scene."

There is a strong analogy between the way the genome stores information and the way a computer stores information. At the most basic level, computers use strings made of bits of binary code: 1s and 0s. Just these two symbolic numbers can be *organ*ized into larger, strand-like structures that are infinitely more descriptive and unique. For example, 8 bits is known as a byte, and there are 256 unique bytes (e.g., 10100101, 00000111, and 254 other combinations of 0s and 1s). Unique permutations become functionally infinite very quickly, since 1024 bytes make a kilobyte and there are more ways to write a unique kilobyte than there are particles in the universe. In the same way that words are used as references to concepts, "byte"-sized identifiers can be assigned as representations of specific pieces of information. Bytes that represent different things, like shades of color, can be assigned to different squares in a grid to create meaningful 2-D representations (see figure 2.2). Computers are basically machines that read and record the associations between pieces of information (like shades of color) and unique bytes. Thanks to kilobytes, megabytes (1,000 kilobytes), and gigabytes (1,000 megabytes), computers can produce stunningly realistic visuals and amazingly powerful simulations, all through the power of ever-expanding combinations of bytes.

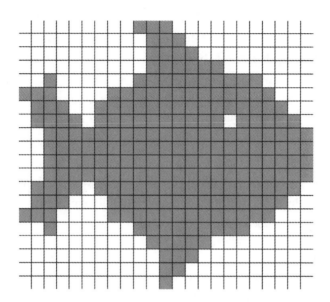

FIGURE 2.2 A simple image of a fish that was created by assigning a color to specific squares in a grid.

So, how do binary code and computers relate to the genome? Well, it is called *bi*nary code because "bi" is Latin for two and there are only two bits, 0s and 1s. As stated above, DNA strands are composed of four different nucleotides, A, T, C, and G, which thus makes the genome what's known as a *quatter*nary code, "quattor" meaning four. The genome's quaternary code is similar enough to the way a computer stores information that researchers have even created DNA "hard drives" that can store any information your computer could store—e-mails, movies, even the operating system itself. These DNA computing systems are currently capable of storing the equivalent of 200 million gigabytes of information in a single gram of DNA.[50] This density of data may seem impressive compared to computer storage, but your entire

50 Yaniv Erlich, and Dina Zielinski, "DNA Fountain Enables a Robust and Efficient Storage Architecture," *Science* 355, no. 6328 (March 2017): 950, https://doi.org/10.1126/science.aaj2038.

genome fits on 3.5 picograms of DNA[51]—that's 1 trillionth of a gram.

When we say that every cell nucleus contains a copy of your genome, it means that (with some exceptions) each of your cells contains 46 strands of DNA (see figure 2.3). Each of these DNA strands is tightly wrapped around many protein molecules. This combination of protein and DNA is known as a chromosome. For a mindboggling sense of the scale at hand, consider that each cell containing your entire genome has an estimated 2 meters (6.5 feet) worth of genetic material.[52] One of our cells tends to be about 10–100 micrometers (0.00001–0.0001 meters) in diameter, which is 100,000-fold shorter than the full length of our genome. Your entire genome fitting into one of your cells is the equivalent of fitting 2 miles of string into a regular sized yo-yo. It is equivalent to fitting the distance between the Earth and outer space into the height of a human. It is quite difficult to properly visualize how tightly DNA is wrapped up in chromosomes.

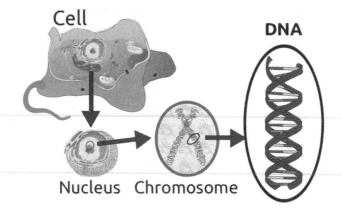

FIGURE 2.3 Almost every cell in your body contains a nucleus, which itself contains 46 chromosomes, each of which are composed of tightly wrapped strands of DNA.

51 "Molecular Facts and Figures," Coralville: *Integrated DNA Technologies*, 2005 & 2011, http://sfvideo.blob.core.windows.net/sitefinity/docs/default-source/biotech-basics/molecular-facts-and-figures.pdf.

52 Steven Chen, "Length of a Human DNA Molecule," *The Physics Factbook*, accessed September 20, 2018, https://hypertextbook.com/facts/1998/StevenChen.shtml/.

One of the most important jobs of the genome is to provide instructions for the creation of new proteins. Although there are approximately 3.5 million proteins that make up each chromosome, this is an unfathomably small number when compared to the total number of vital proteins that your body produces every day, as more than 80 quadrillion (a quadrillion equals one thousand trillion) proteins are made in your body every second.[53] In the time it took you to read this page, your body created at least one protein for every grain of sand on every beach on Earth.[54] Earlier, the genome was described as instructions for powerful cellular tools, and proteins are one major type of these tools. Cells living without proteins would be like you living without cells—it may be possible, but it is a hard concept to grasp. Proteins not only determine how a cell behaves and functions, but they are also a key determinant in how a cell develops[55] (i.e., whether a cell becomes a heart cell, a brain cell, or a skin cell). The creation of proteins from sequences of nucleotides is one form of a process known as *gene expression*. The next chapter will explore some of the details of this vital process.

53 Roland Nilsson, "How Many Proteins Do All Human Ribosomes Together Produce Per Hour?" *Biology Stack Exchange*, November 28, 2016, https://biology.stackexchange.com/questions/53428/how-many-proteins-do-all-human-ribosomes-together-produce-per-hour.

54 Robert Krulwich, "Which Is Greater, The Number of Sand Grains on Earth or Stars in The Sky?" *NPR: Krulwich Wonders*, September 17, 2012, https://www.npr.org/sections/krulwich/2012/09/17/161096233/which-is-greater-the-number-of-sand-grains-on-earth-or-stars-in-the-sky.

55 Mark Ptashne, "Epigenetics: Core Misconcept," *Proceedings of the National Academy of Sciences* 110, no. 18 (April 2013): 7101–3, https://doi.org/10.1073/pnas.1305399110, "Development of an organism from a fertilized egg is driven primarily by the actions of regulatory proteins called transcription factors...Signaling used in development affects expression of genes encoding yet more transcription factors—it does so by changing activities of transcription factors, already present, which target those genes. Retinoic acid (a small molecule) and growth hormone (a protein) are examples of such signaling molecules."

CHAPTER 3

Genome to Gene Expression

In this chapter we will see that the main role of the genome is not just to store intergenerational memories, but to act as a set of instructions—templates for the creation of life. Cells use these instructions to create the massive variety of molecules in your body, known as RNA and proteins. Since DNA was likely not a part of the original lifeforms, RNA and proteins have been suggested to be the original replicators. It is hard to say if RNA or proteins came first; RNA is more self-sufficient and flexible, but proteins are sturdier and functional. Either way, at some point in our evolutionary past these two self-replicating systems joined forces. Together, RNA and proteins created a system of computing (analogous to human computers) that allows them to read and write an instruction manual in the form of DNA—a genetic book of life as it were. This lets RNA and proteins create and maintain massive conglomerations of themselves. The phrase "gene expression" refers to the process of RNA and proteins creating more RNA and proteins. It is logical to consider transcription (the process of creating RNA from DNA) and translation (the process of creating protein from RNA) as a form of molecular reproduction, analogous to the way that living things make copies of themselves. Gene expression is a powerful determinant of cellular behavior, and by extension, human behavior. But every human has a very similar genome, and all the cells in a given individual have the same copy of their genome, so how can cells and humans all act so differently?

THE CENTRAL DOGMA

Like cytoplasm and membranes, proteins are a universal feature of cellular life. Proteins are so fundamental to cellular life that they are theorized to have evolved before the genome.[56] This idea is controversial, since the two systems seem inseparably entangled. In any case, the importance of protein expression cannot be understated. Alzheimer's, Parkinson's, and mad cow disease are just some of the many examples of pathologies that can occur when protein function goes awry.[57] Proteins come in many shapes and sizes and it is estimated that there are millions of unique variants of proteins in your body. These innumerable cellular tools are extremely flexible, and they do a staggering amount of work for our cells.

What follows is a short list of proteins just to give you a very small taste of the tens of thousands of vital functions that they perform:

- hemoglobin—holds oxygen in your red blood cells
- salivary amylase—breaks down sugars in your mouth
- insulin—regulates metabolism of sugars, fats, and other proteins
- actin and myosin—contract and relax your muscles
- NMDA receptor—controls learning and memory in your brain

This is by no means an exhaustive list and each of these proteins almost certainly has many forms and other functions. Without proteins, life as we know it would not exist.

Until quite recently, scientists thought that the primary function of the genome was to provide instructions for protein creation. This concept is known as "The Central Dogma of Molecular Biology." Even if you don't know the details of the theory, the word dogma should immediately make you skeptical. The scientific method is built entirely on the active attempt to falsify

56 Romeu Cardoso Guimarães, "Linguistics of Biomolecules and the Protein-First Hypothesis for the Origins of Cells," *Journal of Biological Physics* 20, (February 1994): 193–99, https://doi.org/10.1007/BF00700436.

57 Larry C. Walker, and Harry LeVine, "Proteopathy: The Next Therapeutic Frontier?" *Current Opinion in Investigational Drugs* 3, no. 5 (June 2002): 782.

a hypothesis. This is because a hypothesis can be supported by thousands of experiments and an immense amount of corroborating evidence and still be proven wrong. Therefore, the best way to ensure the integrity of a hypothesis is by trying to falsify it right off the bat. Then, if it turns out to be wrong you can modify it and try to falsify it again. After many trials of this process you will end up with a very strong hypothesis that is unlikely to be proven wrong by future experiments (even though future experiments will continue to try and make it fail). In other words, being a scientist is all about repeatedly being wrong. Because of this, scientific dogma tends to lead to ignorance and denial.

This "dogmatic" theory, however, does explain and simplify the role of the genome as a cellular instruction book for proteins. The Central Dogma is a sequence that has been described like this: "DNA makes RNA, RNA makes proteins, proteins make us."[58] RNA, or *ribonucleic acid*, is a molecule that is very similar to DNA, but differs in regard to some key features. For example, RNA has a U nucleotide instead of a T nucleotide, but the U sticks to A just as a T would. Unlike RNA, DNA prefers to be a double-stranded molecule and is more stable. Since nucleotides stick to each other, when a single RNA strand contains two or more sequences that match, they can bind together and "lock" the RNA in a folded, single-stranded position, often referred to as a *hairpin* or a *stem-loop* (see figure 3.1).

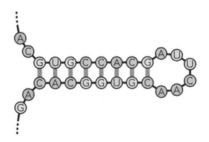

FIGURE 3.1 A strand of RNA folded and bound to itself in a formation known as a "hairpin" or "stem-loop."

---

58 Sarah Leavitt, "Deciphering the genetic code: Marshall Nirenberg," *Office of NIH History*, accessed September 20, 2018, https://history.nih.gov/exhibits/nirenberg/glossary.htm.

Arguably the most important difference between RNA and DNA is that RNA can be read directly by protein-making machinery. The process of DNA → RNA is known as *transcription* and the process of RNA → protein is known as *translation*. RNA and DNA are similar enough that a matching sequence allows a strand of RNA to stick to a strand of DNA and vice versa. A protein known as an *RNA polymerase* uses this pairing ability between RNA and DNA to transcribe a DNA sequence into a piece of RNA, just like you can write a note to remind yourself of a thought. Then, in an *organ*elle known as a *ribosome*, proteins and RNA work together to translate these pieces of transcribed RNA into more proteins.

Again, this works similarly to binary code. Like a group of 8 bits is called a *byte*, a group of 3 nucleotides is called a *codon*. As bytes can be identifiers for concepts (such as colors), codons represent amino acids—the building blocks from which proteins are constructed. Unlike a computer, the genetic code is *degenerate*, which basically means that codons are redundant; there are 64 possible unique codons, but only 20 amino acids that your body creates. In addition, there is also a metaphorical punctuation mark called a *stop codon* that acts like a period to inform the cell to stop transcription. Cells use this genetic language of codons to translate the instructions stored within the Cs, Gs, As, and Us of RNA into all the myriad forms of proteins and RNA in our bodies.

RNA WORLD

There is a wondrous circularity about proteins and RNA making themselves (and more DNA) from DNA. It is clear why it has been suggested that proteins evolved before the genome—because without proteins, DNA would be unusable strands of data storage. RNA has the capacity to replicate itself,[59] which suggests that it could exist and evolve independently from DNA and proteins. Therefore, there is also a well-supported theory that RNA was the first of this trifecta to evolve. Scientists are quite sure that RNA came before

---

59 Thomas R. Cech, "A Model for the RNA-Catalyzed Replication of RNA," *Proceedings of the National Academy of Sciences* 83, no. 12 (June 1986): 4360–63, https://doi.org/10.1073/pnas.83.12.4360.

DNA but are somewhat unsure about whether RNA was the very first self-replicating structure.[60] It is interesting to speculate about a hypothetical "RNA world" that existed before the creation of DNA, but a time without DNA leads to the question: Which came first, RNA or proteins?

It is plausible that proteins came first, because, like RNA, they are also able to self-replicate.[61] On the other hand, RNA has a higher signal fidelity, which means that it stores information more precisely. But proteins are much more stable, so they are more functional and break down less easily. There are good arguments for both cases, but the history of evolution suggests a clear answer—simultaneous evolution through cooperation. As larger structures demonstrate, *organ*ization is a powerful tool. The ribosome is an organelle in which proteins and RNA work together to translate RNA into more proteins. This kind of organization through cooperation happens everywhere in biology. All life forms are called organisms, all organisms are composed of cells, and all cells have organelles.

One might conclude that RNA and proteins coordinated to create the information storage tool that is DNA. The attributes of DNA are certainly a combination of the strengths of RNA and protein. DNA is stable, flexible, and stores information with high fidelity. DNA also stores information about how to make both proteins and RNA. In addition, the double-stranded nature of DNA acts as a built-in backup system: should anything go wrong with one strand of DNA, there is still another one that contains redundant information. Your genome acts like a blueprint in the sense that it is a physical record of abstract concepts that can be used by its reader to create something in the physical world. By itself, the instructions don't do anything. But combined with the appropriate user they become a powerful tool. We cannot travel backwards in time, so we may never know for certain whether RNA or proteins came first. But one thing is for sure, that these two molecular species intricately, effectively, and amazingly cooperate to create all the cellular life we see on Earth.

---

60 Thomas R Cech, "The RNA World in Context," *Cold Spring Harbor Perspectives in Biology* 4, no. 7 (2012): a006742. https://doi.org/10.1101/cshperspect.a006742.

61 David H. Lee et al., "A Self-Replicating Peptide," *Nature* 382, (August 1996): 525–8, https://doi.org/10.1038/382525a0.

READERS AND WRITERS OF THE GENOME

> "…[I]t is becoming increasingly untenable to hold a 'genecentric' view
> of the evolutionary process (especially considering that new discoveries
> in molecular biology keep questioning the very meaning of the term
> 'gene')."

—MASSIMO PIGLIUCCI, geneticist, biologist, and professor of philosophy

This analogy of the genome as a book offers insight to an otherwise complicated topic. Nucleotides (the As, Cs, Gs, and Ts; Us in RNA) are like the letters in the book of the genome, while chromosomes (the complex of DNA wrapped around proteins) are like the chapters or volumes of the book. In any analogy of a book, there must be agents that act as readers and writers. The examination of proteins and RNA as these metaphorical agents induces an uncanny feeling of looking in a mirror. These molecules quite literally read, write, and copy the meaningful, as well as the seemingly meaningless,[62] sequences in DNA.

The genome is often viewed as the foundation of life, but there is a strong consensus that RNA and proteins came first as self-replicating molecules. Could RNA and proteins be considered the first forms of life? Even a type of life that existed before cells? It is hard to imagine RNA and proteins replicating themselves independently from the environment of the cell. But basically anything can perform the most basic act of replication—breaking or splitting into two pieces. Historically, the atom was defined as the tiniest and most unbreakable thing in existence, hence its derivation from the Greek word *atomos*, which means "indivisible." But very recent discoveries have revealed that atoms aren't even close to the most indivisible units of existence. It is now well-established that atoms are made up of many subatomic particles. Biology, chemistry, and physics all seem to suggest that there is no limit to how many times a thing can break into pieces.

But breaking a thing into two pieces is not quite the same as biological self-

---

62 DNA that does not code for proteins is often called "junk" DNA. But such noncoding
sequences have many other functions—no DNA sequence is really "junk."

replication. In addition, the ability to self-replicate is not enough to survive. Environments constantly change, resources run out, and something always gets lost in translation. When information has been passed on too many times it will begin to change and mutate. Mutations that occur in the process of self-replication will be more likely to get "recorded" if they improve replicative effectiveness. This is because a lineage that is better at surviving or replicating will do just that—survive and replicate. But replication is more effective in some substrates than others. Like in a game of telephone, it is much harder to lose the strength of a signal when it is recorded in a relatively inflexible substrate. This is obvious when considered practically: If you want to remember something, you write it down instead of trying to repeat it in your mind over and over again.

Despite these differences, natural selection is substrate independent (see Chapter 1). It is a straightforward mental exercise to show that natural selection will work on any imperfectly self-replicating structure, whether it be DNA, RNA, protein, or even information (see Chapter 6). It stands to reason that RNA and proteins evolved first and then later created DNA to keep track of effective replication methods with greater fidelity, like the way that humans have written records to keep track of detailed information that an individual could not remember by themselves. While written records of this sort hold an immense amount of information, the modern synthesis, or Neo-Darwinism, is too focused on DNA as the sole substrate of heredity. It suggests something even more specific: that genes are the sole substrate of natural selection. But what is a gene exactly?

GENES AND HEREDITY

"A gene is not a DNA molecule, it is the transcribable information coded by the molecule."

—GEORGE C. WILLIAMS, *Adaptation and Natural Selection*

While it is difficult to pinpoint exactly what a gene is, genes are conceptually so closely related to words that biologists use linguistic terms (translation and transcription) to describe the way that genes are handled by RNA and proteins. Darwin himself directly compared the evolution of species with the evolution of language.[63] Words are arrangement of letters, but only specific arrangements of letters are words. In this same way, genes are specific sequences of nucleotides, but only specific sequences of nucleotides are genes. This comparison is quite straightforward; only meaningful or functional sequences of letters or nucleotides can be considered a word or a gene, respectively.

But what about when humans utter "random" strings of letters that mean something or induce a functional result and are not considered words? For example, there are many meaningful and functional ways to express that you have encountered something frightening, humorous, or amazing, like an "ahhh" when you are startled, a "hahaha" when you are amused, or an "ooohhh" when you are impressed. Biologists have encountered this situation with genes as well, because even if a sequence of nucleotides does not look functional in a translational sense (it does not encode for a protein), it is always possible that it is a transcriptionally meaningful sequence (a piece of RNA made from the sequence could be functional), or the sequence itself could have some meaningful effect on the proteins and RNA already in existence (see RNAi in Chapter 7).

Let's put this in terms of everyday human activity. Even if you don't create something "physical" from an instruction book, you may change your behavior based on what you read. Consider one example of a meaningful sequence that does not produce any RNA or proteins that has already been mentioned: the stop codon that signals for the termination of transcription. This is somewhat like reading a book and seeing "The End" or "This book gives you cancer"—you would likely stop reading, or at least hesitate. Nothing physically materialized from the instruction, but your behavior changed.

Due to the parallels between words and genes, the details of both concepts can clarify each other. Genes are popularly defined as the basic physical and functional units of heredity. As discussed in Chapter 1, heredity is what happens when a feature or attribute is copied from one generation to the next. Heredity is one of four major constituents of an organism that allows natural selection to operate (see Chapter 11). As soon as self-replication becomes

63 Darwin, *Origin of Species*, 40.

a heritable trait (i.e., a self-replicator transmits its ability to self-replicate), natural selection begins to operate. Interestingly, the definition of the word *words* can be made more precise when words are considered to be units of heredity just like genes. This does not mean that a word can produce a brand-new individual or generation. Rather, words are the simplest linguistic unit that can take an underlying meaning and replicate it from one mind to another. For example, when you read the word *dog*, a massive amount of information, like "furry, loyal, walks on all fours," can be replicated from the page to your mind. There are some caveats to this, as the word *dog* doesn't truly create information in your head, it simply activates associated information that is already there. However, genetic heritability works in the same way—the process of DNA replication that passes genes from one generation to the next also requires pre-existing "templates" of information to replicate.[64] In other words, strands of DNA aren't assembled *de novo*—the specific sequences of nucleotides in our genes are always copied from existing strands of DNA. As far as scientists can tell, there has never been a gene created entirely from scratch. Our genomes are in the order they are in because the genome of the previous generation was arranged in a similar fashion.

GENE EXPRESSION

"The entire biological edifice, from cells, tissues, and organs to systems and images, is held alive by the constant execution of construction plans, always on the brink of partial or complete collapse should the process of rebuilding and renewal break down."

—ANTONIO DAMASIO, *The Feeling of What Happens*

Genes are known as the fundamental unit of heritability because they are useful representations of how to create functional proteins and RNA that are easily replicated. In the sense that genes are instructions in a book, or diagrams

---

64 Jeremy M. Berg, John L. Tymoczko, and Lubert Stryer, "DNA Polymerases Require a Template and a Primer," In *Biochemistry 5th Edition* (New York: W.H. Freeman), chapter 27.2, 2002.

in a blueprint, they are quite literally the written record of how to create and sustain life. Imagine cooking a five-course meal without a recipe, assembling a car from scratch with no instructions, or learning complex mathematics without a textbook. These are not impossible tasks, they simply require an extraordinary amount of previous experience and conceptual know-how. The same can be said for the role of genes in creating new RNA and proteins. We will see that genes are far from the only heritable aspect of *you*, but they seem to be the most precise records of how to create, either directly or indirectly, all the stuff in your body—proteins, RNA, sugars, fats, and even DNA itself. Gene expression is the way in which all cells (even red blood cells, which have no DNA) create the tools they need to behave and survive. In the same way that one word can have many different meanings, the same gene can produce many different proteins and RNAs based on how, when, and to what extent it is expressed. If your genome is a blueprint, then gene expression is the act of building the things represented by the plans—it is up to the builders to determine how the two-dimensional representation is translated into a three-dimensional space.

Although discussing genes as if they were words in the book of the genome is a useful analogy, the situation is far more complicated than that. From our perspective as human organisms, we see genes as the substrates of life and evolution. But, as this chapter has discussed, RNA and proteins seem more alive or, at the very least, more capable of truly independent self-replication than DNA. The systems at play in your body are cooperative efforts of all three of these players: DNA, RNA, and proteins. It is very difficult to disentangle the role that any one of these molecules plays in our bodily functions. Our lives, and the lives of every complex organism, are only possible because of a constant cycle of production and degradation. This has caused some people to compare the human body to the ship of Theseus—a mythical boat which had its wooden planks replaced so many times that there was no longer an original piece of wood in the ship. We have to ask ourselves: *Is it the same ship?*

Just as cells, tissues, organs, and organisms are dynamic and constantly changing, the human genome is not a static and universal feature of human existence. About 0.3% of the nucleotides in the sequence of the human genome differ from person to person. Where one person might have a C-G pairing, another might have an A-T pairing, or a G-C pairing (DNA is direction specific, so C-G is different than G-C). These variable sites are known as *single-nucleotide polymorphisms*, or SNPs. Although 0.3% sounds small, that ends up being 10 million nucleotides throughout your entire genome. SNPs, the sites of genetic variability in the genome, help to explain why there are subtle differences between people, why there are predispositions to diseases and addictions, and why some people are more resistant to toxins than others.[65] For example, certain SNPs cause diseases like sickle-cell anemia and cystic fibrosis, and create higher risks for diseases like Alzheimer's and cancer. But SNPs are measured across people, not across cells within the same body, and every cell in your body has the same copy of your genome. This leads to an important question, which science writer Sarah Williams asks like this: "How does each cell retain its unique properties when, in its DNA-containing nucleus, it has the same master set of genes as every other cell?"[66]

65 "What Are Single Nucleotide Polymorphisms (SNPs)?" Genetics Home Reference, NIH: U.S. National Library of Medicine, last modified September 18, 2018, https://ghr.nlm.nih.gov/primer/genomicresearch/snp.

66 Sarah C. P. Williams, "Epigenetics," *Proceedings of the National Academy of Sciences* 110, no. 9 (February 2013): 3209, https://doi.org/10.1073/pnas.1302488110.

CHAPTER 4

Evolution and Development

All our cells (and all of us) have nearly identical genetics. Even beyond the comparison from cell to cell or human to human, every single living thing is related to every other living thing. This is because we all share a common ancestor—a preposterously old organism that spawned all generational lineages, which has led to everything that is currently alive. For this reason—and probably other reasons too—all living things look, act, and develop in very similar ways. This is clearly visible in the arm bones of mammals or in the developmental process of vertebrate embryos. It is possible to use this similarity to argue for "intelligent design," but it is more reasonable to see this as a function of the relative "blindness" of evolution. Charles Darwin saw the homology of embryos as being the greatest piece of evidence for natural selection and speciation. The reason that organisms can all look so different and have a variety of different types of cells within them is because of stem cells. These potent cells have the capacity to replicate and turn into any other type of cell in your body, be it a skin cell, a heart cell, or a brain cell. The process of a stem cell becoming another type of cell and losing its replicative capacity is known as differentiation. It is a process highly dependent on when and where a cell is within its developmental and organismal environment, and there are entire scientific fields dedicated to the study of these concepts.

COMMON ANCESTRY

The last chapter ended with the question: "How does each cell retain its unique properties when, in its DNA-containing nucleus, it has the same master set of genes as every other cell?"[67] This question can be asked on a more macroscopic scale as well: How do all life forms look and act so differently when we all share so much of our DNA? These questions fall into the purview of "Evo Devo," a cross between evolutionary biology and developmental genetics. This field studies the relationship between the development of an organism and the evolution of its species as a whole. Creationists (deniers of evolution) are quick to point out that humans are drastically different from other animals. They often echo oppositional arguments such as "a dog could never become a cat, so how can an ape become a human?" But this sort of question gets it all completely backwards.

Evo Devo is essentially the study of common ancestry, which proposes the existence of *a last universal common ancestor*—a hypothetical organism that lived some 3 billion years or more in the past and is the ancestor to all the creatures that live on Earth. In this way, studying the evolution and development of one organism is like illuminating a piece of the invisible, hereditary thread that connects all organisms. This theory does not suggest that life only evolved once on this planet, or even that life originated on Earth. It is entirely possible that life evolved multiple times independently and that other kinds of life simply died off because they were less effective than our lineage. Chapter 3 argued that cooperative *organization* is a well-supported evolutionary strategy, like the way that mitochondria began permanently residing within our cells. It seems plausible that life *did* evolve multiple times, possibly in the form of pre-cellular RNA and proteins, and that the separate lineages of life fused into one indistinguishable lineage. In any case, genetic evidence strongly suggests a shared relationship between all branches on the tree of life. Whether it be a bird, fish, bacterium, or even the mysteriously alien-like tardigrade, humans share at least some of our genes with every single organism discovered on Earth. Genetics and many other pieces of

---

67 Williams, "Epigenetics," 3209.

evidence, including fossils, phylogeny, and studies of fetal development, all point towards an organismal Adam or Eve—an ancient prototypical creature from which everyone is descended. Perhaps you find it hard to imagine a singular origin point, à la the Big Bang, but it is still hard to deny that all creatures share similarities at some level. Even before the theory of evolution and the concept of a last common ancestor, scientists classified organisms into an orderly system based on their outward appearance.

HOMOLOGY IN EVOLUTION

The brilliance of the Evo Devo approach is that it ties together every species under the framework of common ancestry; it makes all life one giant, interconnected family. The strong similarities between all vertebrates were catalogued even before Darwin published his evolutionary theory. As an example of one of these similarities, whether organisms use their arms to grasp, walk, swim, or fly, all vertebrates (creatures that—like humans— have skeletons) have the same structure of forearm bones (see figure 4.1). The idea that all animals have shared design features is termed *homology*. Darwin drew heavily on the concept of homology in his formulation of natural selection. Ironically, the theory of homology originates from a man named Richard Owen, who strongly opposed Darwin. Homology is a current staple in creationist arguments[68] because a universally shared body plan can be seen as evidence for the existence of an intelligent designer. Owen did not oppose evolution itself, he just supported a more Lamarckian-based theory.[69] However, he kept his views on evolution quiet, since creationism was the accepted doctrine of the time and he had a reputation to uphold as the creator of the British Natural History Museum.

---

68 See [Diane Eager, "Homologous Structures? Vertebrate Limbs Have the Same Bone Structure. Is This Evidence for Evolution?" *Ask John Mackay: The Creation Guy,* May 24, 2016, http://askjohnmackay.com/homologous-structures-vertebrate-limbs-have-the-same-bone-structure-is-this-evidence-for-evolution/] as just one example of a homology-based creationist argument.

69 Nicolaas A. Rupke, *Richard Owen: Biology Without Darwin, a Revised Edition* (Chicago and London: The University of Chicago Press, 2009), 148, 176.

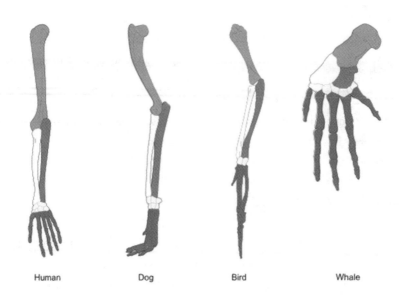

Human   Dog   Bird   Whale

FIGURE 4.1 The similarity between bones in the forelimbs of mammals is one example of the evolutionary concept of homology—that the bodily structures of diverse organisms are related to each other through common ancestry.

Homology is readily observable in both adult animals and developing embryos. It is often exemplified by the pharyngeal arches, also known as "gill slits," which are a universal feature of vertebrate embryonic development. As their nickname suggests, these embryonic structures develop into the gills that fish use to breathe. In humans, they develop into structures in the head and neck, arteries and veins, the various parts of the middle ear, the larynx, and associated nerves. The pharyngeal arches and their resulting anatomy are remarkably similar in structure and function across all types of vertebrate embryos (see figure 4.2). Darwin was quite encouraged by these similarities, to the point that he wrote in one of his letters, "…embryology is to me by far the strongest single class of facts in favour of [my theories]."[70]

---

70 Darwin, "Letters of Charles Darwin," 339.

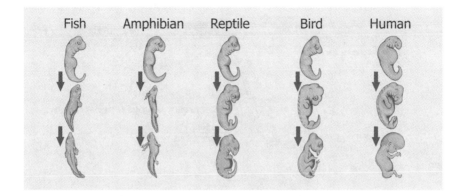

FIGURE 4.2 Homology is evident in the striking similarities seen across embryos from organisms as diverse as fish, amphibians, reptiles, birds, and humans.

There is a fascinating argument about the laryngeal nerve, which innervates the larynx (voice box) and develops from these gill slits. It is called the *recurrent* laryngeal nerve, because it starts in the brain, wraps around the aorta of the heart, and then travels back to the neck. In fish, this nerve has a straight shot from the brain to the gill slits, but this design has become a bit stretched in other animal forms that have evolved more recently. The curious circuitousness of this route is best illustrated in the giraffe, where the recurrent laryngeal nerve travels roughly 6 feet down the neck to the heart and then another 6 feet or so back up the neck to the voice box, where it innervates a target that sits just a few inches away from its point of origin (see figure 4.3). Intelligent design advocates are quick to point out that the laryngeal nerve innervates targets in the region of the heart and, therefore, has a "reason" to travel such great distances.[71] This may be true, but it seems silly for an allegedly omnipotent biological engineer to produce such an inefficiency, instead of simply allocating another nerve to manage these targets. This design is far easier to understand from an evolutionary perspective, as evolution is more akin to tinkering than engineering. In contrast to an intelligent designer, natural selection is not concerned with inefficiencies insofar as they don't have a measurable impact on reproductive fitness.

---

71 Wolf-Ekkehard Lönnig, "The Laryngeal Nerve of the Giraffe: Does it Prove Evolution?" Last modified October 19, 2010, http://www.weloennig.de/LaryngealNerve.pdf/.

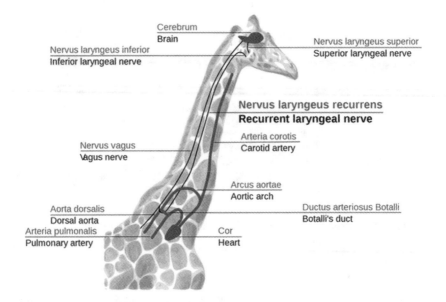

FIGURE 4.3 The recurrent laryngeal nerve of a giraffe travels from its brain down to its heart, loops around its aorta, then travels all the way back up its neck to the voice box. The entire length of the nerve is about 12 feet long, while the distance from its origin to its endpoint is just a few inches.

The conserved utility of the laryngeal nerve only adds more support to the idea that giraffes, humans, and fish all share a common ancestor that had a shorter distance between its voice box and its heart. But, as strong as they may be, comparative anatomy and embryology are no match for genetics as evidence of natural selection. Thanks to the rapid evolution of genome sequencing technology, it is possible to quite literally read and contrast the genes of different organisms. A process called *multiple sequence alignment* compares different genomes to each other by aligning and then scoring the differences between sequences. Multiple sequence alignment can be used to estimate evolutionary distances between organisms and homologous genes. This powerful method of comparative analysis can create informative graphics called *phylogenetic trees*, which represents inferred evolutionary relationships (i.e., how closely related two species are to each other). Multiple sequence alignment is the biological equivalent of running documents through a piece of software to determine if there is any plagiarism. In this analogy, phylogenetic trees differentiate between original creators and plagiarists. Genomic analysis has revealed that evolution is a serial self-plagiarist.

Scientists have created a spatiotemporal map of familial relations for all living organisms—a quantitative tree of life—by sequencing many genes from many different species across many different times (using fossils and predictive models). Despite our relationship to all creatures on Earth and the body plan that humans share with all vertebrates, there remain striking differences between any two human beings—even identical twins aren't truly identical.[72]

The extent to which natural selection can affect embryonic development is somewhat controversial.[73] But, despite arguments about the specifics, the broader picture of development has a lot to teach us about our similarities and differences as human beings. The next sections will briefly review the process of human reproduction and development to explain the variance that exists between individual humans and the cells in our bodies.

A CELLULAR VIEW OF DEVELOPMENT

Like many multicellular organisms, humans replicate through sexual reproduction. This means that our species has sexes, otherwise known as male and female. There is currently a fierce cultural battle raging over how many

---

72 F. Nipa Haque, Irving I. Gottesman, and Albert H C Wong, "Not Really Identical: Epigenetic Differences in Monozygotic Twins and Implications for Twin Studies in Psychiatry," *American Journal of Medical Genetics, Part C: Seminars in Medical Genetics* 151, no. 2 (May 2009): 140, https://doi.org/10.1002/ajmg.c.30206, "The evidence reviewed makes it clear that MZ [monozygotic] twins have substantial differences in obvious phenotypes like disease, and in epigenetic DNA modification patterns. Earlier twin studies were based on the premise that MZ twins are genetically identical, and that phenotypic differences must arise from non-shared environment. However, knowledge of epigenetic mechanisms such as differential DNA methylation, skewed X-inactivation, and imprinting provides a new model to understand MZ twin discordance, and potentially to discover more general mechanisms affecting psychiatric disease susceptibility...nature versus nurture may be recast as nature and nurture in combination, with epigenetic and stochastic factors both mediating and initiating the interactions between genes and the environment."

73 Alex T. Kalinka, and Pavel Tomancak. "The Evolution of Early Animal Embryos: Conservation or Divergence?" *Trends in Ecology and Evolution* 27, 7 (April 2012): 385–93, https://doi.org/10.1016/j.tree.2012.03.007.

sexes and genders there are and how to define the difference between these two terms. There simply isn't space in this book to get into the topic. This section will only consider males and females to keep the discussion as simple as possible. Males have certain cells that are very different from females and vice versa. These sex-specific cells are called *gametes* or, more frequently, *germ cells*—sperm for males and eggs for females. Gametes are special for many reasons. For example, sperm are the smallest cells in the human body while eggs are the largest. These two types of germ cells are some of the exceptions to the rule that every cell in your body contains your entire genome. Sperm and egg cells usually contain just half of your genome—23 out of 46 chromosomes. These two types of cells are also capable of fusing together to create a new, single cell, a *zygote*. Zygotes combine half of the father's genome with half of the mother's genome to create the first cell in a brand new human body.

Every single one of the human cells in your body, including skin cells, heart cells, brain cells, and even gametes themselves, originated from a single zygotic cell. Although the details of human development are extremely complex, it is easy to illustrate how the overall process works (see figure 4.4). First, two germ cells combine into a new cell with a novel genome that is an amalgamation of the parental genomes. Then, this zygotic cell begins to multiply through divisions: one cell splits into two, two cells split into four, four cells split into eight, and so on. At this point the divisions occur uniformly, which means that each "daughter" cell will be identical, and the resulting cellular mass will be same size as the original zygote.

After about 4 days and 4 cellular divisions, the zygote will become a solid ball of 16–32 cells called a *morula*, from the Latin word for mulberry—an indication of the shape of this cellular mass. The next day, the morula becomes a new developmental structure called a *blastula*. This is caused by a separation between the innermost and outermost layer of cells in the morula. The blastula has a remarkably similar anatomy to that of a single cell—a dynamic inner layer of cellular "stuff" swimming in fluid that is separated from the outside world by a protective barrier. This outer layer of the blastula will eventually become all the "non-fetal" aspects that nourish the embryo, such as the placenta, while the inner layer of the blastula will become every part of your body, except for your resident bacterial cells.

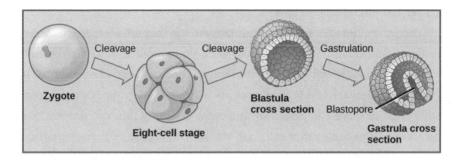

Cleavage   Cleavage   Gastrulation

Zygote   Blastula cross section   Blastopore

Eight-cell stage   Gastrula cross section

FIGURE 4.4 A zygote (the fused combination of a sperm and an egg) undergoes a series of divisions, which leads to the formation of a hollow ball called a blastula. Eventually, the cells in the blastula will differentiate, migrate, and organize themselves into every kind of cell in the human body.

STEM CELL BIOLOGY

The dividing cells that compose both the morula and the blastula are known as *stem cells*. A stem cell is defined by two properties: 1) the ability to perfectly self-replicate, and 2) the capacity to *differentiate*. Differentiation occurs when a cell divides, and each half becomes a new type of cell. In other words, a cell is a stem cell if it can create copies of itself and turn those copies into a variety of other cells types. *Embryonic* stem cells—the cells in the innermost part of the blastula—are pluripotent, which means that they can differentiate into any other type of human cell found in your body. Stem cells, as many know from the news, have amazing powers that can cure disease.

Embryonic stem cells that have an unfortunate association with abortion, because many people think that the only place to find them is in a developing fetus and, therefore, that the only way to get these cells is through abortion. Most of the stigma is unwarranted, because the embryonic stem cells used in research are generally created through in vitro fertilization, or the fusion of sperm and egg in a test tube and not from a developing fetus—aborted or otherwise. But there is good reason to be wary of stem cells, because the features that allow stem cells to cure diseases are very similar to the aspects of cancerous cells that cause tumors.[74]

There are stem cells in every adult human, but they are far more restricted in their differentiation capacity than their embryonic counterparts. Adult stem cells cannot become any cell type in your body; it would be disastrous if you grew a stomach inside your heart, or a heart inside your brain. Instead, adult stem cells are only multi- or unipotent, meaning they can differentiate into a few or just one other cell type, respectively. These cells are important for the maintenance of cellular populations that undergo rapid turnover (e.g., gut cells and skin cells). Other types of adult stem cells are mobilized after an injury and aid in bodily regeneration through differentiation into blood, skin, bone, or scar tissue. The therapeutic potential of adult stem cells is just beginning to be harnessed.

Finally, it is clear why there is so much significance and difficulty in answering the question at the beginning of this chapter: "How does each cell retain its unique properties when, in its DNA-containing nucleus, it has the same master set of genes as every other cell?"[75] Stem cell biology has begun to investigate this question by looking at specific genetic differences between degrees of "stem-ness," or the capacity to self-renew and differentiate. These differences do not lie within the genome itself, as all of the cells in a morula originate from a single progenitor cell and are genetically identical to each other. Instead, it is *when* and *how* each cell expresses specific genes that makes one cell become a part of the placenta and another cell become a part of the fetus. There are many specific causative factors that have been determined to play a role in stemness.[76] Differential gene expression is a vital aspect of all cell biology, not just stem cells (see Chapter 3). This is a very important concept in contemporary research, which is focused on reversing changes in genetic

---

74 Jonghwan Kim, and Stuart H. Orkin, "Embryonic Stem Cell-Specific Signatures in Cancer: Insights into Genomic Regulatory Networks and Implications for Medicine," *Genome Medicine* 3, no. 75 (November 2011), http://doi.org/10.1186/gm291.

75 Williams, "Epigenetics," 3209.

76 Though it sounds farfetched, a particular cocktail of only four proteins is all it takes to reprogram a differentiated cell back to a pluripotent state. For certain cell types only two genes are needed—in some, only one and some chemicals. Danwei Huangfu, et al., "Induction of Pluripotent Stem Cells from Primary Human Fibroblasts with Only Oct4 and Sox2." Nature Biotechnology 26, no. 11 (November 2008): 1269–75. https://doi.org/10.1038/nbt.1502.

expression to perform amazing feats. For example, the creation of stem cells from skin cells, or the transformation of cancerous cells into healthy cells.

The developmental step from morula to blastula is very important, because it is the first time that the cells in your body experience a division that leads to specialized daughter cells. In other words, when a cell in the morula splits in two, each half has a choice to make: move inwards to the hollow cavity and become a part of the fetus or stay on the outer edge of the cellular ball and become a part of the placenta. This is a very important choice, because one path leads to the body of the future organism, while the other path is a "dead end" that only leads to support tissue that never lives a life of its own. This process of differentiation raises many fascinating questions. How do cells know what they should become? How do they know where they are? How do they keep track of the number of divisions they've gone through? There are whole fields of scientific research dedicated to the study of these questions— areas like stem cell biology, cellular and molecular signaling, and circadian rhythms and cellular clocks. These fields are the subject of a host of different textbooks and research articles, but the next chapter will try to compress the answers to these questions into just a dozen or so pages. While such a task feels nearly impossible, these questions are just a means to an end—stepping stones on the pathway to an inverted perspective. This is an attempt to dig so far down into the foundations of biology that we start to move up—a strange inversion of reasoning.[77]

---

77 Dennett, "Darwin's 'Strange Inversion of Reasoning,'" 10061.

CHAPTER 5

Expression in Space and Time

"It turns out that even micro-organisms are highly complex
and intelligent, not simple and mechanical…cells appear
to be units of will, purposeful agents."

—ANDREAS WEBER, *The Biology of Wonder*

In this chapter we will discuss how cells have many, many ways of determining "when" and "where" they are. The various means by which they perform these feats are known collectively as cell signaling. One of the ways that cellular signaling works is through concentration gradients, which rely on diffusive forces to spread molecules from areas of high concentration to areas of low concentration (imagine introverts moving away from the group at a party). One type of molecule that signals through concentration gradients are transcription factors (TFs). TFs are proteins that bind to DNA to affect gene expression. They are very important for all aspects of cellular function and can be a powerful signal of where a cell is spatially. TFs can operate in cyclical feedback loops that act like the mechanisms of a clock or an hourglass to keep track of time, or "where" a cell is temporally. These rhythmic cycles of gene expression are one piece of a complex system of timekeeping known as circadian rhythms. Rhythmic physiology is a universal feature of life that controls almost every aspect of our being. But even red blood cells and things that don't have genes or DNA can operate in a rhythmic fashion. Non-genetic rhythms provide a powerful example of how life can hypothetically operate in the absence of gene expression, even though there don't seem to be any biological processes that are independent from DNA.

GRADIENTS AND CELL SIGNALING

As discussed in the last chapter, stem cells have the amazing capability to differentiate into the variety of cell types that comprise your body. The precise workings of how they do this is still a matter of debate, but many decades of research suggest some possible mechanisms. One potent means of affecting cellular behavior and gene expression is cellular signaling. This is an answer to the two questions posed earlier: "How do cells know where they are?" and "How do cells know what they should become?"

These two questions are really just one question, because spatial relationships inform stem cells about what type of cells they should become. In other words, every cell has a relative idea of where they belong in your body based on the cells that surround them. The development of the morula into the blastula (see Chapter 4) is an excellent example of how this relative cellular positioning works in a simple system. Since the morula is basically a compacted ball of cells, the inside is less accessible than the surrounding fluid. This causes the dispersion of molecules (called a concentration gradient), whereby a hypothetical chemical released by a pregnant woman would be more strongly detectable by the cells on the outside of the morula than those on the inside.

A concentration gradient is essentially the amount of a thing that exists in a particular space. As everything in existence is constantly moving, atoms and molecules are continually bumping into each other. When there are lots of things in a small area they will bump into each other a lot, which begins to push some of the molecules away. Over time, the concentration will decrease as more molecules float away from the areas of high concentration and find their own empty space to inhabit. When a boundary occurs that the molecules cannot cross, they become stuck, and the concentration cannot decrease anymore.

There are a seemingly infinite number of barriers that occur within our bodies; consider skin, fascia, organs, blood vessels, and cell membranes, just to name a few. In the developing morula there are significantly fewer of these boundaries, but the concept is the same. A plausible system that could turn a morula into a blastula can be designed with a hypothetical chemical, PTF (placental transforming factor). To do this, only two simple rules are needed:

1) if a cell remains undisturbed it will become a fetal cell, and 2) if a cell receives a high dose of PTF it will become a placental cell. Given these rules and a gradient of PTF, the cells on the outside will receive high doses and become placental tissue, while the cells on the inside will receive low doses and become fetal tissue. The real situation is much more complicated, but it is a useful thought experiment that shows the power of chemical signaling.

Cells don't just transform during development, they also move in a process known as *cellular migration*. When cells migrate, they can crawl along surfaces or swim through liquid-filled spaces. If we consider the perspective of a single cell within the morula, there are only a few paths it can take depending on its starting position. Whether a cell is at the edge of the ball or in the middle, it only has two options: either stay where it is or migrate away. If a cell in this situation decides to migrate, it needs to choose which direction it will move.

To achieve this sense of direction, cells express protein receptors that react to certain chemicals, such as hormones, neurotransmitters, and ions (one instance of this was discussed in Chapter 2, in the example of the shared bodily response to calcium versus lead). These protein receptors allow a cell to do all kinds of things, but in the context of migration there are three possible reactions to a chemical signals: move towards it, move away from it, or stop moving. This type of cellular sensing is comparable to the way that humans smell molecules in the air: if you smell your favorite food you are likely to move towards it, but if you smell something rancid and rotting you are likely to move away from it. The concentration of a given chemical is a very important aspect of these reactions, as a stronger signal is much more likely to induce a reaction.

In the case of smell, there is no way to tell which direction to move if a scent is too weak to determine its spatial origin. In the same way, cells follow the concentration gradients of the chemicals in their environments—they move away from repulsive signals and towards attractive signals until they can't move anymore or no longer sense a signal. It is also important to mention that different cells have different protein receptors, which determine how they react. In terms of the smell analogy, you will not be motivated to move by even the foulest scent if you can't detect it. Alternatively, you may actively seek out a foul smell if it is coming from something hidden in your house or car.

TRANSCRIPTION FACTORS AND "WHERE?"

The example of PTF in the last section is purely hypothetical, but it is exactly the way in which real biological development proceeds. Experiments in developmental biology have shown that cells not only receive and react to chemical gradients, they can also produce their own. There are some truly fascinating (and sometimes horrifying) examples of these studies on animals like tadpoles. For example, there is a patch of cells in the developing tadpole embryo called *Spemann's organizer.* This *organ*ized group of cells produces a variety of chemical substances that instruct other cells in the immediate vicinity to differentiate (see Chapter 4) into the central nervous system[78] (the spinal cord, brain, and head). Scientists know this because if you take a small piece of this cellular mass and transplant it to the opposite side of the embryo something amazing happens: the resulting tadpole will grow an entirely new, additional, and separate central nervous system. Using this "copy and paste" method (along with some "cutting" too) scientists have determined many of the complex signaling pathways that lead to the development of a fully-grown organism.

One of the primary ways that these signaling mechanisms alter the traits of a cell over long periods of time is through changes in patterns of genetic expression. It is often stated that these changes in gene expression are primarily effected through free-floating proteins known as *transcription factors.*[79] As the name implies, these are protein factors that affect the transcription of DNA into RNA. To make a long story short, transcription factors can alter the way that RNA polymerase (see Chapter 3) interacts with DNA. They can enhance expression by attracting RNA polymerase to transcribe a certain gene, or physically prevent the RNA polymerase from accessing a DNA sequence. If

---

78 Edward M. de Robertis, "Spemann's Organizer and the Self-Regulation of Embryonic Fields." *Mechanisms of Development* 126, no 11–12 (July 2009): 925–41. https://doi.org/10.1016/j.mod.2009.08.004.

79 Ptashne, "Epigenetics: Core Misconcept," 7101, "...[N]ew patterns of gene expression arise in two ways: as a matter of course (some transcription factors activating expression of genes encoding other regulatory proteins, etc.), and in response to signals sent by other cells. Signaling used in development affects expression of genes encoding yet more transcription factors—it does so by changing activities of transcription factors, already present, which target those genes."

a gene is not accessible on a strand of DNA, there is no way to transcribe RNA and subsequently translate protein from that gene. A real-world and straightforward example of this is the role of retinoic acid on the developing embryo. Retinoic acid is a metabolite of vitamin A, which is popularly attributed to carrots and plays a very important role in eyesight.[80] Retinoic acid intake during pregnancy needs to be properly controlled to ensure the health of the fetus. If too much or too little is ingested, serious abnormalities—like craniofacial, central nervous system, and cardiovascular deformities[81]— can occur. But how can the ingestion of a chemical like this affect your cells?

Like the hypothetical PTF example, retinoic acid works by means of concentration gradients. Areas of differing concentrations are arranged by a type of protein called an *enzyme* that can break down the retinoic acid molecule. This is the equivalent of spraying a localized cloud of Lysol to neutralize a bad smell in an area. In this way, a gradient is set up across the length of the embryo so that the posterior portion (by the butt) has a very high concentration, while the anterior portion (by the head) has a very low concentration. Retinoic acid signals to cells through a protein embedded within the outer cell membrane called the *retinoic acid receptor*, or RAR. When the RAR binds retinoic acid, the bound pair of protein and signaling molecule undergo a process called *endocytosis*. Endocytosis is just a fancy way of saying the RAR/retinoic acid complex gets swallowed by the cell. In other words, when the RAR encounters retinoic acid, it loses its access to the outside world and gains access to the things inside the cell, like the nucleus and the DNA contained within it. When the RAR/retinoic acid complex enters the nucleus, it will activate genes that turn the cell into a posterior-type cell. The cells that receive little to no retinoic acid will "automatically" begin to express different genes that turn them into anterior-type cells. Although the actual story is much more complicated, this is a good example of how a whole body can be patterned by chemical gradients.

---

80 George Wolf, "The Discovery of the Visual Function of Vitamin A," *The Journal of Nutrition* 131, no. 6 (June 2001): 1647–50, https://doi.org/10.1093/jn/131.6.1647.

81 Hannah Browne, Gerald Mason, and Thomas Tang, "Retinoids and Pregnancy: An Update," *The Obstetrician & Gynaecologist* 16, no. 1 (2014): 10, https://doi.org/10.1111/tog.12075.

RHYTHMIC EXPRESSION AND "WHEN?"

"Where am I?" is an important question, but it isn't helpful if the cell has no sense of timing. Without knowing *when* it should perform specific actions, a cell is liable to differentiate too soon or too late. What stops a zygote from giving up after only a few divisions? How is a morula consistently 16–32 cells across individuals and vertebrates? Humans use clocks to quantify time and, in the same way, our cells have their own set of molecular clocks. On a deeper level, these cellular clocks are what allow our subjective experience of time to exist. You may have heard of these rhythmic biological cycles, *circadian rhythms*, which means "around the day" in Latin. In many animals, like humans, these rhythms are synchronized by sunlight and determine whether the organism is diurnal (sleeps during the day) or nocturnal (sleeps at night). Circadian timekeeping is also the mechanism that is disrupted when people say they are jet-lagged. In this case, our internal body clocks are literally out of step with the rotation of the sun around the Earth. Circadian rhythms are an extremely important part of a functional organism, which is clear from the massive list of diseases often associated with circadian disruption. Here are of just a few of them: depression, schizophrenia, Alzheimer's, Parkinson's, substance abuse, diabetes, cardiovascular disease, and even cancer.[82]

Every single cell in your body has a circadian rhythm, but this is not enough for them to keep an accurate sense of time. Two clocks will always eventually become asynchronous as one moves just a teensy bit faster than the other. Thanks to the internet and cell phones, most clocks don't need to be synchronized anymore. But you probably know if you have a clock in your car or on your microwave that analog clocks require continual upkeep to stay perfectly on time. In the same way, the cells in your body must constantly correct their timekeeping to stay in step with each other.

Cells synchronize their clocks with chemical methods and with electrical

---

82 Katharina Wulff et al., "Sleep and Circadian Rhythm Disruption in Psychiatric and Neurodegenerative Disease," *Nature Reviews Neuroscience* 11, no. 8 (August 2010): 594, https://doi.org/10.1038/nrn2868.

signals,[83] like the gradients described above and the pulses of electricity your nerves use to communicate. In addition, there is a master clock in the form of a small and important brain region called the *suprachiasmatic nucleus*, or SCN for short. This brain region receives a direct projection from your eyes and acts as a pacemaker to synchronize the rhythms of all the cells in your body to a 24-hour cycle.[84] The SCN is analogous to the atomic clocks of the world that act as centralized timekeepers so that all the other (less accurate) clocks can be synchronized in lockstep. There is never a single moment when gene expression completely stops, but the levels of transcription oscillate in a circadian manner. In other words, the amount of a given RNA or protein will change in predictable ways depending on the time of day.[85] So what are the molecular mechanisms that allow for such intricate timekeeping?

Circadian clocks operate through very elegant feedback loops of gene expression. One example of a timekeeping feedback loop is the cyclical expression and repression of the transcription factors CLOCK, BMAL1, PER, and CRY (see figure 5.1 for a visual schematic of this loop). At the beginning of the day, your cells start expressing copies of CLOCK and BMAL1. When these two proteins pair up they become what's called a *protein dimer*. The CLOCK/BMAL1 protein dimer is a very important transcription factor that controls the expression of many other genes. PER and CRY are just two of the many proteins expressed when the CLOCK/BMAL1 dimer is doing its job. But PER and CRY are special, because when enough copies build up they begin to combine into their own dimer, PER/CRY, which is a repressor of CLOCK/BMAL1 activity. Because CLOCK/BMAL1 causes the expression of PER and CRY, and PER/CRY inhibits the activity of CLOCK/BMAL1, a negative feedback loop occurs whereby PER/CRY can shut off its own expression. This is very similar to the way that a thermostat turns itself

83 Sara J. Aton, and Erik D. Herzog, "Come Together, Right...Now: Synchronization of Rhythms in a Mammalian Circadian Clock," *Neuron* 48, no. 4 (November 2005): 531–34, https://doi.org/10.1016/j.neuron.2005.11.001.

84 Shun Yamaguchi, et al., "Synchronization of Cellular Clocks in the Suprachiasmatic Nucleus." *Science* 302, no. 5649 (November 2003): 1408–12, https://doi.org/10.1126/science.1089287.

85 Brooke H. Miller et al., "Circadian and CLOCK-Controlled Regulation of the Mouse Transcriptome and Cell Proliferation," *Proceedings of the National Academy of Sciences* 104, no. 9 (February 2007): 3342, https://doi.org/10.1073/pnas.0611724104.

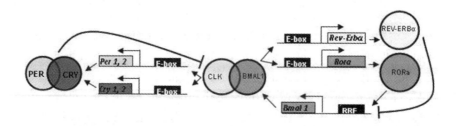

FIGURE 5.1 A graphical representation of the gene expression feedback loop whereby CLK (CLOCK) and BMAL1 inhibit their own expression by driving the expression of their repressors, PER and CRY.

off when it achieves a certain temperature. As more and more PER and CRY proteins are created, they begin to combine into more PER/CRY complexes, which will repress CLOCK/BMAL1 and therefore repress PER and CRY expression. After approximately 24 hours, PER and CRY expression will be totally repressed and all of these proteins will be degraded, including the inactivated CLOCK/BMAL1 dimers. Then, a new physiological day begins as more CLOCK and BMAL1 are created and the cycle restarts. In space and time, this feedback loop works somewhat like an hourglass—each grain of sand counts another iteration of the loop and you can know that a specific amount of time has passed when all the grains have fallen.

ROBUSTNESS OF CLOCKS

Everything in our bodies runs on circadian time—eating, sleeping, exercising, sexual activity, and even learning and memory.[86] Cellular differentiation and the cell cycle (the process in which cells split up their chromosomes and divide) are also strictly regulated and well-timed affairs controlled by circadian rhythms. For example, experiments in petri dishes have shown that stem cells divide and differentiate more readily at certain times of the day. Although there are no detectable transcriptional rhythms in embryonic

---

86 Adriano Dellapolla et al., "Long Days Enhance Recognition Memory and Increase Insulin-like Growth Factor 2 in the Hippocampus," *Scientific Reports* 7, no. 1 (June 2017), https://doi.org/10.1038/s41598-017-03896-2.

stem cells, rhythmic cycles begin as soon as they differentiate.[87] These timing mechanisms may help solve one of the big problems with having stem cells in our bodies—once they start dividing there is always the possibility that they won't ever stop. It only takes one stem cell with a harmful mutation to create a slew of copies of itself (there are many mutations that inhibit the inhibitory mechanisms of stem cells—like cutting the break line on a car). These copies will all contain the same mutation and will all be capable of copying themselves, but incapable of stopping their own growth. Copies that make copies can create a cycle of replication that quickly spirals out of control and the uncontrolled growth of stem cells will occur exponentially; this is how cancerous tumors start to develop.

Researchers have observed that skin is more sensitive to DNA damage from radiation when it is nighttime,[88] and therefore stem cells in the skin somehow operate in a circadian fashion. This could suggest that the skin is an organ involved in the generation and modulation of our circadian rhythms. There has been a presumption that the synchronization of internal clocks to the rhythm of the sun happens only through the eyes and SCN. But the skin is a massive, sunlight-absorbing organ, so it could make sense that our skin somehow plays a role in regulating our rhythmic biology. Scientists are discovering that rhythms are more pervasive in and more fundamental to our biology than we realized.

The example used previously of PER and CRY proteins is just one of many timekeeping systems in our bodies. There are multiple kinds of PER and CRY proteins that have relatively overlapping functions. When a biological system has many semi-redundant pieces as these do, it can be very difficult to disrupt its operation. This is a quality known as *robustness*, or the capacity to perform optimally under unstable conditions. As it allows a system to survive stressful conditions, robustness is strongly selected for by

---

87 Steven A. Brown, "Circadian Clock-Mediated Control of Stem Cell Division and Differentiation: Beyond Night and Day," *Development* 141, no. 16 (August 2014): 3109, https://doi.org/10.1242/dev.104851.

88 Vivek Kumar, Bogi Andersen, and Joseph S Takahashi, "Epidermal Stem Cells Ride the Circadian Wave," *Genome Biology* 14, no. 11 (November 2013): 140, https://doi.org/10.1186/gb4142.

evolution[89] and may be a universal feature of life.[90] For example, if one of the PER or CRY genes becomes mutated and nonfunctional, there are back up genes available that will keep the system operational.

Circadian biology is so well conserved and robust that timed cycles seem integral to all life. Even when organisms live in environments completely detached from the cycles of the sun (such as bacteria that live by geothermal vents in the dark depths of oceans, or eyeless fish that live in pitch-black caves), they still have circadian biology.[91]

Beyond the SCN in the brain and the transcriptional loops of gene expression in all our cells, there is a powerful pacemaker that couldn't possibly be closer to our hearts. Heart rates rest in the 50–100 beats per minute (BPM) range in the average adult human, but hearts can beat as slowly as 26 BPM[92] and as quickly as 600 BPM[93] (in extreme cases). Despite this variability, the heart is an important time-setting device that is intricately linked to circadian time.[94]

The inherently rhythmic nature of pumping blood brings up a good question—what about red blood cells? They have no nucleus and no genes to express. But, amazingly, red blood cells still have their own clocks, which

---

89 J. Arjan G. M. de Visser et al., "Perspective: Evolution and Detection of Genetic Robustness," *Evolution* 57 (9): 1959–72, https://doi.org/10.1111/j.0014-3820.2003.tb00377.x.

90 Jörg Stelling et al., "Robustness of Cellular Functions," *Cell* 118, no. 6 (September 2004): 675, https://doi.org/10.1016/j.cell.2004.09.008.

91 Andrew David Beale, David Whitmore, and Damian Moran, "Life in a Dark Biosphere: A Review of Circadian Physiology in 'Arrhythmic' Environments," *Journal of Comparative Physiology B: Biochemical, Systemic, and Environmental Physiology* 186, no. 8 (June 2016): 947–68, https://doi.org/10.1007/s00360-016-1000-6."

92 World Record Academy, "Slowest Heart Rate: Daniel Green Breaks Guinness World Records Record," accessed September 22, 2018, http://www.worldrecordacademy.com/medical/slowest_heart_rate_Daniel_Green_breaks_Guinness_World_Records_record_214157.html/.

93 Lovely Chhabra et al., "Mouse Heart Rate in a Human: Diagnostic Mystery of an Extreme Tachyarrhythmia," *Indian Pacing and Electrophysiology Journal* 12, no. 1 (January 2012): 32, https://doi.org/10.1016/S0972-6292(16)30463-6.

94 Darwin Jeyaraj et al., "Circadian Rhythms Govern Cardiac Repolarization and Arrhythmogenesis," *Nature* 483, 7387 (March 2012): 96–101, https://doi.org/10.1038/nature10852.

are based on repeated cycles of a precisely timed chemical reaction.[95] This is an interesting piece of evidence that DNA is not a necessary feature of living systems, and it moves us a bit further from the gene-centric view of the central dogma and the modern synthesis of evolution.

---

95 John S. O'Neill, and Akhilesh B. Reddy, "Circadian Clocks in Human Red Blood Cells," *Nature* 469, no. 7331 (January 2011): 498–504, https://doi.org/10.1038/nature09702.

CHAPTER 6

The Heritability of Experience

This chapter will describe genes and DNA as an amazing system of heritable memory. The genome is a sort of written record that can be inherited and, therefore, exist long past the death of any individual RNA, protein, cell, or human. It is truly magnificent that great thinkers such as Darwin and Mendel were able to produce detailed descriptions of evolution and heritability without any idea that DNA or genomes existed. It actually makes quite a bit of sense when we consider that the gene-centric view of evolution is not nearly the full story. Humans and other organisms cannot exist in their current forms without DNA, but it is important to focus on the interplay between genes, the organism, and the environment to get a complete picture of heritability and evolution. This becomes very clear when we consider the zombified proteins called prions. Prion diseases can be genetic, but often they are simply the spread of a protein folding configuration—essentially the inheritance of a structure, a shape, an idea. The heritability of ideas is a well-established science known as memetics—the study of ideas as individual, but ambiguous, units known as memes. Viruses show us that the line between living things and pure information, or memes, is a lot fuzzier than we often think. Viruses are a clear example of a DNA sequence that can produce a transient body in order to infect other organisms. The infection of a new organism creates a dormant piece of pure information within a new genome. Perhaps it is for this reason—that viruses can exist somewhat independently of a body—that many scientists and philosophers have a hard time accepting viruses as living things. The confusion surrounding the division between pure information and life is a perfect place to begin the dive into epigenetics.

(Non-)Genetic Inheritance

Genes and heredity were briefly reviewed in Chapter 3. But both are worth taking a closer look at in this chapter, since genes are just the tip of the iceberg when it comes to inheritance. Gregor Mendel—the monk who determined the precise likelihood of trait heritability—was also mentioned previously (see Chapter 1). Gregor Mendel found that certain bodily traits were controlled by the expression of two different copies of one gene, which led him to create the distinction between *dominant* and *recessive* traits.

Dominant traits occur when your body doesn't need both copies of a gene to present a specific bodily function, structure, or characteristic. For example, if you got a gene from your mom that makes brown pigment in your eye, it doesn't matter if you got a gene from your dad that produces blue pigment because the brown will wash out any traces of blue. An observable trait is called a *phenotype*, a concept that includes various aspects of who you are, such as eye color, height, and even lactose intolerance. A recessive gene is only observable in your phenotype when you get two copies of a non-dominant gene. If you get one dominant and one recessive gene, the dominant but not the recessive gene will be phenotypically observable. This is why it is possible to be a carrier for a disease—even if you don't express a particular recessive gene in your phenotype, your children could if they get a second copy of the recessive gene from their other parent.

Mendel described the phenotypic aspect of this without knowledge of chromosomes, DNA, or the genome. Due to this amazing feat he is often called the father of modern genetics. Genetic heritability is an interesting, but confusing topic, since genetics is still taught using Mendelian principles, which were created before DNA was even discovered. This makes for all sorts of issues, like the difference between genotype (genetic makeup) and phenotype (observable traits), or the difference between behaviors inherited from your parents versus behaviors you received from your surroundings. This debate, often referred to as "nature vs nurture," misses the point entirely because it assumes that all inheritance must pass through the gate-keeper of the gene. But there are plenty of obvious examples that show the non-genetic heritability of traits and experiences—our nurture informs our nature and vice versa.

To be perfectly clear, the concept of "non-genetic" heritability is quite misleading. Because of our complex organization as multicellular, multi-level systems, it is difficult (if not impossible) to imagine our existence without genetics. Gene expression underlies everything that humans are and everything that we can become. Therefore, it is silly to try and pretend like "non-genetic" heritability is somehow separate from genetics.

This is where we finally bring the concept of epigenetics into the picture. Rather than separating genes from the environment or nature from nurture, why not study the interplay between the two systems instead? After all, genes cannot exist without an environment, and genes themselves can play the role of an environment![96]

Epigenetics is a bit hard to define due to the ambiguity inherent in the epi- (meaning above, on, or in addition to) prefix; everything and anything can technically be considered "in addition" to genetics. Sarah Williams, a science writer, defines epigenetics as "chemical flags, or markers, on genes that are copied along with the genes when the DNA is replicated. Without altering the sequence of DNA's molecular building blocks, epigenetic changes can alter the way a cell interacts with DNA."[97]

This definition makes some people very uncomfortable in its implication that pretty much anything related to gene expression is epigenetic. Mark Ptashne, a molecular biologist, is one of them. He has a different interpretation: "For as long as I can remember, [epigenetics] has been used to imply memory: A transient signal or event triggers a response that is then perpetuated in the

---

96 Augustine Kong et al., "The Nature of Nurture: Effects of Parental Genotypes," *Science* 359, no. 6374 (January 2018): 424, 427, https://doi.org/10.1126/science.aan6877, "...[T]he genome and the environment are not independent and models that fail to account for this are thus incomplete... the genomes of close relatives, parents and siblings, can affect the proband through their contributions to the environment...We introduced the concept of genetic nurture and through the study of the nontransmitted [genes] demonstrated that genetic nurturing effects exist, and can have a substantial impact on variance explained." These "nontransmitted genes" are sort of like 'super-recessive' traits that have effects on phenotype but aren't transmitted from the genome of the parent to the offspring at all!

97 Williams, "Epigenetics," 3209.

absence the original signal."[98] It will become clear that Williams's definition is better suited to explain the concept of epigenetic inheritance, or how these chemical flags and marks are transferred through DNA replication, while Ptashne's definition is more closely related to the concept of "non-genetic" inheritance.[99]

In part two of this book, epigenetic will be used to describe both epigenetic inheritance and non-genetic inheritance. As of September 22, 2018, the Roadmap Epigenomics project website (essentially the epigenetic version of the human genome project) defines epigenetics as any "stable, long-term alterations [...] in gene activity and expression," whether those alterations are heritable or not. The confusion between heritable and non-heritable epigenetics raises some very interesting questions that we will return in upcoming chapters. Either way, epigenetic mechanisms are intricately linked to the concepts of timekeeping, rhythm, and memory—both heritable and not.

PRIONS AS A HERITABLE PHENOTYPE

Let's continue with our examples of non-genetic inheritance. Earlier in Chapter 3 the central dogma was discussed—the idea that information flows from DNA to RNA to protein. According to this theory, DNA can make RNA, and RNA can make DNA, but proteins can never transfer information

---

98 Ptashne, "Epigenetics: Core Misconcept," 7102–3.

99 In [Russell Bonduriansky, Angela J. Crean, and Troy Day, "The Implications of Nongenetic Inheritance for Evolution in Changing Environments," *Evolutionary Applications* 5, no. 2 (November 2011): 193, https://doi.org/10.1111/j.1752-4571.2011.00213.x] the authors define "non-genetic inheritance" as "...the transmission to offspring of components of the parental phenotype or environment... such as the transmission of epigenetic variation (i.e., DNA-methylation patterns, chromatin structure, or RNA), parental glandular secretions (e.g., milk), nutrients (e.g., yolk), hormones, or behaviors to offspring, and encompasses phenomena such as maternal/paternal effects, vertical (parent–offspring) indirect genetic effects, vertical components of niche construction, and cultural inheritance." This definition is extraordinarily broad, but Ptashne's definition of epigenetics is even broader. The use of the term "epigenetics" in this book refer to Ptashne's definition (which, admittedly, is quite an extreme extension of the concept of "non-genetic inheritance," because it can describe basically anything).

to RNA, DNA, or other proteins.[100] It would be inconceivable to think that proteins and RNA could exist without DNA if the central dogma were true. It is both lucky and unfortunate that these rules are completely shattered by an epidemic that has become world famous: mad cow disease.

Mad cow disease is just one pathology among a group of disorders called *prion diseases*. Prion diseases are very deadly, and they are the only group of diseases with a single cause that can be infectious, genetically heritable, and sporadic (sporadic means that they can just happen for no apparent reason). Although prion diseases can be genetically heritable, it is also possible to inherit them *without any influence from our genetic code*. In order to understand how, we need to know some details about this class of diseases. A prion is a protein that has folded into the wrong shape. As discussed in Chapter 3, proteins are made of strings of amino acids that are encoded for by three nucleotides of DNA or RNA called a *codon*. But proteins are massively complicated molecules and they require a very specific folding pattern to unlock their potential as powerful, flexible, and functional cellular tools. Every cell has built-in protein folding mechanisms and repair systems even though proteins tend to fold on their own using the electrical charges of their constituent amino acids and the type of environment they are in. For example, proteins tend to *denature* or unfold without water, but when they are rehydrated, proteins can generally refold themselves without outside help.

Very rarely, a genetic mutation will interrupt or alter a codon, which can change the amino acid sequence of a protein and potentially disrupt its natural folding pattern. Given just the right mutation these proteins may become immune to degradation and start forming clumps of misfolded protein debris. If the cell cannot clear away these rampant prion proteins, they will fill up the cell and result in cellular death. Prions are terrifyingly zombie-esque because they can convert normally folded proteins into the undying prion form—no genetic mutations required. This contagion spreads throughout all the tissues of the body from just the physical contact of a prion with a normal protein. Some prion diseases move quickly, some move slowly, but they all inevitably lead to death. Not only do dying cells rupture, further spreading the prions

---

100 Francis H. C. Crick, "Central Dogma of Molecular Biology," *Nature* 227, no. 5258 (August 1970): 561–63, https://doi.org/10.1038/227561a0.

throughout the body, but anyone else who happens to ingest or get one of the prions of an infected person into their body will likely fall victim to the spread of protein misfolding.

Let's look at another horrifying aspect of prion proteins—that they can be sporadic. It is extraordinarily rare, but a protein can misfold into a prion at any time, for no discernable reason. Even though prions can arise from gene mutations, the way that the misfolding pattern spreads is entirely non-genetic. This is a beautiful, if horrific, instance of a self-replicating pattern. The prion misfolding pattern gives these proteins a form of "molecular memory"—which may be referred to as "epigenetic" inheritance—as they can remember the states of previous "generations" of proteins. Because of this, well-known prion researchers have proposed *the prion hypothesis*.[101] They claim that if prion proteins can be made from scratch in a test tube with no cells involved, then they are capable of undergoing evolution by natural selection, just like RNA or DNA.[102] This is reminiscent of the theories that RNA and proteins were the first self-replicating molecules (see Chapter 3).

To summarize, the phrase "epigenetic inheritance" is often used in two distinct ways. In one usage, the prefix epi- means "above" or "on top of" and this refers to chemical markers on DNA that alter the expression of the underlying genes. In another usage, the prefix epi means "in addition to" and this refers to a concept that Mark Ptashne describes as, "A transient signal or event [...] perpetuated in the absence the original signal."[103] In a sense, this is the most basic form of memory—what is sometimes called "non-genetic inheritance."

Prion diseases are a fascinating and terrifying example of how heritable phenotypes can be *independent of genetic influence*. In addition, the spread of prions is an instance of how information can replicate. Although prions are associated with the physical shape of a protein, prion diseases are more of a conceptual force than a physical thing. Prion diseases are caused by the

---

101 James Shorter, and Susan Lindquist, "Prions as Adaptive Conduits of Memory and Inheritance," *Nature Reviews Genetics* 6, no. 6 (June 2005): 435, https://doi.org/10.1038/nrg1616.

102 *Ibid.*

103 Ptashne, "Epigenetics: Core Misconcept," 7102–7103.

spreading pattern of protein folding, not simply the physical shape of the prions. In a way, prions show how information has a life of its own.

MEMETIC INHERITANCE

Prion diseases are very much like viruses in the sense that they are infectious patterns of information. Like prions, viruses blur the classic distinction between living and nonliving matter. There happens to be no scientific consensus about what constitutes a "living" organism, but this book has already touched on some features that seem to be universal across all cellular life forms, like:

- an internal milieu of cytoplasmic material,
- an outer barrier in the form of a fatty membrane,
- self-replication and generational information transfer in the form of nucleotides, and
- a functional capability to balance internal and external forces using proteins.

Viruses do self-replicate with nucleotides and they do have a protein shell that protects their DNA or RNA, but they don't really have their own specific internal liquid. Instead, they steal cytoplasm from the cells that they infect. They also don't have a fatty membrane surrounding them as they are not cells—they're just simple bundles of protein and nucleotides. For this reason, viruses provide some interesting evidence that the creation of DNA was the result of evolutionary cooperation between proteins and RNA.[104] If we do consider viruses to be alive, then they are examples of living organisms on the planet *right now* composed of nothing more than RNA and protein.[105]

Viruses and prions are certainly alive according to NASA, which defines

---

104 Bob Holmes, "First Glimpse at the Viral Birth of DNA," *New Scientist*, April 18, 2012, https://doi.org/https://doi.org/10.1016/S0262-4079(12)60990-7.

105 Teryl Frey, "RNA Viruses," accessed September 17, 2018, http://www2.gsu.edu/~biotkf/bio475/475lecture6.htm/.

life as, "a self-sustaining chemical system capable of Darwinian evolution."[106] In their discussion of this definition, the professor of chemistry Steven Benner and his colleagues state that this is a powerful definition that avoids many issues with previous attempts to categorize life.[107] However, they stipulate that if a living being was discovered that was composed purely out of information (à la the nanites in Episode 50 of *Star Trek: The Next Generation*), NASA would have to change this definition of life.[108]

An extension of this idea can be found in *The Selfish Gene*. In this book, author Richard Dawkins coined the term *meme* to describe a functional unit of self-replicating information: the informational parallel to a gene.[109] Dawkins wanted the word meme to draw attention to the fact that ideas replicate, spread, and have a type of survival of their own—essentially, that ideas are subject to Darwinian evolution by natural selection in the same way as genes. Unfortunately, when Dawkins introduced the concept of a meme as being analogous to a gene, he did not provide a framework for the study of *memetics*, a field analogous to genetics. Many people began to study memes, but interest quickly waned and the primary publisher of papers about these replicative ideas, *The Journal of Memetics*, shut down. This led to a 30-year limbo for the field of memetics, during which time basically no research was done. Despite this setback, the idea that natural selection applies to much more than just genes is starting to take hold. In other words, the meme about memes is replicating.

Consider where Eva Jablonka and Marion Lamb take memes in their book, *Evolution in Four Dimensions*, in which they argue that ideas,

---

106 "About Life Detection," NASA, Astrobiology at NASA: Life in the Universe, accessed September 22, 2018, https://astrobiology.nasa.gov/research/life-detection/about/.

107 Steven A. Benner, Alonso Ricardo, and Matthew A. Carrigan, "Is There a Common Chemical Model for Life in the Universe?" *Current Opinion in Chemical Biology* 8, no. 6 (October 2004): 673, https://doi.org/10.1016/j.cbpa.2004.10.003.

108 *Ibid*, 674.

109 Richard Dawkins, *The Selfish Gene* (Oxford: Oxford University Press, 1976), 192. "We need a name for the new replicator, a noun that conveys the idea of a unit of cultural transmission, or a unit of imitation. 'Mimeme' comes from a suitable Greek root, but I want a monosyllable that sounds a bit like 'gene'... it could alternatively be thought of as being related to 'memory,' or to the French word même. It should be pronounced to rhyme with 'cream.'"

behaviors, and epigenetics constitute separate dimensions of evolution that are independent from, but cooperative with, the effects of natural selection on genes.[110] In support of this, research has repeatedly shown that cultural evolution has a strong and measurable effect on genetic evolution.[111] Despite their clear capacity to replicate and evolve, memes are rarely considered to have "biological" existence. This puts memes in a similar camp to biological viruses. For this reason, it is no surprise that we talk about how memes go viral on the internet; viruses seem to be the perfect conceptual bridge between biological and memetic evolution.

VIRUSES: PURE INFORMATION OR LIFE?

Viruses are amazing molecular machines that are much tinier than even the smallest cells. When the term *virus* is mentioned, we often think of the flu, chickenpox, or herpes as "external" invaders, but viruses are more inherently associated with human life than we often realize. Even after recovering from a viral infection there will always be a piece of that virus encoded within your DNA.[112] It has been estimated that approximately 4 to 8% of the human genome is made up of *endogenous retroviruses* (ERVs), which are basically viral nucleotide sequences that have become a permanent part of the lineage of humanity.[113]

These ERVs don't just sit silently in the genome either—their expression has been implicated in diseases like autoimmune disorders and breast cancer.[114] But ERVs don't only harm our health, they can also be extremely

---

110 Eva Jablonka, and Marion J. Lamb, *Evolution in Four Dimensions: Genetic, Epigenetic, Behavioral, and Symbolic Variation in the History of Life* (Cambridge: The MIT Press, 2006), 1–576.

111 Kevin N. Laland, *Darwin's Unfinished Symphony: How Culture Made the Human Mind* (Princeton: Princeton University Press, 2017), 1–464.

112 Viral infections not only leave a piece of themselves behind, they can also activate older viruses that are often the true cause of diseases.

113 Paul N. Nelson et al., "Human Endogenous Retroviruses: Transposable Elements with Potential?" *Clinical and Experimental Immunology* 138, no. 1 (August 2004): 1, https://doi.org/10.1111/j.1365-2249.2004.02592.x.

114 *Ibid*, 2, 7.

useful for human survival. For example, they play a very important role as an interface between a pregnant mother and her fetus through the regulation of placental development and function.[115] It has been suggested that viruses are not only necessary for the existence of placental mammals, but also for the existence of life in general.[116]

It is likely that RNA and proteins were two types of self-replicating life forms before viruses ever existed (see Chapter 3). Having said that, the role that viruses played in the creation of multi-molecular, multi-cellular, and DNA-based life should not be understated. Gene expression requires the information in a DNA sequence to be read, copied, and translated into a new molecule. As discussed in previous chapters, there are many factors that bring this process to fruition, including RNA and proteins (like RNA polymerase and transcription factors). However, not all sequences of DNA are created equally. Every gene has an element known as a "promoter," which attracts the transcription machinery to the gene. Promoters act as advertisers for the associated gene—their job is to draw the attention of the readers and writers of DNA so that the gene can be expressed. In other words, every gene is constantly trying to convince RNA and proteins to translate (or just transcribe) it from a static sequence of nucleotides into a functional, three-dimensional object, like a strand of RNA or a protein. A gene will never be expressed without a promoter, and, as the next chapter will describe, viruses are somewhat like the rogue advertising agents of the cellular world.

Viruses are diverse, but extremely simple overall. They tend to be nothing more than a few pieces: a protein *capsid*, which is a simplistic and protective shell; a protein called a *polymerase*, which carries out most of the functions related to replicating the viral genome; and a sequence of nucleotides, either RNA or DNA, that encodes for the previously mentioned viral proteins (see figure 6.1 for what it looks like when these viral components are assembled into

---

115 David Haig, "Retroviruses and the Placenta," *Current Biology* 22, no. 15 (August 2012): R609–13, https://doi.org/10.1016/j.cub.2012.06.002.

116 Luis P. Villarreal, "Viruses and the Placenta: The Essential Virus First View," Acta Pathologica, *Microbiologica et Immunologica Scandanavica*, 124, no. 1–2 (January 2016): 27, https://doi.org/10.1111/apm.12485,"As the virosphere provides no 'virus-free' habitat for any life form, all living forms have adapted to their own viral habitat... So powerful and ancient are viruses, that I would summarize their role in life as 'Ex Virus Omnia' (from virus everything)."

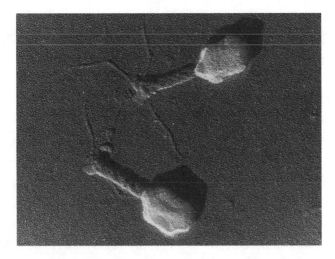

FIGURE 6.1 Viruses (specifically bacteriophages) as imaged with an electron microscope.

a unified whole). In a much more direct way than the human genome, a viral genome can be thought of as a self-contained model of the entire viral form. Within its RNA or DNA, a virus contains all the instructions necessary to create an entirely new body for itself and to replicate those same instructions. The string of viral nucleotides must also contain within it a promoter, in addition to the physical proteins that are encoded by the viral genome. This is similar to an advertiser that advertises their own advertisements. The simplicity and self-contained nature of viruses makes them phenomenal tools for biological engineering and medicine. Since they are ardent self-promoters, it is easy to replace the disease-causing aspects of their genetic content and re-tool their highly effective promoters. This allows researchers to express whatever genes they desire—a very common research technique.[117]

Viruses, like all other organisms, have circadian-esque features in the sense that they go through periods of dormancy between rounds of infection—a

---

117 I personally used viral promoters quite frequently in my graduate work to force neurons to express various factors. For example, a genetic editing tool known as "CRISPR," [Ben L. Callif et al., "The Application of CRISPR Technology to High Content Screening in Primary Neurons," *Molecular and Cellular Neurosciences* 80, no. 1 (April 2017): 170–79, https://doi.org/10.1016/j.mcn.2017.01.003]. Ironically, CRISPR originally evolved in bacteria to fend off viral invasion.

rhythmic process that has been described as epigenetic.[118] Since viruses are extremely simple and go through these cycles of "wakefulness" and "sleep," they don't technically need their own bodies to survive; dormant viruses are nothing more than a string of letters in the book of the genome (sort of).[119] But as soon as something disturbs their sleep, like a mutation or a new virus invading the host, sleeping viruses can awaken and rebuild their physical bodies from a purely genetic form. When the wrong (or right, depending on your perspective) protein manages to leak out of a dormant viral gene, it is like the virus is suddenly awake again. A new physical body means that it has all the tools necessary to replicate.

This is eerily reminiscent of the idea of ancient spells, which sit quietly as words in a book until someone utters the mystical syllables and unleashes the magic contained within. This comparison leads us further from the translations of epigenetics as "on top of genetics" (gene expression) or "in addition to genetics" (non-genetic inheritance) and closer to epigenetics as what happens "above" the level of genetics. And this is where the major resistance to the idea arises—like a spellbook transforms ideas into reality, epigenetics allows conscious intentions to influence evolution in a manner that is straightforwardly Lamarckian. Although it sounds somewhat mystical, there's really nothing magical about it; our conscious choices have an undeniable effect on reality and interdimensional information transfer happens all the time—concepts that we will return to in Chapter 11.

For now, it is a certainty that the memetic, "pure information" aspect of a virus is subject to the same forces of natural selection as a physically expressed virus. By the dogma of the gene-centric view of evolution it is *only*

---

118 Villota-Salazar, "Epigenetics," 350. "Another similar and biologically balanced circuit that gives rise to two epiphenotypes is responsible for the shift from the lysogenic to the lytic phase of replication in the Lambda phage. The Lambda replication cycle is controlled by two mutually repressing proteins encoded by the viral genes cro and cl. During the lysogenic phase, the protein encoded by cl blocks the expression of cro by binding to two of the three operator sequences that regulate the system, thereby keeping the lytic state inactive and promoting its own expression. This state is strongly protected from environmental fluctuations, which allows it to be transmitted across many generations."

119 *Ibid*. Technically, these "dormant" viruses express proteins and RNA that can maintain their dormancy in a stable state despite environmental perturbations.

the representative "pure information" stored in DNA that is subject to natural selection, not the physically expressed virus itself. This may be a confusing concept, but Chapter 11 will introduce the concept of a *Level of Description* (LoD) that can help us distinguish the various dimensions that natural selection can operate in. In addition, the upcoming second part of the book will dig into the details of epigenetics and discuss the theories of Lamarck in terms of a new framework of evolutionary theory. This integrative approach leads to some powerful implications about human memories, lives, and identities.

Intermission

Let's do a quick review of the concepts introduced so far in Chapters 1 through 6 before things get more complicated and philosophical.

Chapter 1 examined a very brief history of evolutionary thought, from Lamarck and Darwin to the modern synthesis of biology.

Chapter 2 touched on the role of cells in animal physiology, the inner workings of cells, and how cells are related to the human genome.

Chapter 3 introduced some aspects of gene expression, including the central dogma, the heredity of genes, and the role of RNA and proteins.

Chapter 4 surveyed the concepts of a common ancestor, homology, human development, and stem cells.

Chapter 5 considered one of the ways that cells know *where* they are (concentration gradients), the special type of protein called transcription factors, and how cells know *when* they are (circadian rhythms).

Finally, Chapter 6 covered the various forms of inheritance and how they cannot be wholly explained by genetics. Chapter 6 ended with a discussion of how viral life seems to straddle the line between living and inanimate information.

Taken together, the first six chapters are intended to show that a human being is much more than a homogenous mass of "personhood" or a pile of DNA. What an individual considers to be their "self" is a massively complex and ever-changing system composed of an uncountable number of smaller things, like nucleotides, proteins, cells, organs, and even other organisms.

These preceding chapters are also meant to highlight the fact that while genetics is necessary for life, DNA is nowhere near the main character of this story. Instead, it seems likely that proteins and RNA were the first life forms, long before DNA ever existed. Perhaps at some point in life's ancient evolutionary past these two self-replicating molecules began to cooperate, much in the same way that the cells within our bodies cooperate with bacteria and mitochondria. RNA and proteins may have collaborated to create a database that contains an untold number of instructions for replicating and reproducing themselves.

In this analogy, RNA and proteins are the creators and users of the computer that is the genome. Just like humans use computers and technology to make our lives easier and our cities organized, RNA and proteins use the genome to better themselves and their surroundings.

In his book *The Selfish Gene*, Richard Dawkins likens humans to survival machines built and controlled by genes.[120] Humans are clearly machines built by and composed of much tinier living things, but it is also clear that genes are just the instructions for self-replication. Ironically, in the same book, Dawkins himself created a concept, the meme,[121] that validates the paradigm shift away from genes as the main carriers of inheritance. But memes, RNA, and proteins aren't the only main characters in the story that is evolution.

Part two will dive into the idea that evolution by natural selection applies to many more systems than just those of a biological nature. First, there is a still a bit more biology to get into. Things are about to get a lot more interesting and complicated.

---

120 Dawkins, *The Selfish Gene*, ix.

121 *Ibid*, 192.

CHAPTER 7

Epigenetics

Here we will finally broach the subject of epigenetics—a phrase that literally means "on top of genetics." This topic is the perfect interface between genetics, heritability, and phenotype. Epigenetics is a means by which the environment can change the genetic expression of an organism in a way that its offspring can inherit. Epigenetics can also be literally translated as "in addition to genetics," in which case it describes types of completely non-genetic heritability—specifically, the memory of events that happened in the past. But, this chapter will use the stricter definition of epigenetics as "mechanisms that operate by altering the structure of chromosomes," chromosomes being the combination of DNA and the proteins that it wraps around ("on top of" rather than "in addition to"). These changes can physically block genetic sequences to prevent their expression. But this definition is a bit too strict, because there are clear examples of epigenetic processes like RNAi (RNA interference) that aren't directly related to chromosomal structure. It is possible that all these epigenetic mechanisms arose to control transposable elements (TEs)—essentially, sequences of DNA that literally jump in and out of the genome. The extreme ambiguity and variety of epigenetic mechanisms allow them to perform amazing feats that were thought to be biologically impossible. Indeed, a third way to translate epigenetics is "above genetics," which is suggestive of the miraculous implications of the concept and the way the word will be used for the remainder of the book (after this chapter).

Epigenetics: A Brief Introduction

> "I guess that I see epigenetics (including environmental epigenetics)
> as continuing to learn about inheritance, rather than anything
> fundamentally new and different?"[122]
>
> —DAVID PENNY, professor of theoretical biology

Armed with the knowledge contained in part one, you are now prepared to tackle the concept of epigenetics. The epigenetic perspective has existed since the 1930s and 40s, but in the last 30 years it has seen a drastic explosion of research interest and public popularity.

Epigenetics has such a capacity to reconfigure biology that it has been compared to quantum mechanics—the physics that completely obliterated our understanding of objective reality. Just like quanta replaced the particulate truth of reality with "a field of possibilities,"[123] this book intends to replace the particulate understanding of genes with the concept of epigenetic *organa*.

Epigenetics is a marvelously ambiguous term and, just like quantum mechanics, it has been co-opted by popular mystical thinkers. Deepak Chopra, for example, has used epigenetics to make statements like this: "Regardless of the nature of the genes we inherit from our parents, dynamic change at this level [of epigenetics] allows us almost unlimited influence on our fate."[124]

---

122 Note: The question mark is part of the original quotation—an indication of the confusion and resistance that surrounds epigenetics.

123 Richard A. Jorgensen, "Epigenetics: Biology's Quantum Mechanics," *Frontiers in Plant Science* 2, (April 2011): 2, https://doi.org/10.3389/fpls.2011.00010. "The original concept of the atom, the fundamental entity of Newtonian mechanics, had held that the atom was an indivisible particle. This concept was transformed...by quantum mechanics which redefined the atom as a 'field of probabilities' of subatomic particles existing in four dimensions (three spatial dimensions and time)....the original concept of the gene, the fundamental entity of Mendelian genetics, was that it was also particulate and indivisible, a concept that has also been transformed...by molecular biology, looking through the prism of epigenetics, into what might be referred to as a 'field of possibilities'..." See the Epilogue for more information on the relationship between quantum mechanics and epigenetics.

124 Deepak Chopra, and Rudolph Tanzi, "You Can Transform Your Own Biology," *The Chopra Center*, accessed September 16, 2018, https://chopra.com/articles/you-can-transform-your-own-biology/.

Not everyone agrees with Deepak,[125] but this book is an attempt to make a more rigorous argument in favor of a similar (though more restrained) point of view—that epigenetics unlocks a doorway of possibilities for the evolution of biology, consciousness, and the universe. Whether or not this is an overstatement, the evidence certainly suggests that epigenetic mechanisms increase the pace of evolutionary adaptation[126] (see *speciation* in Chapter 11). Epigenetics also promises to uncover the answers to many longstanding questions, like why some people are left-handed and why handedness is associated with a range of diseases.[127]

This chapter is devoted to the biological details of a stringently defined version of epigenetics as "chemical flags, or markers, on genes that are copied along with the genes when the DNA is replicated."[128] But the rest of the book will dive into more philosophical and speculative ideas. Specifically, the revolutionary potential of a broader definition of epigenetics as "non-genetic inheritance," or the ways in which "a transient signal or event triggers a response that is then perpetuated in the absence the original signal."[129]

CHROMOSOMES AND CHROMATIN

Let's get back to chromosomes, the structures that are formed when the DNA of the genome wraps tightly around millions of proteins known as *histones*. If you are familiar with chromosomes you may be aware of a *karyotype* (shown in figure 7.1)—a kind of diagnostic imaging that visualizes the genome as pairs of chromosomes. Karyotyping requires a genetic sample from just one of your cells, which means that it can be done before you are fully developed

---

125 Rutherford, "Pseudo Gene Genies."

126 Chikara Furusawa, and Kunihiko Kaneko, "Epigenetic Feedback Regulation Accelerates Adaptation and Evolution," *PLoS ONE* 8, no. 5 (May 2013): 1, https://doi.org/10.1371/journal.pone.0061251.

127 Sebastian Ocklenburg et al., "Epigenetic Regulation of Lateralized Fetal Spinal Gene Expression Underlies Hemispheric Asymmetries," *eLife* 6 (February 2017): 2, https://doi.org/10.7554/eLife.22784.

128 Williams, "Epigenetics," 3209.

129 Ptashne, "Epigenetics: Core Misconcept," 7102–3.

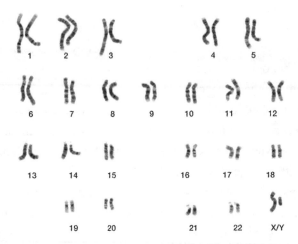

FIGURE 7.1 An image of a karyotype—a diagnostic tool used to visualize the shape of the 46 chromosomes found in each of our cells.

or born. One immediate consequence of karyotype visualization is the knowledge of your sex. If you're a human, having an X and a Y chromosome means you are a male, while having two X chromosomes means you are a female (as stated in Chapter 4, things are not quite this simple. But that is the subject of another book). A karyotype also makes it easy to see if there are noticeable disruptions or variations in chromosomal pattern. For example, extra copies of chromosomes—like the triplicate chromosome 21 in Down syndrome—are visible in a karyotype.

While the karyotype is a useful way of visualizing chromosomes, only actively replicating cells organize the genome into these paired chromosomes. However, this does not mean that the shape of chromosomes is unimportant. Adrian Bird, a researcher at the forefront of epigenetic research, considers the field to be the study of how cellular machinery signals and organizes dynamic changes in chromosomal shape. He defines epigenetics like this: "the structural adaptation of chromosomal regions so as to register, signal or perpetuate altered activity states."[130] The physical and structural organization of the genome is the most important aspect of when, why, and how much each gene is expressed. And again, the question returns: "How does each cell

---

130 Adrian Bird, "Perceptions of Epigenetics," *Nature* 447, no. 7143 (May 2007): 398, https://doi.org/10.1038/nature05913.

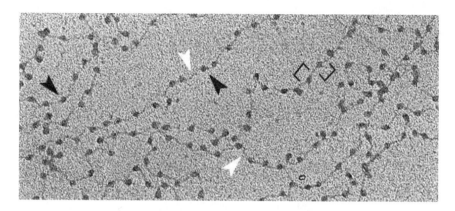

FIGURE 7.2 An image of decondensed chromatin taken with an electron microscope. When DNA is wrapped around histone proteins to create nucleosomes, it has a characteristic "beads on a string" pattern. This image clearly depicts this pattern—the black arrowheads point to the nucleosomes, or beads, and the white arrowheads point to the naked DNA, or string. Each arrowhead is ~25 nanometers long—that's 0.000025 millimeters!

retain its unique properties when, in its DNA-containing nucleus, it has the same master set of genes as every other cell?"[131] This chapter will describe the specific mechanisms that allow these differences to occur.

Within a chromosome, DNA wraps around histone proteins like a string around a yo-yo. This organization of DNA plus protein is called *chromatin*—a physical organization that provides our genomes with a very visible and ordered arrangement reminiscent of beads on a string. Just like DNA has nucleotides as its basic unit of organization, chromatin is made up of repeating structures called *nucleosomes*. A nucleosome is always composed of 146 nucleotides of DNA wrapped around 8 histone proteins. In between each nucleosome there is a region of *linker DNA* that holds two adjacent nucleosomes together. These linkers tend to be about 80 nucleotides long, which means that all 3.2 billion nucleotides of your DNA are arranged into 14 million segments, each of which is approximately 226 nucleotides long. Figure 7.2 shows that this regular organization truly does make the genome look like beads on a string, where the DNA is the string, and the nucleosomes are the points at which the string "winds through" the beads that are histone proteins (see figure 7.2).

131 Williams, "Epigenetics," 3209.

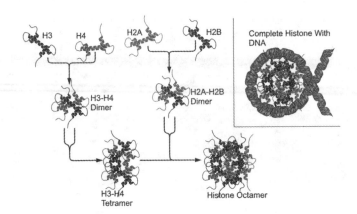

FIGURE 7.3 A depiction of the four kinds of histone proteins (H2A, H2B, H3, & H4), how they combine to create histones, and what it looks like when DNA is wrapped around a histone.

Previously (see Chapter 2), two generic types of free-roaming proteins were discussed: *polymerases*, which catalyze the transcription of DNA into RNA (and the replication of DNA sequences onto new DNA), and *transcription factors*, which alter the expression of specific genes. Just like a transcription factor, chromatin structure can block a polymerase's access to a gene. Chromatin is analogous to a papyrus scroll (DNA) wrapped around a dowel (histone proteins)—to read the writing on the papyrus the scroll needs to be unrolled. Nucleosomes (8 histone proteins plus 146 nucleotides of DNA; see figure 7.3) can pack tightly together to physically block a segment of DNA, which prevents RNA polymerase from transcribing any genes in that region.

When chromatin is tightly packed and inaccessible, it is called *heterochromatin*. Heterochromatin is opposed to *euchromatin*, which is loosely wrapped and therefore accessible to polymerases and other factors (see figure 7.4). These dualistically opposed states—open (euchromatin) and closed (heterochromatin)—represent a powerful control point for genetic expression. Polymerases and DNA-binding molecules cannot access the DNA contained within heterochromatin, in the same way that physical barriers prevent the diffusion of concentration gradients in specific directions (see Chapter 5).

Using the definition given by Adrian Bird, epigenetics is the study of how cellular machinery signals and organizes these hetero- and euchromatic states. This definition is too restrictive and simplistic for the larger purposes of this

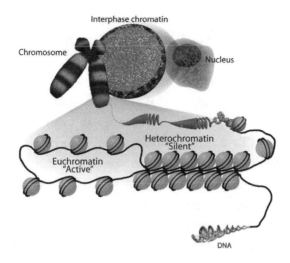

FIGURE 7.4 Chromosomes are composed of regions of heterochromatin—tightly packed, "silent" DNA—and euchromatin—loosely packed, active DNA.

book, but this simplicity is convenient in the sense that chromatin states are essentially "on" and "off" switches for specific genes, or even specific parts of genes. This chapter will use Bird's definition to stay focused on chromatin for now. But, the rest of the book uses epigenetics to mean *any non-genetic system of memory or heritability.*

CELLULAR REGULATION OF CHROMATIN STATES

"Can acquired phenotypes, not encoded in the DNA sequence, be inherited and transmitted across generations?... [E]pigenetic states can be transmitted by chromatin mechanisms for many generations, possibly indefinitely... the doors to a world of Lamarckian inheritance are flung wide open."

—VINCENZO PIRROTTA, professor of molecular biology and biochemistry

Chromatin states and gene expression are one of the reasons that stem cells can differentiate into the myriad other cell types in our bodies (see Chapter 4). Even individual cells of the same type[132] seem to have a unique, physical chromatin organization[133]—a special 3-dimensional way of expressing a shared genome. These epigenetic chromatin states are tightly controlled phenomenon that can respond to the experiences of the organism—a powerful and defining feature of the broader sense of epigenetics that will be used throughout the remainder of this book. This responsive control involves an interplay between DNA, protein, and RNA that is exceptionally complex. This chapter only scratches the surface of the details; new chromatin regulators and epigenetic signaling mechanisms are being discovered every day.[134] Despite the complexity of these systems it is worth exploring a few prominent examples. This will provide a scientific context for some of the more speculative claims in upcoming chapters, and provide a personal context about the underlying mechanisms of gene expression happening in your body right now.

The most well-studied regulator of chromatin states is methylation. As the name suggests, methylation is the attachment of a chemical called a "methyl group" to either the histone proteins that DNA wraps around, or the DNA itself. Methylation is a highly flexible mark that can signal many subtleties, so keep that in mind as you read through this shallow overview. Methylation is often taught as being the primary inhibitor of gene expression because the two best examples of it are repressive in nature.

The first of these examples is the process of stem cell differentiation, which has been explored previous chapters (see Chapters 4 and 5). A vital part

---

132 In this case "type" means different kinds of fully differentiated cells, like skin cells, brain cells, blood cells, or heart cells. The differences between these various types of cells are somewhat analogous to the differences between species (say, a human versus a dog), while the differences between cells of the same type are more comparable to the differences between individual humans. This is a special feature of the *organum* that will be discussed in Chapter 12. Organa organize themselves into groups based on shared form, but each individual organum is a unique organization of smaller organum. Although the difference between a heart and a brain cell may seem obvious, it can be just as hard to define the distinct boundaries between cell types as it is to define an organ (see Chapter 2).

133 Takashi Nagano et al., "Single-Cell Hi-C Reveals Cell-to-Cell Variability in Chromosome Structure," *Nature* 502, no. 7469 (October 2013): 59–64, https://doi.org/10.1038/nature12593.

134 For examples of just a few of the well-studied chemical modifications of chromatin, see ["Histone Modifications: A Guide," Epigenetics, Abcam, accessed September 23, 2018, https://www.abcam.com/epigenetics/histone-modifications-a-guide].

of differentiation is turning off so-called pluripotency genes, which provide the capability to turn into any kind of cell. If the expression of pluripotency genes is not controlled, stem cells can cause a variety of difficult to cure and treatment-resistant cancers.[135]

The second well-known example of methylation as a repressive process is known as X-chromosome inactivation. In most cases, males have one X chromosome and one Y chromosome, and females have two X chromosomes. Redundant gene expression can be a good thing, and it is a necessary feature of robustness (see Chapter 5). This is why there are two copies of every chromosome (except the X chromosome in most males). However, in a truly robust system the copies have different, but overlapping functions. Too many exact copies of a gene can cause things to go awry, like the mental retardation caused by the extra copy of chromosome 21 in Down syndrome. If females expressed two copies of every gene on the X chromosome, men and women would be even more different than they already are. In order to avoid this, one of X chromosomes in females undergoes "inactivation" so that there aren't two active copies of every X-chromosome gene. This process is mediated in part by methylation,[136] and the level of methylation can be used as a diagnostic to tell which chromosome is inactive.[137]

So how does methylation achieve this all-important and reliable genetic silencing? It is thought that methylation represses genetic expression by changing the chromatin state from open to closed—it simply flips the "on/off" switch of a gene to "off." Interestingly, methylation can occur both on the histone proteins and on the C (cytosine) nucleotides in a DNA sequence. In some organisms, methylation can also occur on the A (adenine) nucleotide

---

135 Tracy Seymour, Alecia Jane Twigger, and Foteini Kakulas, "Pluripotency Genes and Their Functions in the Normal and Aberrant Breast and Brain," *International Journal of Molecular Sciences* 16, no. 11 (November 2015): 27288–301, https://doi.org/10.3390/ijms161126024.

136 Howard Cedar, and Yehudit Bergman, "Programming of DNA Methylation Patterns," *Annual Review of Biochemistry* 81 (February 2012): 104–105, https://doi.org/10.1146/annurev-biochem-052610.

137 George L. Chen, and Josef T. Prchal, "X-Linked Clonality Testing: Interpretation and Limitations," *Blood* 110, no. 5 (September 2007): 1414, https://doi.org/10.1182/blood-2006-09-018655.

in a DNA sequence.[138] It is thought that methylation physically regulates how nucleotides associate with histone proteins, which affects the availability of a gene for expression.[139] There are also fascinating examples of methyl-binding proteins that can attach to methylated DNA and physically block RNA polymerase from transcribing a gene, just like a transcription factor. These proteins are not transcription factors because they do not bind to a specific DNA sequence. Rather, they bind to any sequence of DNA with a particular pattern of methylation. They might be considered a type of "epi-transcriptional factor." A phenomenal example of one of these epi-transcriptional proteins is MeCP2, which binds to methylated DNA and will be discussed in greater detail in Chapter 10.

Acetylation, or the addition of acetyl groups, is the second most well-studied regulator of chromatin states. Acetyl groups are somewhat like methyl groups, but they only occur on histone proteins, not directly on DNA sequences. Acetylation acts as an important electromagnetic repellant that force histones away from both DNA and other histones. Acetyl groups are meant to keep nucleosomes loosely wrapped so that gene expression can occur freely. In this way, acetylation is the functional opposite of methylation—if methylation is the "off" part of the switch, then acetylation is the "on."

But these epigenetic marks are not so simplistic, because they interact with each other to control gene expression. For example, MeCP2 and other methyl-binding proteins not only block RNA polymerase directly, they also recruit additional proteins that deacetylate histones and further enhance repression.[140] This is somewhat like having a dimmer switch on your lights that makes it harder to turn up the brightness as the lights get dimmer. Since methylation passively degrades over the course of many cell divisions, it is also interesting to speculate that it could act as a timing mechanism for

---

138 Lakshminarayan M. Iyer, Dapeng Zhang, and L. Aravind, "Adenine Methylation in Eukaryotes: Apprehending the Complex Evolutionary History and Functional Potential of an Epigenetic Modification," *BioEssays* 38, no. 1 (December 2015): 27–40, https://doi.org/10.1002/bies.201500104.

139 Cedar and Bergman, "DNA Methylation Patterns," 101.

140 *Ibid*.

keeping track of cellular division[141] as discussed in Chapter 5.

There are hundreds of known factors that interact with methylation, but there is still so much about these complicated epigenetic systems that is not yet known. In this section, methylation has been discussed in contexts where it represses gene expression. But some strange and seemingly contradictory results suggest that methylation on different parts of a gene can have different effects. For example, the promoter of a gene (the part that attracts the transcription machinery; see Chapter 6) is inhibitory,[142] while methylation on the body of the gene (the part that encodes for the subsequent RNA or protein) can actually enhance expression.[143] A complete treatment of all the ins and outs of methylation, including the various types, functions, and placements could fill several books; it is my hope that you have enough detail from this brief introduction to understand the basic concept.

RNA AND PLANT EPIGENETICS

RNAs play just as big a role in epigenetic mechanisms as methylation and acetylation. There are many varieties of RNA, just like there are many kinds of proteins (i.e., transcription factors, polymerases, methyl-binding proteins, etc.). So far, RNA has been described as if it is transcribed from DNA and then translated into proteins. In biological reality, only one type of RNA—*messenger RNA* (mRNA)—follows this specific track of the central dogma, from DNA to RNA to protein. The regulation of mRNA is one way to affect gene expression without modification of the underlying DNA sequence. Tightly controlled transport of mRNA allows cells to decide the specific locations where certain proteins will get expressed.[144] This can work

141 Feng C. Zhou, "DNA Methylation Program During Development," *Frontiers in Biology (Beijing)* 7, no. 6 (December 2012): 486, https://doi.org/10.1007/s11515-012-9246-1.

142 Peter A. Jones, "Functions of DNA Methylation: Islands, Start Sites, Gene Bodies and Beyond," *Nature Reviews Genetics* 13, no. 7 (July 2012): 484.

143 *Ibid*, 484.

144 Guoning Liao, Lisa Mingle, Livingston Van De Water, and Gang Liu, "Control of Cell Migration Through Mrna Localization and Local Translation," *Wiley Interdisciplinary Reviews: RNA* 6, no. 1 (January 2015): 2, https://doi.org/10.1002/wrna.1265.

in a similar manner to the retinoic acid example discussed in Chapter 5, whereby the precise local concentration of a protein has a powerful effect on nearby cells. Cells can also control *when* mRNA is expressed by responding to specific cues in the environment to induce the translation of specific proteins. Developing cells use this on-demand protein translation to determine their overall "body" shape and migration behavior, often in response to various types of concentration gradients[145] (see Chapter 5).

Since each mRNA is a relatively unique string of nucleotides, cells have intricate mechanisms for affecting specific mRNA sequences in targeted ways. For example, animals, plants, and fungi (and even some of the ancient archaeaon mentioned in Chapter 2) all share cellular machinery called *RISC* (RNA-Induced Silencing Complex).[146] RISC is a cooperative complex of proteins and RNA that degrades specific mRNAs in a process called RNA *interference*, or RNAi. Cells use this process to regulate the kinds and amounts of mRNA that can be translated into their subsequent proteins. This is a very important task that prevents runaway protein production and maintains cellular harmony, and there are many kinds of RNA that play a role in this process. You don't have to remember any of these, but here's a short, incomplete list (in no particular order) to give you a sense of the complexity of RNA: siRNA, miRNA, piRNA, rasiRNA, tasiRNA, tncRNA, hcRNA, scnRNA.[147] Each of these types of RNA have unique structures and functions, but they are all a part of the RNAi process. These examples are also all "non-coding" RNA, or *ncRNA*, in that they do not produce proteins.

The RNAi system works because these ncRNAs are complementary to the targeted mRNA sequence. In other words, as discussed in Chapter 2, nucleotides can physically connect with their complementary partner like puzzle pieces, A to T (A to U in RNA) and C to G, which creates the strong

---

145 See [Akira Nukazuka et al., "Semaphorin Controls Epidermal Morphogenesis by Stimulating MRNA Translation via EIF2α in Caenorhabditis Elegans," *Genes and Development* 22, no. 8 (February 2008): 1025–36, https://doi.org/10.1101/gad.1644008] as just one example of this.

146 Ashley J. Pratt, and Ian J. MacRae, "The RNA-Induced Silencing Complex: A Versatile Gene-Silencing Machine," *Journal of Biological Chemistry* 284, no. 27 (July 2009): 17897, https://doi.org/10.1074/jbc.R900012200."

147 *Ibid.*

bonds seen in the double-helical structure of DNA. In RISC, the ncRNAs are attached to an enzymatic protein that will degrade only specific mRNAs which are complementary to the attached ncRNA. The enzymatic protein is somewhat like a missile, while the ncRNA is like a guidance system that tells the missile where to go.

RNAi is a highly conserved system, which means that it is found in a broad range of multi-cellular and even singled-celled organisms. However, plants represent one of the most popular systems to study both RNAi and epigenetics, because they have distinctive and extensive epigenetic systems. For example, plants have a specialized RNA polymerase (the same kind of protein that transcribes DNA into RNA) that allows their RNA to direct the methylation of their DNA.[148] In some plants, RNA can also directly affect chromatin structure through modifications (like the methylation and acetylation described in the previous section) that enhance or inhibit the expression of specific genes.[149] In addition, plants have regulatory mechanisms that control the demethylation of DNA.[150] In certain plants, these processes allow RNA to have extremely tight regulatory control over gene expression. Despite their lack of locomotion, plants can compete evolutionarily with animals and microorganisms partly because of their powerful epigenetic mechanisms.

Specific types of RNA can manipulate transcription through DNA methylation and control translation through RNAi. These complex systems of gene expression regulation are thought to be an evolutionary response to overly redundant genes and virus-like DNA sequences called *transposons*. Transposons, also known as *transposable elements* (TEs), are fascinating case studies of the flexibility and power of gene expression. When they are active, TEs will make copies of themselves all over a genome by cutting (or copying) and pasting their nucleotide sequence into other chromosomal regions. This can be a serious

---

148 Bruno Huettel et al., "RNA-Directed DNA Methylation Mediated by DRD1 and Pol IVb: A Versatile Pathway for Transcriptional Gene Silencing in Plants," *Biochimica et Biophysica Acta - Gene Structure and Expression* 1769, no. 5–6 (March 2007): 358–74, https://doi.org/10.1016/j.bbaexp.2007.03.001.

149 Daniel Holoch, and Danesh Moazed, "RNA-Mediated Epigenetic Regulation of Gene Expression," *Nature Reviews Genetics* 16, no. 2 (January 2015): 71–84, https://doi.org/10.1038/nrg3863.

150 Huettel, "RNA-Directed DNA," 359–360.

problem if the TE pastes itself into a genetic sequence and disrupts a vital function. While TEs are not technically epigenetic, they were a key piece of evidence that led to our current understanding of epigenetic mechanisms.

It has been suggested that epigenetic mechanisms are an evolutionary response to TEs—an attempt to control TE behavior.[151] However, the full extent of the relationship between TEs and epigenetic evolution is unclear.[152] TEs compose approximately *half* of all human DNA sequences and it has been suggested that they play an important role in species change (also known as *speciation*; see Chapter 11). The next section will run through a quick overview of these amazing DNA sequences that can literally "jump" in and out of the genome.[153]

TRANSPOSABLE ELEMENTS AND VIRUSES

As stated in the last section, TEs are DNA sequences that can literally jump out of their position within a chromosome. Some kinds of TEs perform this "jump" without removing their original sequence in a "copy-and-paste" fashion, while others move entirely by "cutting and pasting" themselves. The idea of "mobile genetic elements" was so absurd that it took nearly four decades after their original discovery by cytogeneticist Barbara McClintock for the broader scientific community to even consider the concept. But once other

---

151 Mélanie Rigal, and Olivier Mathieu, "A 'Mille-Feuille' of Silencing: Epigenetic Control of Transposable Elements," *Biochimica et Biophysica Acta - Gene Regulatory Mechanisms* 1809, no. 8 (April 2011): 456, https://doi.org/10.1016/j.bbagrm.2011.04.001. "Because TEs represent highly dynamic genomic components and because there are potentially deleterious consequences of TE mobilization, evolutionary forces have likely driven the production of various epigenetic mechanisms to ensure TE silencing."

152 Nina V. Fedoroff, "The Suppressor-Mutator Element and the Evolutionary Riddle of Transposons," *Genes to Cells* 4, no. 1 (January 1999): 11, https://doi.org/10.1046/j.1365-2443.1999.00233.x. "[Transposons] are both prevalent and ubiquitous, often comprising as much as a third, and in some cases, more than half, of the genomes of higher plants and animals, including humans. However, their evolutionary role remains enigmatic: do they drive genome evolution or has evolution struggled to eliminate, control and contain transposons?"

153 Nina V. Fedoroff, "Transposable Elements, Epigenetics, and Genome Evolution," *Science* 338, no. 6108 (November 2012): 765, https://doi.org/10.1126/science.338.6108.758."

scientists got over their disbelief, it was considered to be such an important discovery that it earned her a Nobel Prize.[154]

Some of these moving nucleotide sequences (TEs) prefer to insert themselves near or within genes.[155] A mobile TE can interfere with the normal function of a gene if it disrupts an important part of the DNA sequence, like a protein coding region or a promoter. TEs can also cause breakage and nonfunctional recombination of chromosomes.[156] Recombination can occur in many ways and it is a very important aspect of DNA repair and reproduction. Since most humans have two copies of each chromosome (except for sex chromosomes and the occasional chromosomal disorder), there is almost always a backup if one stretch of genes fails for some reason. In the case of a damaged DNA strand, cells will perform a type of repair known as *recombination*—a process in which a broken strand of DNA is swapped or replaced with a functional copy. Recombination also occurs during sexual reproduction when matching chromosomes from the male and female are "shuffled" to create a new organism with a random, unique chromosomal organization (see figure 7.5).

In addition, recombination is a process that is required to create antibodies, which are a major part of the immune system. Antibodies are relatively large and numerous proteins that stick strongly to a specific target molecule. These target molecules tend to be small pieces of an invading pathogen, like a virus, bacteria, or fungus. Antibodies are one part of a system that is designed to recognize what is "self" and what is "not self." There are practically an infinite number of possible antibodies, but they only work if they are very specific and do not stick to anything within your own body. If they don't function properly they can cause autoimmune disorders such as arthritis, multiple sclerosis, or type 1 diabetes. Recombination is a vital part of the function and evolution of organisms that allows for extremely rapid adaptation in response to changes in the environment.

---

154 It must have been extremely satisfying to be recognized with the Nobel Prize in Physiology and Medicine in 1983 after decades of derision from her colleagues.

155 Rita Rebollo, Mark T. Romanish, and Dixie L. Mager, "Transposable Elements: An Abundant and Natural Source of Regulatory Sequences for Host Genes." *Annual Review of Genetics* 46, no. 1 (August 2012): 26, https://doi.org/10.1146/annurev-genet-110711-155621.

156 Rigal, "Epigenetic Control of Transposable Elements," 452.

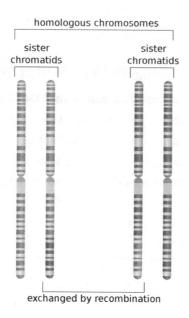

homologous chromosomes

sister chromatids

sister chromatids

exchanged by recombination

FIGURE 7.5 Recombination is a process whereby a portion of a chromosome is swapped with or copied from a homologous chromosome.

As discussed earlier in this chapter, genetic redundancy can lead to problems when expression is not tightly controlled. Because of this, TEs can cause serious issues as they create a great deal of redundancy when they copy and paste themselves all over the genome. It has been argued that epigenetic systems evolved to control redundant gene sequences, like TEs, and to protect important genes from recombination events (like sexual reproduction).[157] There is strong evidence that multiple copies of a gene can cause an epigenetically-mediated decrease in gene expression, as the cell will methylate all the copies of the gene to inhibit redundant expression.[158] TEs are structurally and functionally similar to viruses, to the point that some ERVs (endogenous retroviruses; see Chapter 6) can actually be considered TEs. Viruses and TEs both operate within the three-dimensional space of cells, but most of their existence is spent in information storage as a dormant

157 Fedoroff, "The Evolutionary Riddle of Transposons," 16.

158 John R. Edwards et al., "DNA Methylation and DNA Methyltransferases," *Epigenetics & Chromatin* 10, no. 1 (May 2017): 23, https://doi.org/10.1186/s13072-017-0130-8.

sequence of DNA. Like memes, TEs and viruses wait as inert, abstract ideas—poised to express and copy themselves when the time is right. It was Barbara McClintock who first described how TEs operate in cycles of dormancy and activity, [159] just like viruses (see Chapter 6).

Since TEs jump in and out of genomes, they can use viral and bacterial DNA as vehicles to copy themselves into new organisms.[160] This is conceptually comparable to the way that an idea can move from mind to mind over long distances through various forms of media, like television or radio. Although they are often described as "parasitic" or "selfish" DNA,[161] TEs are also like viruses in that they play very important roles in our bodies. For example, there are TEs that produce RNA polymerases that are necessary for the process of RNA interference (RNAi).[162]

In addition, it is theorized that organisms can intentionally awaken dormant TEs to accelerate the pace of evolution under stressful conditions.[163] This is thought to work because active TEs can jump out of the genome and preferentially insert themselves in sites of active gene expression. This is a form of rapid mutation that can lead to recombination and change in the functional products of gene expression (like RNAs and proteins). Even though TEs can be helpful, it is vital for our cells to keep TE activity in check. One important reason for this is that unregulated TE activity may cause some of the problems associated with aging.

As discussed in Chapter 5, cells have mechanisms that allow them to keep track of time and how many divisions they have gone through. Interestingly, some cells will never stop dividing, while others undergo a process known as senescence, or what is more commonly referred to as aging (see Chapter 12). Like many of the topics covered already, epigenetics has a powerful influence

---

159 Barbara McClintock, "Topographical Relations Between Elements of Control Systems in Maize," *Carnegie Institution of Washington Year Book* 61 (1962): 448–461.

160 Laurent Keller, *Levels of Selection in Evolution* (Princeton: Princeton University Press, 1999), 124.

161 *Ibid*.

162 Rebollo, "Transposable Elements," 26–27.

163 Richard A. Jorgensen, "Restructuring the Genome in Response to Adaptive Challenge: McClintock's Bold Conjecture Revisited," *Cold Spring Harbor Symposia on Quantitative Biology* 69 (2004): 350–351, https://doi.org/10.1101/sqb.2004.69.349.

over the process of aging. As cells age, heterochromatin becomes euchromatin and vice versa, which causes "transcriptional noise." In other words, as you age, genes that keep you healthy and young become silent, while genes that are disruptive and destructive become active.[164] It is well established that the RNAi pathways and TEs are important for the process of aging, but there are confusing and conflicting results that prevent any strong conclusions from being made yet. Despite the many unknowns in the systems related to aging, scientists have increased the lifespans of worms through epigenetic modification of histone marks[165] (see Chapter 8). See the Epilogue for more information about the relationship between epigenetics and aging.

The examples presented in this chapter are intended to serve as an introduction to the interplay between genes and their expression mechanisms. The upcoming chapters will continue to explore epigenetics in the context of evolution and heritability—and the discussion is about to get a lot less scientific and a lot more speculative.

164 Jason G. Wood, and Stephen L. Helfand, "Chromatin Structure and Transposable Elements in Organismal Aging," *Frontiers in Genetics* 4 (December 2013): 7-9, https://doi.org/10.3389/fgene.2013.00274.

165 Eric L. Greer et al., "Transgenerational Epigenetic Inheritance of Longevity in Caenorhabditis Elegans," *Nature* 479, no. 7373 (November 2011): 365–71, https://doi.org/10.1038/nature10572.

CHAPTER 8

Collective Memory

"Inheritance must be looked at as merely a form of growth…"

—CHARLES DARWIN, *The Variation of Animals and Plants Under Domestication*

As I mentioned at the beginning of Chapter 7, the rest of the book will no longer be using the word epigenetics in the restricted sense of changes in gene expression through the alteration of chromatin marks. Instead, from now on it will mean *any non-genetic system of memory or heritability*. In this sense of the word, epi- no longer means what physically happens "on top of" genes, but rather, what happens at the levels "above" genes. Epigenetic inheritance is a powerful concept that leads to many hard-to-believe conclusions, because it is easy to overlook that heritability is essentially a form of memory. Memory is a tool that provides an organism with a template for where it has been, so it can best choose where it needs to go in the future—to survive. Even though genetic and epigenetic mechanisms are surely a form of memory or information storage, natural selection is often described as blind. And although there does not seem to be a single designer in or outside of nature, the process of evolution produces designs that are highly reminiscent of the artifactual mechanisms created by humans. For example, non-genetic memory systems like circadian rhythms strongly resemble the mechanisms of a clock or a watch (or do human artifacts resemble evolutionary designs?). There are many examples of non-genetic and epigenetic memory systems within our bodies right now. Some of these systems even seem to store information over the course of a lifetime that can be inherited by one's offspring, which is exemplified by the concepts of inherited fears and traumas. The interplay between our many concurrent levels of memory indicates how evolution progresses and has implications for the role that we as individuals play in the collective future of our species. Let's dive in.

Evolutionary Blindsight

> "A junkyard contains all the bits and pieces of a Boeing 747,
> dismembered and in disarray. A whirlwind happens to blow through
> the yard. What is the chance that after its passage a fully assembled
> 747, ready to fly, will be found standing there?"
>
> —FRED HOYLE, *The Intelligent Universe*

For quite a while now, scientists have taken a gene-centric view of evolution (see Chapter 1). In this view, natural selection is driven by the replication, competition, and survival of genes, while genomes and the bodies that contain them (i.e., living organisms) are nothing more than vehicles (see Chapter 12 for more details about this idea). According to this logic, genes are not conscious and intentional agents, and the evolution of life proceeds in a blind and unguided way. On a larger scale, this means that the universe has no designer and, therefore, there is no design in nature.

This perspective is succinctly summed up in the title of Richard Dawkins's 1986 book, *The Blind Watchmaker: Why the Evidence of Evolution Reveals a Universe Without Design.*[166] The "watchmaker" refers to a creationist argument in which the elaborate design of a human creation—a watch—is compared to the complexity of biology. This is an attempt to suggest that living things are too complicated to have arisen through a natural process such as evolution. The line of reasoning goes something like this: If you are walking along the beach and discover a pocket watch with all of its intricate gears and timekeeping mechanisms, you would immediately assume that this piece of machinery was designed by an intelligent being. This position is somewhat convincing on an intuitive level—perhaps an intelligent designer really did build all the forms of life on Earth? After all, biological organisms are intricate collections of vast numbers of miraculous parts and mechanisms, and they do perform the function of keeping time (see Chapter 5). But living things are drastically more complex than a pocket watch, and the watchmaker argument does not

---

166 Richard Dawkins, *The Blind Watchmaker: Why the Evidence of Evolution Reveals a Universe Without Design* (New York: W. W. Norton & Company, 1986).

stand up to the rigors of either science or logic.

Dawkins turns the watchmaker argument on its head by replacing God with the process of natural selection as the disembodied designer of biological life. In Dawkins's description, evolution is a "blind watchmaker" because—unlike the process of design by an omnipotent God—the process of evolution designs in an unconscious and unguided way. But this explanation merely replaces one God with another and has the unfortunate effect of turning Neo-Darwinian evolutionary theory into a secular religion. In Dawkins's framework, it is the process of evolution that *creates* the designs we see in nature; evolution becomes the disembodied *designer* of the universe. But Dawkins goes even further and claims that natural selection operates solely on genes, which gives them near total control over the direction of evolutionary progress. In a way, genes are the new pantheon of gods in the scientific dogma of evolutionary theory.

Daniel Dennett, a brilliant philosopher of consciousness and evolution, has also argued against the necessity of God as the supreme designer of living things. In his book *Darwin's Dangerous Idea*, he completely sidesteps the strawman logic of the watchmaker argument and avoids Dawkins's mistake of deifying evolution. He does this by claiming that evolution is not the designer of life, because design does not necessarily require a designer.[167] He states that any argument invoking an "intelligent designer" will necessarily lead to an infinite regression, whereby that intelligent designer will need another intelligent designer above it.[168] In this same way, if natural selection is a designer, it must have been designed by some other process or thing.

Dennett concisely and convincingly argues that complex systems are always more reasonably explained by "cranes" rather than "skyhooks." When we reframe the watchmaker scenarios in terms of a hook we may encounter hanging from the sky, rather than a watch found on the ground, a different intuitive claim emerges. In this case, we do not assume that a hook just happens to be hanging from the sky, completely unattached to anything above. Instead we assume the hook must be attached to something that is holding it there, such as a crane, i.e., something sensible comes to mind and we don't assume

---

167 Dennett, *Darwin's Dangerous Idea*, 135–136.
168 *Ibid*, 70.

it's a free-floating hook. In other words, any level of complexity, no matter how miraculous, can be broken down into simple processes that have built on one another. We thus escape an infinite regression that relies on a mystical explanation (although a new natural regression emerges, as we will see in the case of *organa*).

As far as evolution goes, Dennett tends to agree with the sentiment in Francisco Ayala's quote: "Natural selection does not have foresight; it does not anticipate the environments of the future."[169] Where I am going in this book breaks with this view—for me, design without a designer makes sense, but design without foresight does not.[170] Design is literally defined as a plan, purpose, or intention, and these concepts only exist in the context of a possible and somewhat predictable future. This is not a claim that natural selection can predict the future—natural selection does not need to be a conscious, self-aware entity to create intentional designs with foresight. Design can exist without a designer, and foresight can exist without conscious awareness. How is this possible?

Consider the phenomenon of "blindsight." This strange and mind-bending malady is caused by damage to the back of the brain—and specifically the occipital lobe—the region in which visual sensations are processed into more complicated forms and concepts. Sufferers of blindsight cannot see, hence the *blind* in blindsight. But when they are asked to guess on a task or walk through an obstacle course they perform far better than chance and as if they could see quite a bit, even though they report total blindness. There are even examples

169 Francisco J. Ayala, "Design Without Designer: Darwin's Greatest Discovery," *Proceedings of the National Academy of Sciences* 104, suppl. 1 (May 2007): 8572, https://doi.org/10.1017/CBO9780511804823.005.

170 Dennett does seem to see the foresight of human beings, but as a kind of foresight not shared by other species or the process of natural selection itself. As he says in [Dennett, "Darwin's 'Strange Inversion,'" 10064–65], "Such representations make possible highly efficient, guided, foresighted trajectories in design space... Our 'godlike' powers of comprehension and imagination do indeed set us apart from even our closest kin..." This exceptionalism seems to stem from a functional pragmatism— humans look like we're better designers. But if we were able to take a few steps back and more directly view the evolutionary history of entire species, we would likely see a much different picture. Other organisms have more intentional foresight than we give them credit for. Indeed, our inability to see other beings as intelligent lifeforms doesn't exactly support Dennett's argument that humans have "...godlike powers of comprehension and imagination..."

of blindsight patients who behave as though they had normal eyesight, yet they lack awareness of their functional vision—the *sight* in blindsight.[171] This is just one example of (fore)sight, and an ability to look ahead without conscious awareness.

Stay with me here. Research in the field of epigenetic inheritance and memory provides evidence of a kind of "evolutionary blindsight"—an unconscious (or superconscious[172]) plan that natural selection imposes on anything that evolves[173] (the category of "things that evolve" will come to be called *organa* in Chapter 12). This section has referred to "design without a designer" and "design without foresight," but seeing evolution through the lens of blindsight allows us to conceptualize intentional designers that aren't necessarily aware of what they are doing. Even beyond this, the natural world is filled to the brim with marvels of design created by designers (also known as "agents") that do have some form of foresight! For example, bees build hives, spiders build webs, and bowerbirds build incredible huts for their mating rituals (see figure 8.1), even if these animals don't know about the evolutionary pressures that drive them to create such designs. Such phenomenal creations do not arise from nothing—these natural builders must have some form of memory in order to plan these stunning feats of engineering.

---

171 The underlying brain mechanisms that allow this to happen are fascinating, and I encourage you to learn more about it if you are interested.

172 I believe that evolution is a kind of "superconscious" entity. I have no intention of making this a religious idea, but it is a very similar conception to the mythological idea of a deity—an inconceivably large and self-aware agent that seems to impact us in the same way that we might impact our individual cells. Science will likely never be able to truly explore this in a meaningful way.

173 Fascinatingly, it has been suggested that natural selection itself can evolve, and, therefore, seems to impose an evolutionary plan on itself! Such a self-referencing system should even have the capacity to increase its own capacity for foresight and design. As stated in [Momme von Sydow, *From Darwinian Metaphysics towards Understanding the Evolution of Evolutionary Mechanisms: A Historical and Philosophical Analysis of Gene-Darwinism and Universal Darwinism* (Göttingen: Göttingen University Press, 2012.), 432, 433], "However, if one conceded that there are—internal or external—dimensions of variation that are on average more adaptive than others, it becomes...highly plausible that to some degree also mutational variation is not totally blind, but may, to some extent, be adapted itself... It is advocated that variation needs not always be equally blind and wasteful but may gain a certain sight...in an evolving world it may even be necessary that evolution be able to evolve from blindness to sight."

FIGURE 8.1 Bowerbirds collect colorful trinkets, sticks, branches, and stones to build beautiful and intricate huts. I suggest you search for colorized versions of these photos—the Bowerbird is quite an impressive interior designer.

Thinking of other creatures as conscious agents with desires, beliefs, motivations, and memories is known as *the intentional stance* (see Chapter 10). Many people take issue with this line of thought because there isn't really a way to tell if insects and birds have awareness like human beings. It is much harder to deny that humans have conscious awareness and, despite our obvious consciousness, our work as designers is a great example of evolutionary blindsight—humans have been creating tools and civilizations since long before we knew about evolution by natural selection. Clocks, airplanes, and skyscrapers are just some examples of the designs created by humans, and I'm sure you can think of others.

Some of the more amazing design work of humanity has been performed on other animals—what is known as *artificial selection or domestication*. Domestication is a simple and excellent example of many small human foresights adding up to large unconscious evolutionary foresight. This process is dependent on the relationship between micro- and macro-evolutionary changes—the way that many small changes can add up over hundreds of generations to create entirely new forms of life. Species change, also known as speciation (see Chapter 11), is tightly linked with domestication, like the way we continue to selectively breed amazing varieties of dog species. It wasn't too long ago that dogs didn't exist at all; in the evolutionarily recent past, there were only "wild" wolf populations. As wolves interacted with humans over thousands of generations, the methylation patterns on their DNA changed to the point that they have evolved into another species.

If you'll recall from Chapter 7, TEs (transposable elements or transposons) are sequences of pseudo-viral DNA that physically jump in and out of the genome. As a fascinating aside, TEs account for many of the genetic sequences that have changed methylation patterns from wolves to dogs.[174] This is a strong piece of evidence that suggests that TEs may increase the rate of evolution and species change through large and precise mutations to important regions of gene expression. In Chapter 11, we will dive much deeper into the connections between species change, epigenetics, and conscious influences over evolutionary change. For now, let's explore the relationship between epigenetics, evolution, and memory.

MEMORIES OF THE FUTURE

"… [M]emory of the here and now also includes memories of the events that we constantly anticipate… memories of the future."

—ANTONIO R. DAMASIO, *The Feeling of What Happens*

It may seem counterintuitive, as we associate them with the past, but memories are actually quite useless unless they have predictive value. It is prudent at any level to learn about the past to prepare for the future, because—as we know well at the human scale—history repeats itself. Working with this concept more abstractly, we see that our responses to environmental stimuli have a kind of unconscious foresight (blindsight) based on previous experiences.

Here's where it gets really cool. Epigenetic inheritance provides a mechanism for our history to inform the evolutionary path that our species will take in the future. Scientists like Mark Ptashne prefer the word epigenetic to mean any system of memory that does not require genes[175]—epi- meaning "in addition to" as opposed to "on top of," like its use in the last chapter to

---

174 Ilana Janowitz Koch et al., "The Concerted Impact of Domestication and Transposon Insertions on Methylation Patterns between Dogs and Grey Wolves," *Molecular Ecology* 25, no. 8 (April 2016): 1850, https://doi.org/10.1111/mec.13480.

175 Ptashne, "Epigenetics: Core Misconcept," 7102–03.

discuss chromatin marks and DNA methylation. Neither of these definitions refers to controversial ideas. Prions, circadian rhythms in red blood cells, and many other cell-signaling processes are clear and indisputable examples of non-genetic memory. These systems are forms of information storage that can guide future behaviors based on past events (see Chapters 5 and 6). The idea that information stored by these epigenetic memories can be transmitted to future generations to influence the progression of evolution, however, is currently a matter of a fierce debate.[176] Let's explore the evidence.

The capacity to pass on traits to your offspring is one of a few necessary elements for natural selection to occur (see Chapter 11). It is not contentious that epigenetic mechanisms contain a form of memory. As discussed in Chapter 7, chemical modifiers called *methyl groups* can be attached to both histone proteins and the DNA wrapped around them to create an epigenetic memory system for gene expression. In addition, it is not controversial that epigenetic changes can be inherited by subsequent generations. For example, as strands of DNA are replicated their methylation patterns are reproduced on the newly synthesized strands. The quarrel seems to arise around the idea that specific epigenetic memories are heritable—like the intergenerational transmission of fears or food preferences. Any apprehension is reasonable because the possibility of inheriting epigenetic memories in the specific sense leads to all sorts of disturbing and remarkable implications.

Another aspect of the controversy is that most biological research is performed in non-human systems, so it is unclear what can be translated from this research and applied to humans. The next section and the rest of the book will present the conclusions of studies from a whole range of organisms (in mammals like humans and rats all the way down to microorganisms like yeast). These non-human experiments will be tied together with experiments on humans when possible, but the field is still quite new.

Please take caution as you read where I take you next, because a great deal

---

176 Russell Bonduriansky, "Rethinking Heredity, Again," *Trends in Ecology and Evolution* 27, no. 6 (June 2012): 334, https://doi.org/10.1016/j.tree.2012.02.003. "Although the existence of nongenetic inheritance is not in doubt, some putative mechanisms of nongenetic inheritance remain poorly understood, and controversy persists over the role and importance of nongenetic inheritance in shaping phenotypic variation and influencing the dynamics and course of evolution."

of it is speculative. Even if everything written here is dead wrong, it will have been a fun and challenging thought experiment about the nature of humanity, evolution, and reality as a whole.

THE INHERITANCE OF MEMORY

> "…[I]nheritance of parents' life and consciousness in children is absolutely true, but you will see, people will not understand it for a long time!"
>
> —ANDRZEJ SZYSZKO-BOHUSZ, chess champion and professor of pedagogy

The first example of the inheritance of epigenetic memory comes from fruit flies and worms. For a long time, it was thought that the worm *C. elegans* contained no detectable DNA methylation. This was an unfortunate oversight, because it is a very popular model system in scientific studies. Such a drastic difference between *C. elegans* and other organisms could call into question all the experiments ever done on these worms. Luckily, *C. elegans* do have a form of DNA methylation, but it is different enough from other organisms that it was undetectable until recently.[177] The previous chapter briefly described that scientists have slowed the aging of worms through the modification of chromatin marks. What wasn't mentioned is that the increased lifespan caused by these changes was heritable for up to three generations.[178] Because the next generation exists within us from the time that we are born in the form of *gametes* (also known as "germ cells"—sperm and eggs in humans; see Chapter 4), this finding avoids one of the strongest criticisms of evidence that supports epigenetic inheritance: that manipulating an organism will affect the gametes that will eventually become its children. If such an effect can be shown to operate in humans, it is highly likely that the experiences of your great-grandparents are directly affecting you today.

---

177 Eric L. Greer et al., "DNA Methylation on N6-Adenine in C. Elegans," *Cell* 161, no. 4 (April 2015): 868, https://doi.org/10.1016/j.cell.2015.04.005.

178 Greer, "Epigenetic Inheritance of Longevity," 365.

In yeast, this transgenerational inheritance of epigenetic memory can last even longer than three generations. Researchers have shown this with a clever experimental tool called a "reporter gene." A reporter gene is meant to produce an observable change in a cell, usually through the forced expression of a fluorescent signal. A group of researchers edited a fluorescent reporter gene into a heterochromatic region of the yeast genome. As discussed in Chapter 7, heterochromatin is an inaccessible or "closed" part of a chromosome. So, when a reporter gene is inserted into a heterochromatic region it will not be expressed and, therefore, will not glow. However, the yeast would start to glow when treated with a chemical that inhibited the deacetylation of histones. If you remember from Chapter 7, acetylation is an epigenetic mark that repels histones from each other and makes the nearby genes easier to express while deacetylation does the opposite (represses gene expression). When deacetylation was prevented in the genetically modified yeast, it stopped the constant process of inhibition. This inhibition of inhibition uninhibited the expression of the fluorescent reporter in the heterochromatic region. To put this much more simply: when they applied an epigenetic chemical, the yeast started to glow. Now that's some cool science in of itself, but not the most amazing result of the experiment. Even when they washed the chemical away, the fluorescent phenotype was heritable for up to 200 generations![179] This plainly shows how experiences can be heritable even after many cellular divisions. There is no strong evidence for this kind of longevity in our human epigenetic memory, but there is also no strong evidence of its absence.

---

179 Karl Ekwall et al., "Transient Inhibition of Histone Deacetylation Alters the Structural and Functional Imprint at Fission Yeast Centromeres," *Cell* 91, no. 7 (December 1997): 1022, https://doi.org/10.1016/S0092-8674(00)80492-4.

ANCESTRAL FEARS

> "Because snakes have never posed a threat to most of us, being so
> fearful of them does not make sense. Try telling that, however, to
> people with ophidiophobia [the fear of snakes]."
>
> —LYNNE A. ISBELL, *The Fruit, the Tree, and the Serpent*

Although humans cannot consciously remember specific events from 200
generations ago, we may have a form of memory that extends hundreds of
million years into the past. The snake detection hypothesis posits that humans
have unconscious memories of snakes mediated by brain structures shared
across all primates.[180] According to this hypothesis, snakes have played a key
role in the emergence of primate vision and are therefore built directly in to
the way we perceive the world. In support of this idea, the most common
cause of human fears and phobias are spiders and snakes.[181] Fearful or aversive
memories are powerful behavioral motivators, and many non-scientific
commentators have pinned our fears to one part of the brain: the amygdala.

Many people have called the amygdala the fear center of the brain, but this
is a drastic oversimplification that assumes a great deal about the relationship
between our feelings and awareness in our behaviors. Joseph LeDoux is a
researcher who has studied the neuroscience of emotion and the amygdala for

---

180 Lynne A. Isbell, *The Snake, the Tree, and the Serpent*, (Cambridge and London:
     Harvard University Press, 2009), 5. "The fear of snakes likely has an even longer
     evolutionary history than 60 million years. I can say this because the molecular
     evidence suggests that modern placental mammals evolved around 100 million years
     ago, and, as you will see, all modern placental mammals today share a common set of
     brain structures that help them avoid objects, such as predators, that are dangerous
     to their survival."

181 Vanessa LoBue, David H Rakison, and Judy S. DeLoache, "Threat Perception
     across the Life Span: Evidence for Multiple Converging Pathways," *Current
     Directions in Psychological Science* 19, no. 6 (December 2010): 375, https://doi.
     org/10.1177/0963721410388801. "Snakes and spiders are potent symbols of evil
     and fear—from the evil serpent in the Garden of Eden to modern-day movies like
     Arachnophobia and *Snakes on a Plane*. Part of the reason that these depictions are so
     powerful is the fact that snakes and spiders are two of the most common objects of
     human fears and phobias throughout the world, even in highly industrialized countries
     in which direct contact with these animals is relatively rare. Why, then, are we so
     afraid of them?"

over forty years. He is an avid proponent of the idea that our conscious fears and the underlying neural mechanisms are not necessarily one and the same. LeDoux does not mean that the amygdala plays no role in the emotion called fear, but as he puts it, "Be suspicious of any statement that says a brain area is a center responsible for some function. The notion of functions being products of brain areas or centers is left over from the days when most evidence about brain function was based on the effects of brain lesions localized to specific areas."[182] It is also important to be suspicious because almost everything we know about the brain comes from studies of non-human animals who are unable to speak and, therefore, cannot provide information about the subjective experiences associated with said brain centers.

LeDoux stresses that the amygdala is primarily a group of brain cells tasked with threat detection. Although the neural circuitry is complex, the way this threat detection works is quite familiar from a behavioral standpoint. Humans easily create associations between two experiences, especially when one of them is aversive. In other words, if you have a friend or family member that insults you every time you see them, you may begin to feel bad when you're around them. This feeling will stick with you, even in the absence of a constant stream of insults. In neuroscientific studies, the classical example of this associative power is fear conditioning. This is an experimental model in which an animal, like a rat, is given a shock while a sound simultaneously plays through loudspeakers. Rats will learn that the sound predicts the shock after a few repetitions of this association. So even when you play the sound and *don't* shock the rat, it will freeze in anticipation of a pain that will never come. The amygdala plays a well-defined role in this specific process. It combines the sensory information of the shock felt in the skin with the sensory information of the sound heard through the ears.[183] This is called "Pavlovian conditioning"—and that name may ring a bell—as the most famous example is Pavlov's dogs, which were trained to salivate every time they heard a specific sound. Pavlov achieved this simple behavioral trick by

---

182 Joseph E. LeDoux, "The Amygdala is Not the Brain's Fear Center," *Psychology Today*, August 10, 2015, https://www.psychologytoday.com/us/blog/i-got-mind-tell-you/201508/the-amygdala-is-not-the-brains-fear-center/.

183 Joseph E. LeDoux, "The Amygdala," *Current Biology* 17, no. 20 (October 2007): R871, https://doi.org/10.1016/j.cub.2007.08.005.

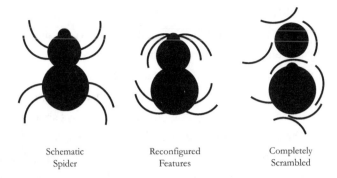

Schematic   Reconfigured   Completely
Spider   Features   Scrambled

FIGURE 8.2 Infants will pay more attention to a schematic drawing of a spider than they will to similar images in which the pieces are either reconfigured or completely scrambled.

ringing a bell whenever he fed the dogs. After a while, the dogs associated the bell with mealtime even when there was no food around.

Humans are not born with fears of snakes and spiders, but we may be primed to learn these fears more quickly than other associations. When adults, children, or even monkeys are trained to react in a specific way to a series of photographs they all respond more quickly to snakes and spiders than they do to innocuous stimuli, like flowers, frogs, or even things that look like snakes (e.g., caterpillars). It doesn't matter if there is no conscious fear of these threats, primates still react more quickly to a snake than to a rabbit.[184] Even five-month-old infants spend more time examining a schematic drawing of a spider than similarly configured images[185] (see figure 8.2). How can such young infants have a "perceptual template" of a threat that they have likely never seen before? Using fear conditioning in rats, scientists are beginning to show that enhanced reactions to threatening stimuli are likely a result of epigenetic heritability—quite literally an inherited (but unconscious) memory of your ancestor's experiences with snakes and spiders.

Kerry Ressler is a scientist who, according to the website *Grantome*, has received nearly 20 *million* dollars in grant funding to perform his research in the combined fields of epigenetic inheritance, stress, and trauma (as of

184 LoBue, "Threat Perception Across the Life Span," 376–77.

185 David H. Rakison, and Jaime Derringer, "Do Infants Possess an Evolved Spider-Detection Mechanism?" *Cognition* 107, no. 1 (April 2008): 381–93, https://doi.org/10.1016/j.cognition.2007.07.022.

September 20, 2018). In an elegant experiment, Ressler induced olfactory fear conditioning in rats, which is a version of Pavlovian conditioning that pairs a smell with an aversive stimulus—in this case, a shock. His results are astounding: when a male rat was fear conditioned with a smell, its children, grandchildren, and great-grandchildren became more sensitive to that specific odor. This means that the offspring could more easily detect small amounts of that smell and showed a more intense reaction when that odor was associated with an aversive stimulus.[186] These results mirror the enhanced sensitivity that human infants display in response to snakes and spiders. Ressler's experiment is especially powerful because he showed changes in the specific neuroanatomical pathways associated with the odor in question. He also ran a version of his experiment using in vitro fertilization to show that these changes in behavior and brain physiology were not the result of parental care (see Chapter 9). This transgenerational inheritance of a specific experience provides strong evidence for heritable "perceptual templates" and epigenetic memories.

STRESS AND TRAUMA

Pavlovian conditioning relies on the amygdala to associate a threatening stimulus or experience with a non-threatening one. For a conceptual grouping to occur, however, the two events need to happen without a time lag in between them. For example, if you hear a car horn when you wake up and then two hours later you get hit by a car, the amygdala is not capable of linking the car horn with the accident. But the amygdala is just a small piece of our three-pound human brains.

A much bigger part of our brains is a large grouping of neurons called the prefrontal cortex (PFC), which is often described as the region that makes us uniquely human (though many other animals share this brain region, albeit in much less developed forms). The PFC links events that are separated by

---

186 Brian G. Dias, and Kerry J. Ressler, "Parental Olfactory Experience Influences Behavior and Neural Structure in Subsequent Generations," *Nature Neuroscience* 17, no. 1 (December 2013): 89–96, https://doi.org/10.1038/nn.3594.

timespans too long to be associated by the amygdala. It may do this with a mental representation of an event or object that can then be used as a reminder to the amygdala,[187] a kind of "instant replay." This ability to keep track of recent sensations, experiences, and thoughts is called working memory. You have undoubtedly experienced this amazing power of the PFC firsthand, as there is no way you could read this book without working memory—it links the words you're reading now to the words you read a minute ago. The PFC is thought to be distinctly human because it allows us to create and remember symbols that are stable representations of concepts, sensations, events, objects, etc. For instance, symbols (like words) can represent basically anything! This is because the PFC not only links things through time, it creates connections in conceptual space. In other words, two seemingly disconnected things, like an apple and an orange, can be associated through conceptual groupings (i.e., round, sweet, grows on trees, etc.) by the PFC and related brain regions.

While the PFC is an amazing and powerful evolutionary tool (and, naturally, a powerful tool for day-to-day life), this neural circuitry can easily backfire. Since it is not bound by the physical rules of space and time, the PFC can create associations that end up mentally crippling us with uncontrollable anxieties, doubts, and fears. We call such pathological overgeneralizations phobias and anxiety disorders. These mental disorders are essentially irrational and stubborn connections—objects, experiences, and sensations that are conditioned, usually by a single event, to produce a negative (and oftentimes, incapacitating) response. For example, somewhere between 10 and 30 percent of military veterans who served in wartime situations develop PTSD (post-traumatic stress disorder).[188] PTSD was considered a matter of "weakness of will" until recently, but it is now understood that violence, abuse, and natural disasters can be mentally and physically disruptive. Even just the witness of intensely adverse events can cause secondary traumatic stress, which is PTSD from indirect exposure to trauma. It is also now apparent that many

187 Marieke R. Gilmartin et al., "Prefrontal Activity Links Nonoverlapping Events in Memory," *Journal of Neuroscience* 33, no. 26 (June 2013): 10913, https://doi.org/10.1523/JNEUROSCI.0144-13.2013.

188 Jamie L. Gradus, "Epidemiology of PTSD," National Center for Post-Traumatic Stress Disorder, Department of Veterans Affairs, last modified March 30, 2017, https://www.ptsd.va.gov/professional/PTSD-overview/epidemiological-facts-ptsd.asp/.

of the leading causes of death in adults can be traced back in some way to childhood trauma,[189] in what is being called "the hidden epidemic."[190] Perhaps it is an epidemic because traumatized people are prone to perpetuate more violence and abuse: "trauma breeds further trauma: hurt people hurt other people."[191] The language in this quote suggests that mental states can "breed" memetically (see Chapter 6) and the idea that behavioral states are heritable will be revisited in Chapter 10.

In addition to the interpersonal aspects, trauma and exposure to trauma appear to be epigenetically heritable. It has been known for some time that PTSD has a genetic component.[192] PTSD is the result of severe stress, but not everyone who experiences severe stress ends up with inescapable flashbacks of their traumatic experiences. This is a concept known as *resilience*—the idea that some people are more prepared to handle severe, unpredictable stress. Similarly, we all face general stressors, but some of us seem to be more resilient to the pressures of daily life.

When we undergo stressful conditions, a part of the brain releases a hormone called cortisol. Cortisol then activates a protein receptor found all over the body called the *glucocorticoid receptor*, or GR for short. Cortisol and the GR rapidly prepare our bodies to operate in the face of stress, but too much cortisol release or over-expression of the GR can lead to serious problems. It does not seem like there is a direct link between SNPs (see Chapter 3) in the GR gene and the prevalence of PTSD, however resilience can be explained by genetic differences in the cellular pathways related to

---

189 Vincent J. Felitti, et al., "Household Dysfunction to Many of the Leading Causes of Death in Adults: The Adverse Childhood Experiences Study," *American Journal of Preventive Medicine* 14, no. 4 (May 1998): 245–58.

190 Ruth A. Lanius, Eric Vermetten, and Clare Pain, *The Impact of Early Life Trauma on Health and Disease: The Hidden Epidemic* (Cambridge: Cambridge University Press, 2010), title.

191 Bessel A. Van der Kolk, *The Body Keeps the Score: Brain, Mind, and Body in the Healing of Trauma* (New York: The Penguin Group, 2014), 348.

192 Michael J. Lyons, et al., "Do Genes Influence Exposure to Trauma? A Twin Study of Combat," *American Journal of Medical Genetics* 48, no. 1 (May 1993): 22–27, https://doi.org/10.1002/ajmg.1320480107.

cortisol-GR signaling.[193] In addition, studies of holocaust victims and their children and grandchildren have not only provided evidence that epigenetic regulation of the GR contributes to resilience, but that traumatic memories themselves are heritable.[194]

Some descendants of holocaust survivors even seem "as if they have actually inherited the unconscious minds of their parents,"[195] because they suffer from the same anxiety, depression, and nightmares about the holocaust. Similarly, male survivors of a Dutch famine in the mid-1940s tended to have obese children more frequently than those who were not affected by the food shortage.[196]

While the hereditary trauma associated with the holocaust seems to extend for several generations, the obesity that resulted from the Dutch famine was only detectable in the children, and not the grandchildren, of famine survivors. As compared to evolution in the gene-centric view, this is a very important aspect of epigenetics—epigenetic changes, unlike mutations, are readily reversible. Keep this in mind as you read through the next chapter, because we will be diving into the relationship between epigenetics, illness, and disease. Things may get bleak until Chapter 10.

193 Ivone Castro-Vale et al., "Genetics of Glucocorticoid Regulation and Posttraumatic Stress Disorder—What Do We Know?" *Neuroscience and Biobehavioral Reviews* 63, (April 2016): 143–157, https://doi.org/10.1016/j.neubiorev.2016.02.005

194 Rachel Yehuda et al., "Influences of Maternal and Paternal PTSD on Epigenetic Regulation of the Glucocorticoid Receptor Gene in Holocaust Survivor Offspring," *American Journal of Psychiatry* 171, no. 8 (August 2014): 878–79, https://doi.org/10.1176/appi.ajp.2014.13121571.

195 Natan P.F. Kellermann, "Epigenetic Transmission of Holocaust Trauma: Can Nightmares Be Inherited?" *Israel Journal of Psychiatry and Related Sciences* 50, no. 1 (January 2013): 33.

196 Marjolein Veenendaal, "The Fetal Origins of Adult Disease, the Evidence and Mechanisms" (PhD diss., University of Amsterdam, 2012), 95–102.

CHAPTER 9

The Sickness Within Us

This chapter explores the epigenetic relationship between physical and mental health. The heritability of trauma and stress discussed in the last chapter seems to lead to a vicious, intergenerational feedback loop. The stresses that your ancestors endured can cause stresses in your body, which can lead to physiological changes and disorders. For example, PTSD causes changes in the expression of the GR and cortisol, which can lead to heritable decreases in stress resilience. Similarly, addiction has a strong epigenetic component, which leads to extremely high rates of heritable addictive behavior, even though there is no underlying genetic predisposition for these behaviors. Since mental and physical health are intrinsically linked by epigenetically heritable disorders, we must rethink the current definition of sickness. Diseases are often thought to arise from pathogenic invaders, like bacteria, parasites, or viruses. However, our bodies are crawling with microorganismal critters that don't always cause us harm. It makes more sense to think of diseases as imbalances in homeostatic processes—literally disorders. This means that health and healing are nothing more than restoring balance in disrupted biological processes. Trying to fight off invaders rather than restore balance can lead to even more stress and imbalance. To truly find balance, it is vital to have a clear sense of self—after all, how can invaders be recognized if there are no clear boundaries of what is being invaded? This concept leads us directly to the connection between epigenetics, heritability, and identity.

MENTAL HEALTH

Heritable epigenetic memories based on experience can be difficult for some members of the scientific community to accept. For example, David Haig has written extensively about epigenetics to express his resistance to the idea. In his words, "long-term evolutionary information has accumulated largely, if not entirely, through changes in the DNA sequence, rather than in its epigenetic modifications...the level of achievable adaptive precision is limited by the fidelity of replication."[197] When Haig says "the fidelity of replication," he means the ability to faithfully recreate aspects of your being into your offspring. This is like the difference between a written and spoken game of telephone—errors are less likely when copying a written text rather than a spoken phrase or story.

It was mentioned in the last chapter that heredity is a necessary aspect of natural selection. On the other hand, inheritance that is too faithful will stop evolution and natural selection entirely. If a replicator replicates with too much accuracy, its ancestors will never change, since every generation of offspring will be exactly the same as the original replicator. When Haig says "the level of achievable adaptive precision," he means that epigenetic inheritance is not specific enough to convey anything useful for the survival of an organism. But, as the examples in the last chapter show, humans seem to inherit the mental dispositions of our recent descendants who experienced a severely traumatic event like a famine,[198] the holocaust,[199] or World War II[200]—these examples are pretty specific. In addition, humans and animals maintain inherent knowledge of the specific threats posed to their ancestors, like snakes, spiders, or scents. Haig essentially denies the utility of heritable epigenetic information because genetics has a larger impact on evolution. Genetics certainly play an irreplaceable role in all these examples, but

---

197 Haig, "Epigenetics and the Lamarckian Temptation," 421.

198 Veenendaal, "Origins of Adult Disease," 95–102.

199 Kellermann, "Epigenetic Transmission of Holocaust Trauma," 33.

200 Torsten Santavirta, Nina Santavirta, and Stephen E. Gilman, "Association of the World War II Finnish Evacuation of Children with Psychiatric Hospitalization in the next Generation," *JAMA Psychiatry* 75, no. 1 (November 2017): 21–27, https://doi.org/10.1001/jamapsychiatry.2017.3511.

epigenetic mechanisms are equally necessary to integrate experience and the environment into the longer-term storage of DNA sequences. Haig's argument that epigenetics in evolution plays a limited role is somewhat like the denial of macro-evolution—the denial that many small, imprecise changes lead to big, directed changes.

There is a parallel between this logic and the way society treats mental health. Many bureaucrats, and even some doctors, seem to deny the direct and powerful effects that mental health can have on physical health. It may seem obvious that physical health came before mental health—that the body came before the mind—because humans so clearly feel like our consciousness sits at the pinnacle of evolution and being. Also, no one remembers their own fetal development, so surely the body came first, right? Similarly, scientists have argued that epigenetics could not possibly have come before genetics, because how could there be evolution and replication without the high fidelity of DNA?[201]

But as was discussed in Chapter 3, genetics was not an essential element of the original replicators. As you progress through these final chapters, it will hopefully start to make sense that the "physical" may not have come before the "mental" in the history of evolution. The ease with which memes and viruses move from body to body hints at the idea that a constant physical form may not be a necessary aspect of natural selection. Either way, it seems impossible to disentwine RNA from DNA from proteins. In this same way, mental health is hard to distinguish from physical health. Despite this, it seems impossible to avoid the conceptual separation between "mental" and "physical" health disorders.

---

201 Ptashne, "Epigenetics: Core Misconcept," 7102. "[Chromatin and the chromatin modifying] enzymes that impose such modifications lack the essential specificity: All nucleosomes, for example, 'look alike,' and so these enzymes would have no way, on their own, of specifying which genes to regulate under any given set of conditions. I ignore DNA methylation in the remainder of this article because its possible role in development remains unclear, and it does not exist in, for example, flies and worms—model organisms the study of which has taught us much of what we know about development." We have already seen that methylation does indeed exist in worms, and, as is shown in [Frank Lyko, Bernard H. Ramsahoye, and Rudolf Jaenisch, "Development: DNA methylation in Drosophila melanogaster," *Nature* 408, no. 6812 (November 2000): 538–40, http://doi.org/10.1038/35046205], the same is true of flies.

The U.S. Department of Veterans Affairs website is but one example; as of September 25, 2018, it has the disorders associated with PTSD split into the following groups: "neurocognitive problems," "other issues," "substance use disorders," and "physical health conditions." These arbitrary divisions show how disconnected our brain is considered to be from our bodies, because "neurocognitive problems" *are* physical health conditions. In the same vein, the "other issues" category on the Veterans Affairs website includes such things as anger, aggression, and grief—these "other issues" are essentially feelings,[202] which are well established as effectors of physical health.[203]

PTSD offers a good case study of the relationship between emotional and physical wellbeing. Simply witnessing an extreme event can lead to severe stress, which has been linked to decreased longevity and earlier onset of age-related diseases.[204] This correlation between perception, stress, and disease states is just one instance of how feelings can lead directly to physical maladies, and new research is uncovering the biological mechanisms that link mental and physical disorders. An example that was already discussed in Chapter 8 is the GR—the receptor for the stress hormone cortisol. The GR has been repeatedly implicated in childhood abuse[205] and a variety of mental health conditions, including ADHD, memory impairment, anxiety, and depression.[206] It is a good thing that the GR plays a particularly important role in PTSD and stress

---

202 See "Consciousness" in Chapter 11 for more on the concept of feelings, like how it differs from emotions and the role it plays in conscious awareness.

203 "Is Broken Heart Syndrome Real?" American Heart Association, accessed September 25, 2018, http://www.heart.org/HEARTORG/Conditions/More/Cardiomyopathy/Is-Broken-Heart-Syndrome-Real_UCM_448547_Article.jsp/.

204 Anthony S. Zannas et al., "Correction: Lifetime Stress Accelerates Epigenetic Aging in an Urban, African American Cohort: Relevance of Glucocorticoid Signaling," *Genome Biology* 16, 1 (December 2015): 266, https://doi.org/10.1186/S13059-015-0828-5; Elissa S. Epel et al., "Accelerated Telomere Shortening in Response to Life Stress," *Proceedings of the National Academy of Sciences* 101, no. 49 (September 2004): 17312, https://doi.org/10.1073/pnas.0407162101.

205 Patrick O. McGowan et al., "Epigenetic Regulation of the Glucocorticoid Receptor in Human Brain Associates with Childhood Abuse," *Nature Neuroscience* 12, no. 3 (February 2009): 342–48, https://doi.org/10.1038/nn.2270.

206 Olena Babenko, Igor Kovalchuk, and Gerlinde A. S. Metz, "Stress-Induced Perinatal and Transgenerational Epigenetic Programming of Brain Development and Mental Health," *Neuroscience and Biobehavioral Reviews* 48: 76, 80–81, 83, https://doi.org/10.1016/j.neubiorev.2014.11.013.

resilience, because having a discernible physical mechanism underlying these mental issues is helping researchers and physicians to see the link between brain chemistry, bodily function, and mental health. In addition, the GR has been shown to be epigenetically and heritably regulated[207] by methylation and RNAi activity[208] (epigenetic mechanisms that were discussed in Chapter 7).

PTSD is not the only psychiatric disorder proposed to have a basis in epigenetic inheritance.[209] A majority of PTSD sufferers also have addiction problems,[210] which has a strong heritable component as well; a family history of substance abuse makes you eight times more likely to be an addict yourself.[211] Addiction has even been described as a complex form of PTSD,[212] which strongly suggests a vicious intergenerational cycle of stress, trauma, PTSD, and addiction.

---

207 A fascinating example of this in birds is discussed in Chapter 11, in which the experience of a stressor (specifically, mites in their nest) causes a change in GR expression which leads to altered phenotypes in the offspring (increased height). In this example, it is the *subjective experience* of stress, rather than any objective stressor, that causes the change in future generations.

208 Babenko, "Transgenerational Epigenetic Programming," 76, 78, 80.

209 It has even been suggested that epigenetic inheritance plays a defining role in *all* psychiatric disorders. Take, for example, this quote from [Miklos Toth, "Mechanisms of Non-Genetic Inheritance and Psychiatric Disorders," *Neuropsychopharmacology* 40, no. 1 (2015): 137, https://doi.org/10.1038/npp.2014.127]: "It is expected that both non-gametic and gametic non-genetic inheritance contribute to the high incidence of psychiatric disorders. Therefore, one may also expect that the two forms of non-genetic inheritance carry symptom-specific information simultaneously that, together with genetic traits, will explain the complex and variable phenotypes of psychiatric disorders."

210 Sherry H. Stewart et al., "Functional Associations Among Trauma, PTSD, and Substance-Related Disorders," *Addictive Behaviors* 23, no. 6 (December 1998): 797–799, https://doi.org/10.1016/S0306-4603(98)00070-7.

211 Kathleen R. Merikangas et al., "Familial Transmission of Substance Use Disorders," *Archives of General Psychiatry* 55 (1998): 977.

212 Claudia J. Dewane, "The Legacy of Addictions: A Form of Complex PTSD?" *Social Work Today* 10, no. 6 (December 2010): 16.

ADDICTION

> "Consigning users to a penal system that combines a plentiful supply
> of drugs and the incentive to use them is not a convincing prescription
> for amelioration."[213]

Every year the U.S. spends over $600 billion for the costs of drug abuse as it relates to productivity and crime, according to the National Institute of Health's website on September 25, 2018. Now more than ever, it is clear that incarceration inevitably compounds the stressors that lead to addiction and relapse.[214] Yet, addiction continues to be treated as a crime rather than a mental/physical disorder, despite the staggering expense of imprisonment and all the available evidence.

Research has shown that addictive drugs have an immense amount of power over conscious human behavior. Drug addiction hijacks the neural circuitry that controls habits,[215] which are a kind of automatic behavior that everyone has experienced in day to day life. For example, there are many things that you likely do without thinking at all, like brushing your teeth, fidgeting when you are nervous or bored, or thinking about other things as you drive down the freeway. At the start of an addiction, an individual willingly takes drugs because they feel good when they use the addictive substance. But eventually this behavior becomes so ingrained that it evolves into a habit; the PFC (prefrontal cortex) no longer processes information as it relates to the drug. Instead, older structures that lie deeper in the brain begin to control behavior associated with the drug, which starts the habitual cycle of addiction. Addiction has even been described as a compulsion, or something that is extremely difficult to stop doing, like the compulsive behaviors of OCD

---

213 Thomas Lewis, Fari Amini, and Richard Lannon, *A General Theory of Love* (New York: Knopf Doubleday Publishing, 2000), 213.

214 Dane O'Leary, "Why Imprisonment Is More Harm Than Help to Addicted Offenders," Skywood Recovery, accessed September 25, 2018, https://skywoodrecovery.com/why-imprisonment-is-more-harm-than-help-to-addicted-offenders/.

215 Barry J. Everitt, and Trevor W. Robbins. "Neural Systems of Reinforcement for Drug Addiction: From Actions to Habits to Compulsion," *Nature Neuroscience* 8, no. 11 (November 2005): 1485, https://doi.org/10.1038/nn1579.

(obsessive compulsive disorder) sufferers.

Drug addiction is a serious problem in the U.S. that is steadily getting worse (see figure 9.1). A large part of this trend is the especially problematic opioid epidemic, which accounted for nearly 70% of drug-related overdose deaths in 2017, according to the National Institute of Health's website on September 25, 2018. Opioids are extremely strong anti-nociceptive agents, which means that they block pain. But opioids also produce many other effects when ingested, like euphoria, extreme dependence, and death.[216]

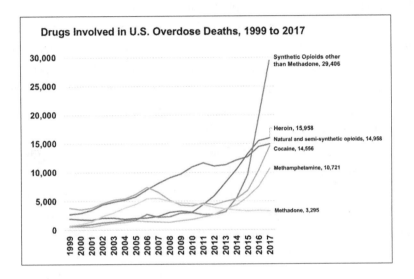

Drugs Involved in U.S. Overdose Deaths, 1999 to 2017

FIGURE 9.1 A graph of overdose deaths over time. Deaths from synthetic opioids like fentanyl have skyrocketed since 2013.

Opium is the most organic form of an opioid, a drug humans have harvested from poppy plants for at least 6,000 years, as is evidenced by ancient burial sites that contain large amounts of poppy seed capsules.[217] There are also very old conceptual associations between poppies and a dreamless, death-like slumber. For example, the Latin name for poppies is *Papaver somniferum*,

---

216 Ramsin Benyamin et al., "Opioid Complications and Side Effects," *Pain Physician* 11 (2008): S106, https://doi.org/11:S105-S120.

217 Suzanne Carr, "Exquisitely Simple or Incredibly Complex: The Theory of Entoptic Phenomena," (MA diss., University of Newcastle upon Tyne, 1995), chapter 4, http://www.oubliette.org.uk/.

which literally means the "sleep-inducing" or "hypnotic" poppy. Opioids are evidence that plants are powerful determinants of human behavior—the synthetic opioids running rampant today (like heroin and fentanyl) are mind-blowingly addictive and deadly. Although organic opioids never caused such widespread problems, naturally occurring opioids of the poppy plant (like morphine and codeine) are also quite strong and addictive.

Morphine is so powerful that a single, ten-day exposure to the drug in adolescent rats causes changes in the behavior of their future offspring[218]—a disturbing, but interesting example of intergenerational epigenetic memory. Consider that this experimental model is intended to simulate the use of morphine for short-term injury, and more habitual use (as with addiction or dependency) would likely lead to even greater changes. These experiments have found that just a single exposure to morphine can enhance the rewarding properties of the drug in the next generation and may make subsequent offspring more aggressive.[219]

Opioids are going through an unfortunate revival of popularity, which is causing a public outcry. Fortunately, this is leading to more research funding. Cigarette smoking in the U.S. recently caused a very similar negative feedback loop of popularity, outcry, and evidence of harm (see figure 9.2). Even despite the clear risks of smoking, as of September 25, 2018, the Center for Disease Control and Prevention's website stated that 15% of adults in the U.S. still smoked in 2016. Although the percentage of smokers has dropped precipitously over the last several decades, a new trend has emerged known as vaping, in which users inhale a vapor produced from a liquid nicotine solution. The nicotine solution is often heated with an electronic battery, which is why these vaporizers are often called e-cigarettes. There are many claims that e-cigarettes are safer than regular cigarettes, which is likely true. However, vaping is being shown to have its own risks, such as a correlation

---

218 Fair M. Vassoler, Siobhan J. Wright, and Elizabeth M. Byrnes, "Exposure to Opiates in Female Adolescents Alters Mu Opiate Receptor Expression and Increases the Rewarding Effects of Morphine in Future Offspring," *Neuropharmacology* 103 (April 2016): 112, https://doi.org 10.1016/j.neuropharm.2015.11.026.

219 Nicole L. Johnson et al., "Adolescent Opiate Exposure in the Female Rat Induces Subtle Alterations in Maternal Care and Transgenerational Effects on Play Behavior," *Frontiers in Psychiatry* 2 (June 2011): 7, https://doi.org/10.3389/fpsyt.2011.00029.

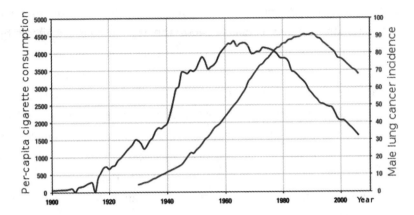

FIGURE 9.2 U.S. cigarette consumption and male lung cancer rates graphed on the same plot (cigarette consumption is measured by the line that starts in 1900, while lung cancer rates are measured by the line that starts in 1930). The rates of smoking rise and then fall, and the rates of lung cancer mimic this pattern ~20 years later.

between e-cigarette use and asthma.[220] Research has also demonstrated in rats and mice that *in utero* exposure to nicotine can cause asthma-like symptoms and an ADHD-like phenotype.[221] In the theme of epigenetic inheritance, these changes are heritable for up to three generations.[222] The multi-generational effect of nicotine is further supported by studies in worms, which have shown alterations of specific RNAi systems in their children, grandchildren, and great-grandchildren.[223] It is tempting to suggest that the ever-increasing rates of ADHD and asthma are transgenerational effects from the high rates of

---

220 Jun Ho Cho, and Samuel Y. Paik, "Association between Electronic Cigarette Use and Asthma among High School Students in South Korea," *PLoS ONE* 11, no. 3 (March 2016): 1–13, https://doi.org/10.1371/journal.pone.0151022.

221 Virender K. Rehan et al., "Perinatal Nicotine-Induced Transgenerational Asthma," *American Journal of Physiology Lung Cellular and Molecular Physiology* 305, no. 7 (October 2013): L501–7, https://doi.org/10.1152/ajplung.00078.2013; Jinmin Zhu et al., "Transgenerational Transmission of Hyperactivity in a Mouse Model of ADHD," *Journal of Neuroscience* 34, no. 8 (February 2014): 2768–73, https://doi.org/10.1523/JNEUROSCI.4402-13.2014.

222 *Ibid.*

223 Faten A. Taki et al., "Nicotine Exposure and Transgenerational Impact: A Prospective Study on Small Regulatory MicroRNAs," *Scientific Reports* 4, no. 2713 (December 2014): 13, https://doi.org/10.1038/srep07513.

smoking in the 50s, 60s, and 70s. Young adults in the height of the smoking craze would have had approximately two to three generations of children by now—a timeframe perfectly aligned with the epigenetic evidence described above. It has been suggested that asthma rates have risen too quickly in the last several decades to be explained by evolution through genetic mutation alone.[224]

Many people also claim that the so-called psychedelic drugs induce transgenerational effects. Ayahuasca, a Native American ritual plant medicine, is said to unlock memories from long-dead ancestors.[225] Unfortunately, peer-reviewed research into these topics is scarce thanks to the continuing war on drugs—because of the legal persecution of these plant-based substances, it is very hard to get federally funded grants to study them, let alone access to them for research purposes. As epigenetics becomes more accepted and popular, the effects and utility of psychedelic compounds will become clearer. When the medicinal mechanism of drugs like LSD, psilocybin, marijuana, DMT, etc. can be easily explained, research on their transgenerational effects will hopefully become easier to conduct.

As this section shows, all drugs are likely to have powerful intergenerational effects that can be explained by epigenetic mechanisms. It does not seem unreasonable to suggest that humans alive today can feel these effects within ourselves and our society. Humans have had relationships with these compounds (and with the plants that produce them) for even longer than we have had written records of our existence.[226] From the brief examples described above, it is clear that opioids and nicotine can have effects on the behavior and biology of both the users, their future offspring, and even their grandchildren and great-grandchildren. Similarly, drugs like cocaine have been shown to produce a kind of tolerance in the offspring of male rats through alteration of PFC function and gene expression.[227]

224 Eleanor Bull, ed., *A Simple Guide to Asthma* (Oxfordshire: CSF Medical Communications Ltd., 2005), 23.

225 Rachel Harris, *Listening to Ayahuasca: New Hope for Depression, Addiction, PTSD, and Anxiety* (Novato, CA: New World Library, 2017), 232.

226 Carr, "Entoptic Phenomena," Chapter 4.

227 Fair M. Vassoler et al.,"Epigenetic Inheritance of a Cocaine-Resistance Phenotype," *Nature Neuroscience* 16, no. 1 (January 2013): 42–47, https://doi.org/10.1038/nn.3280.

These results suggest that at some point in the near future, an "epigenotype" of addiction could be created, much like there is an "epigenotype" for certain kinds of malignant breast cancer.[228] This epigenetic version of a genotype—the genetic makeup of an organism—could act as a marker of predisposition to drug abuse, the success of therapeutic intervention, and the risk of addiction in future generations. It is a scary thought that chemical biomarkers in our bodies can predict not only our behavioral tendencies, but the behavioral tendencies of our children. This leads directly to a debate about free will, which will be touched on in Chapter 12. Let's build to this idea by examining the influence that epigenetics can have on our concept of physical sickness.

Is Illness an Invasion?

"Healing is balance, and balance is about self-reflection."

—KATHLEEN HARRISON, ethnobotanist

Illnesses, or pathologies, are often described as the effect of a *pathogen*: a bacterium, fungus, virus, prion, etc. that infects you and causes a war in which your body fights off the illness as if it were an invading army. Mental health and addiction are conceptually separated from "physical" sickness in the sense that their causes aren't usually described as pathogens or bodily invaders.

But in a very real sense, drug addiction is the invasion of the body by a foreign substance that is almost always produced by, or derived from, plant material. Opium, marijuana, and nicotine are just a few examples of plant-based drugs that have powerful effects on our behavior and ultimately the behavior of our offspring. Similarly, the most popular drug, alcohol, is produced by fermented plants. This is a very interesting instance of biological "coordination," in which the digestion of plant material by microorganisms results in an intoxicating and powerful substance. Neither the plants nor the microorganisms may have intended it, but it is nonetheless an example of the

228 J. Keith Killian et al., "A Methyl-Deviator Epigenotype of Estrogen Receptor-Positive Breast Carcinoma Is Associated with Malignant Biology," *American Journal of Pathology* 179, no. 1 (July 2011): 55. https://doi.org/10.1016/j.ajpath.2011.03.022.

cooperative manipulation of human behavior. Fermented beverages are just one of the startling and underappreciated ways that microorganisms effect human physiology, thoughts, and feelings.

While addiction can be framed as an invasion of the body by plant-derived chemicals, some mental health disorders can be linked to an invasion of pathogens. A common example of this is the cat-derived parasite, *Toxoplasma gondii*, which may exert a potent influence over human cognition. As of September 20, 2018, the Centers for Disease Control and Prevention's website stated that this microorganism affects approximately 10% of the U.S. population, but in hotter, more humid countries the prevalence of infection can be as high as 95%. Many studies have found links between *Toxoplasma* infections and mental health issues, like bipolar disorder,[229] depression,[230] self-harm, and suicide.[231] These results are controversial, since some larger studies have not found any connections between *Toxoplasma gondii* and depression.[232]

Despite the negative results in this instance, it is generally accepted that microorganisms like bacteria are a commanding presence in the human body. As discussed before, every human is coated with bacteria on our skin, inside our bodies, and even within every one of our cells (see mitochondria in Chapter 2). A fascinating new area of research has begun examining what is known as the "gut microbiome"—the diverse and vital world of the bacterial species that live within our stomachs and intestines. The relationship between the gut, microorganisms, and mental health is mediated by a vital chemical called serotonin.

---

229 Brad D. Pearce, Deanna Kruszon-Moran, and Jeffrey L. Jones, "The Relationship Between Toxoplasma gondii Infection and Mood Disorders in the National Health and Nutrition Survey," *Biological Psychiatry* 72, no. 4 (August 2012): 290–95, https://doi.org/10.1016/j.biopsych.2012.01.003.

230 Cosme Alvarado-Esquivel et al., "Toxoplasma Gondii Infection and Depression: A Case—Control Seroprevalence Study," *European Journal of Microbiology and Immunology* 6, no. 2 (April 2016): 85–89, https://doi.org/10.1556/1886.2016.00010.

231 Marianne G. Pedersen et al., "*Toxoplasma Gondii* Infection and Self-Directed Violence in Mothers," *Archives of General Psychiatry* 69, no. 11 (July 2012): 1123–30, https://doi.org/10.1001/archgenpsychiatry.2012.668.

232 Karen Sugden et al., "Is *Toxoplasma Gondii* Infection Related to Brain and Behavior Impairments in Humans? Evidence from a Population-Representative Birth Cohort," *PLoS ONE* 11, no. 2 (February 2016): 1–14, https://doi.org/10.1371/journal.pone.0148435.

Serotonin is a very important, ancient, and evolutionarily conserved neurotransmitter that has been implicated in a wide range of diseases—from depression and anxiety[233] to cardiovascular health.[234] Every psychedelic drug and most antidepressants target the body's serotonergic system in some way or another. This system is strongly linked to the production of energy from the sun and it plays a major role in circadian physiology[235] (see Chapter 5). One way that serotonin is connected to circadian rhythms is through its natural derivative, melatonin—a chemical that is shared across all animal lineages and controls the sleep-wake cycle of every vertebrate.[236]

As it so happens, 95% of the serotonin in our bodies is produced in our gut[237]—a process that is modulated in part by bacteria.[238] This suggests that the microbiome plays a central role in both mental and physical health. Studies have already shown that imbalances in the gut microbiome can create problems like cardiovascular disease and irritable bowel syndrome.[239] Beyond disease and dysfunction, the experience commonly described as a

233 David Baldwin, and Shauna Rudge, "The Role of Serotonin in Depression and Anxiety," *International Clinical Psychopharmacology* 9 Suppl. 4 (January 1995): 41–45, https://doi.org/10.1097/00004850-199501004-00006.

234 Bo Jian et al., "Serotonin Mechanisms in Heart Valve Disease I: Serotonin-Induced Up-Regulation of Transforming Growth Factor-Beta1 via G-Protein Signal Transduction in Aortic Valve Interstitial Cells," *The American Journal of Pathology* 161, no. 6 (January 2003): 2111–21, https://doi.org/http://dx.doi.org/10.1016/S0002-9440(10)64489-6.

235 Emily Deans, "Sunlight, Sugar, and Serotonin," *Psychology Today*, May 9, 2011, https://www.psychologytoday.com/us/blog/evolutionary-psychiatry/201105/sunlight-sugar-and-serotonin/.

236 Melatonin plays an important role in invertebrates as an antioxidant molecule. It may also regulate some rhythmic processes of invertebrates as well, like circadian swimming, as discussed in [KlaIke J. Schippers, and Scott A. Nichols, "Deep, Dark Secrets of Melatonin in Animal Evolution," *Cell* 159, no. 1 (September 2014): 9–10, https://doi.org/10.1016/j.cell.2014.09.004].

237 Doe-Young Kim, and Michael Camilleri, "Serotonin: A Mediator of the Brain-Gut Connection," *The American Journal of Gastroenterology* 95, no. 10 (October 2000): 2698, https://doi.org/10.1111/j.1572-0241.2000.03177.x.

238 Jessica M. Yano et al., "Indigenous Bacteria from the Gut Microbiota Regulate Host Serotonin Biosynthesis," *Cell* 161, no. 2 (April 2015): 264, 271, https://doi.org/10.1016/j.cell.2015.02.047.

239 Andrew B. Shreiner, John Y. Kao, and Vincent B. Young, "The Gut Microbiome in Health and in Disease," *Current Opinion in Gastroenterology* 31, no. 1 (January 2015): 70, https://doi.org/10.1097/MOG.0000000000000139.The.

"gut feeling" may be our microbiome attempting to communicate with us. Interestingly, invading bacterial pathogens can also communicate, both with our bodies and with each other, by using our own serotonin.[240]

Pathogens do not necessarily have to be physical invaders either. Addiction and mental health can be conceptualized as invasions of pathological memes. For example, alcohol consumption,[241] cigarette smoking,[242] obesity,[243] and depression[244] are literally contagious—they spread through social networks in the same way that you can infect your friends and family with the common cold.

And, while the description of addiction and mental health as "invading pathogens" makes sense, it misses the point entirely—sickness is never technically caused by invasion, but by imbalance (a concept that will be discussed in the next section). But it is easy to describe illness this way, because many symptoms of health issues are linked to the invasion of pathogens. For example, it has been suggested that infectious microorganisms can cause cancer,[245] and there are even examples of contagious cancer in other animals[246]—almost as if the cancer is *itself* the invading pathogen. However,

---

240 Leslie D. Knecht et al., "Serotonin Activates Bacterial Quorum Sensing and Enhances the Virulence of Pseudomonas Aeruginosa in the Host," *EBioMedicine* 9 (May 2016): 162, https://doi.org/10.1016/j.ebiom.2016.05.037,

241 J. Niels Rosenquist et al., "The Spread of Alcohol Consumption Behavior in a Large Social Network," *Annals of Internal Medicine* 152, no. 7 (April 2010): 430–32, https://doi.org/10.7326/0003-4819-152-7-201004060-00007.

242 David J. Blok et al., "The Role of Smoking in Social Networks on Smoking Cessation and Relapse among Adults: A Longitudinal Study," *Preventive Medicine* 99 (February 2017): 108, https://doi.org/10.1016/j.ypmed.2017.02.012.

243 Nicholas A. Christakis, and James H. Fowler, "The Spread of Obesity in a Large Social Network Over 32 Years," *New England Journal of Medicine* 357, no. 4 (July 2007): 377–78, https://doi.org/10.1056/NEJMsa066082.

244 J. Niels Rosenquist, James H. Fowler, and Nicholas A. Christakis. "Social Network Determinants of Depression," *Molecular Psychiatry* 16, no. 3 (March 2010): 279, https://doi.org/10.1038/mp.2010.13.

245 Alistair J. Lax, and Warren Thomas, "How Bacteria Could Cause Cancer: One Step at a Time," *Trends in Microbiology* 10, no. 6 (June 2002): 293–99, https://doi.org/10.1016/S0966-842X(02)02360-0.

246 Claudio Murgia et al., "Clonal Origin and Evolution of a Transmissible Cancer," *Cell* 126, no. 3 (August 2006): 477, https://doi.org/10.1016/j.cell.2006.05.051; Ruth J. Pye et al., "A Second Transmissible Cancer in Tasmanian Devils," *Proceedings of the National Academy of Sciences* 113, no. 2 (January 2016): 374, https://doi.org/10.1073/pnas.1519691113.

despite the many correlative links between pathogens and illnesses, perfectly healthy humans are constantly bombarded by things that can be considered "pathological invaders," like bacteria, fungi, and parasites. Even our very own DNA is chockfull of viral sequences and seemingly harmful, selfish genes like TEs (see transposable elements in Chapter 7). How can disease be considered an invasion when our bodies are constantly occupied by enemy forces? Indeed, human cancers are just one of many diseases that are not thought to result from pathogenic disruptions. Similarly, the diseases that occur due to a *lack* of important bacteria also cannot be explained as an "invasion of pathogens."

To make matters more complicated, everything discussed so far in this chapter, including mental health, addiction, and the spread of pathogens, is epigenetically heritable at some level. For example, there is strong evidence that cesarean delivery of a baby can cause long-term health issues for the child, because beneficial bacteria that live in the vagina need to colonize the newborn baby—a process that is disrupted by surgical delivery.[247] Consider that this transmission of the bacterial microbiome from parent to child is a means of inheritance that cannot possibly be explained by the gene-centric, Neo-Darwinian view of heritability. In a similar vein of thought, *Demodex folliculorum* is a type of microscopic mite that lives on the face of nearly every single human being.[248] It is not known if they play a role in health or physiology, or if they are simply our evolutionary co-habitants. These mites get passed down in a heritable and epigenetic fashion from generation to generation, just like the bacteria found in the gut or the vagina. *Demodex* mites peacefully colonize human faces and are generally not disruptive, except in rare cases like rosacea and other skin diseases when they may overpopulate and cause a reaction on the skin.[249]

---

247 Neu, "Cesarean Versus Vaginal Delivery," 321–31.

248 Thoemmes, "Human-Associated Demodex Mites," 5.

249 Stanisław Jarmuda et al., "Potential Role of Demodex Mites and Bacteria in the Induction of Rosacea," *Journal of Medical Microbiology* 61, part 11 (November 2012): 1507–8, https://doi.org/10.1099/jmm.0.048090-0.

HOMEOSTASIS AND IMMUNITY

> "…[L]ife requires an environment that is not at thermodynamic
> equilibrium. This statement is almost certainly true for all life,
> including artificial life…Organisms all require the disequilibrium."[250]

If sickness, illness, and disease are not inherently caused by invasive pathogens, how can human health disorders be categorized? The language used to describe disease can give us a clue, like the phrase "health dis*order*" in the last sentence. You may have seen the previous 249 instances of the morpheme (an indivisible unit of meaning in language) *organ* in this book as in *organ*ism, *organ*elle, and *organ*ic. These descriptions of healthy life as organized groupings of "stuff" are prevalent in our language and hint at a key distinction between "living" and "nonliving" matter.

You can certainly imagine real-world examples of hundreds to thousands of living organisms,[251] but despite our intuitive understanding of the concept, the precise definition of "life" is hotly contested. Although there are many ways to approach the distinction between "living" and "inanimate," this book has homed in on a very specific definition of life: a process that self-sustains and *organ*izes disorder into order. In other words, evolution by natural selection, and quite possibly life itself, only exists because of imbalance. As the quote at the beginning of this section suggests, the very process of living can be defined as the internal organization of external disequilibrium.

The way that life internally balances this energetic disequilibrium is called *homeostasis*, which is an integral part of biological organisms. All life operates through continuous, rhythmic cycles (see Chapter 3)—protein and

---

250 Benner, "Life in the Universe?" 674.

251 To take this a step further, it has been suggested that human consciousness requires other living organisms to exist at all. In other words, the very foundations of our self-aware cognition are built upon our relationship to other forms of life. [Andreas Weber, *The Biology of Wonder: Aliveness, Feeling, and the Metamorphosis of Science* (Gabriola Island, B.C.: New Society Press. 2016), 141, 188] puts it like this: "To understand ourselves, we have to recognize ourselves in other living creatures. To be mirrored is a central element in the formation of human identity… Our distinct thought categories are possible because there exists in other natural beings a form of absoluteness of what life is about, of what the existential possibilities of reality can be."

RNA synthesis and degradation; metabolic intake of food and excretion of waste; the cycles of sleep, rest, and wakefulness; birth, death, and rebirth. It is becoming a popular idea in medicine and healing that every single disease—no exceptions—is caused by a disruption of homeostasis. This means that "curing" diseases is quite literally restoring balance to one or more organismal processes. This homeostatic balancing act also occurs *between* organisms, such as in interpersonal relationships, teamwork, and competition, a concept I will return to in the next chapter. Defining disease in terms of homeostasis makes it clear why mental health, stress, and trauma are so intricately connected to "physical disease"; thoughts and feelings, like our bodies, can be organized or disorganized, balanced or imbalanced.

Going further, diseases are not just a breakdown of balance, they are a very specific lack of homeostasis—an inability to recognize and balance what constitutes our "selves." Our bodies have intricate mechanisms (like antibodies and other aspects of the immune system) that constantly determine what belongs in our body and what is defined as an invader (see Chapter 7). These mechanisms are designed to recognize and fix disruptions of homeostasis that lead to pathological imbalances. For example, everyone has mutations that could lead to cancer but not everyone has tumors—because our immune systems are exquisitely tuned to destroy cancerous cells.[252]

There are even many mental disorders, like depression, that have been described as a dysfunction of the immune system.[253] A failure of the immune system like this can be thought of as an imbalanced balancing mechanism, something analogous to getting dizzy because you've spun around too quickly. When this happens, it is because the fluid in your ears that determines your

---

252 Paul Knoepfler, "Why Literally Everyone Has Cancer and What This Means For You," *Science 2.0*, August 23, 2011, https://www.science20.com/confessions_stem_cell_scientist/why_literally_everyone_has_cancer_and_what_means_you-81937. "…[O]ur immune systems are far better at finding and destroying cancer than we ever imagined. Indeed, from this perspective cancer may frequently be an immune disorder more than anything." There is a depressing irony in the fact that the most commonly used cancer treatment—chemotherapy—is a powerful suppressant of the immune system.

253 Brian E. Leonard, "The Concept of Depression as a Dysfunction of the Immune System," *Current Immunology Reviews* 6, no. 3 (August 2010): 205–212, http://doi.org/10.2174/157339510791823835.

balance has itself lost balance (in a way, consciousness itself is a balancing mechanism meant to balance balancing mechanisms; see Chapter 11 for more on this self-referential idea).

In examining sickness and internal disorder, this chapter has been very focused on the negative aspects of epigenetic and memetic heritability of diseases, but it is not all bad—there are up sides to epigenetic and memetic inheritance. Trauma, addiction, and illness can be heritable, but the effects of these things can also be reversed by experience. For example, depression and smoking are contagious across social networks, but so are happiness[254] and the cessation of smoking.[255] Relieving stress through psychological intervention can improve survival outcomes for breast cancer patients,[256] which suggests that cancer survival is a somewhat contagious heritable trait. In addition, resilience to stress may be just as heritable as stress and trauma, a topic that the next chapter will begin to explore.

---

254 Edward M Hill, Frances E. Griffiths, and Thomas House, "Spreading of Healthy Mood in Adolescent Social Networks," *Royal Society Open Science* 4, no. 9 (August 2015): 4, https://doi.org/10.1098/rspb.2015.1180.

255 Blok, "Smoking in Social Networks," 109.

256 Barbara L. Andersen et al., "Psychologic Intervention Improves Survival for Breast Cancer Patients," *Cancer* 113, no. 12 (December 2008): 3454, https://doi.org/10.1002/cncr.23969.

CHAPTER 10

Who Are You, Really?

"Identity should not be understood as solely subjective, but rather as intersubjective…
The gift, the gift of being seen, of being mirrored, is a biological necessity."

—ANDREAS WEBER, *The Biology of Wonder*

In this chapter, we will use the definition of sickness as an imbalance of "normal" bodily processes to reconsider the concept of identity. Even though we often think of illness as a bodily invasion, humans are constantly swarmed with "non-human" microorganisms. We even have a type of bacteria, mitochondria, in nearly every one of our "human" cells. In addition, viruses and transposable elements (TEs) make up a massive portion of our DNA—possibly over 50%. You likely already know that family history and upbringing have powerful influences on our identities, but interpersonal interactions with non-family members also shape who we are and who we can become. Memetic heritability (the transfer of memes, or ideas, from person to person) creates an interconnected web of human consciousness, so, in a very real sense, humans cannot exist in isolation. There is no way to escape the societal and memetic bonds that keep us tethered to our consciousness and the people around us—our identity as individuals is a total illusion. You do not exist as an entity separated from your surroundings or the universe, as you cannot escape reality. Even if you could somehow define yourself as an individual, your body is constantly being recycled and constantly changing in response to the environment. The most personal information, like our perceptions, can be stored and transmitted to future generations through epigenetic mechanisms. If our conscious perceptions are heritable, then our identities are heritable as well. If our identities don't end with our bodies, our conscious existence needs to be reconsidered in light of epigenetics and evolution.

FAMILIAL IDENTITY

> "...[M]an is generated from man; and thus it is the possession
> of certain characters by the parent that determines the development
> of like characters in the child..."

—ARISTOTLE, *On the Parts of Animals*

The last chapter showed a somewhat bleak view of non-genetic heritability through the examples of inherited fears, stress, and social isolation. It certainly seems like we should be mired down by the addictions and traumas of our ancestors. But, as stated at the end of Chapter 8, epigenetic changes are reversible.

The love, attention, and nurturance that parents provide for their children is a perfect example of our ability to overcome our predispositions. Studies with rat pups show what may be possible in humans. For example, young rat pups have more positive behavioral outcomes later in life when their mother takes the time to groom and lick them as children.[257] These changes in behavior have been linked to epigenetic modifications, like differences in methylation and acetylation of the GR gene[258] (see Chapters 8 and 9). This leads to decreased levels of cortisol signaling and an enhanced resiliency to stress. Rat pups that are well cared for in childhood also end up becoming more attentive mothers themselves.[259] This creates a feedback loop whereby good parents are likely to lead to more good parents in future generations.

On the other hand, maternal separation and a lack of attention during development can unfortunately lead to problems, such as a lack of resilience to stress and inattentive parents in future generations.[260] Even so, these

---

257 Frances Champagne, and Michael J. Meaney, "Chapter 21 Like Mother, like Daughter: Evidence for Non-Genomic Transmission of Parental Behavior and Stress Responsivity," *Progress in Brain Research* 133 (January 2001): 287, https://doi.org/10.1016/S0079-6123(01)33022-4.

258 Ian C. G. Weaver et al., "Epigenetic Programming by Maternal Behavior," *Nature Neuroscience* 7, no. 8 (August 2004): 852, https://doi.org/10.1038/nn1276.

259 Champagne, "Like Mother, Like Daughter," 287.

260 Tamara B. Franklin et al., "Epigenetic Transmission of the Impact of Early Stress across Generations," *Biological Psychiatry* 68, no. 5 (September 2010): 408, 413, https://doi.org/10.1016/j.biopsych.2010.05.036.

negative behavioral changes can be reversed later in life through an increase in the amount of methyl precursor in the diet, since these epigenetic changes are partially mediated by methylation[261] (see Chapter 7).

Rhythmic "inheritance" is another simplistic epigenetic mechanism by which biological circumstances can be mediated. For example, the steady heartbeat of a mother provides a stable cycle for infants to synchronize their own circadian physiology (see Chapter 5). Whether a mother is left or right handed; a human, a gorilla, or a chimpanzee; she will cradle her baby in her left arm so that the head of her infant is directly positioned on her heart.[262] Infants born prematurely become much healthier with a rhythm to guide them. They will sleep and breathe better if they sleep on their mother's chest or are provided with a "breathing" teddy bear in the ICU that simulates their mother's heartbeat, they will sleep and breathe better.[263] This "rhythmic heritability" acts as a form of epigenetic inheritance that allows new organisms to easily adjust to the tempo of the novel, external environment.

Familial inheritance of this kind is one of the most powerful and important aspects of human identity. Many examples of epigenetic inheritance across generations have already been discussed, like the way that bacteria from the vaginal canal colonize a newborn baby. Similarly, it is well-established that breastfeeding transfers important antibodies to an infant epigenetically.[264] This acts as a maternally-derived immune system that protects the baby from infections and diseases until it is old enough to create its own immunity. The antibodies in breastmilk not only fight off invaders, they also control intestinal homeostasis in newborns by precisely dictating the diversity of the baby's microbiome.[265] In other words, a mother's immune system regulates

---

261 Ian C. G. Weaver et al., "Reversal of Maternal Programming of Stress Responses in Adult Offspring through Methyl Supplementation: Altering Epigenetic Marking Later in Life," *Journal of Neuroscience* 25, no. 47 (November 2005): 11052–53, https://doi.org/10.1523/JNEUROSCI.3652-05.2005.

262 Lewis, *A General Theory of Love*, 196.

263 *Ibid*, 85.

264 Eric. W. Rogier et al., "Secretory Antibodies in Breast Milk Promote Long-Term Intestinal Homeostasis by Regulating the Gut Microbiota and Host Gene Expression," *Proceedings of the National Academy of Sciences* 111, no. 8 (February 2014): 3074, https://doi.org/10.1073/pnas.1315792111.

265 *Ibid*.

the bacterial growth in the gut of her infant to influence its health. This is particularly fascinating because the gut microbiome plays an important role in all aspects of adult immune function.[266] So, in a very direct way, the bacteria in the body of a mother select the bacteria that will live in the bodies of her children.

The epigenetic inheritance of the microbiome has astounding implications. For instance, the types of bacteria that live in our guts are correlated with the expression of certain personality traits,[267] which suggests that personality itself may have epigenetically heritable components. Another fascinating example of this is flavor preference—children prefer the taste of foods that they were exposed to in the womb or through their mother's breast milk.[268] What you like to eat is dependent on what your mother ate during pregnancy and lactation, and what your mother liked to eat may have been influenced by the bacteria in her gut.[269]

These examples are very interesting, but familial heritability has been long recognized despite the newly discovered epigenetic mechanisms. It is no surprise that humans look, think, feel, and act like our parents and grandparents. The specifics of epigenetic inheritance simply extend this ancestral identity past the well-established one or two generations of inheritance and allow us to be containers to some degree for the experiences of our great-grandparents and their ancestors.

---

266 Belkaid, "Microbiota in Immunity," 121–141.

267 Han Na Kim et al., "Correlation between Gut Microbiota and Personality in Adults: A Cross-Sectional Study," *Brain, Behavior, and Immunity* 69 (March 2018): 382–83, https://doi.org/10.1016/j.bbi.2017.12.012.

268 Julie Aa Mennella, Coren P. Jagnow, and Gary K. Beauchamp, "Prenatal and Postnatal Flavor Learning by Human Infants," *Pediatrics* 107, no. 6 (June 2001): E88, https://doi.org/10.1016/j.pestbp.2011.02.012.Investigations.

269 In fact, the bacteria in your gut might be more invested in your health than you are! As it says in [Joe Alcock, Carlo C. Maley, and C. Athena Aktipis, "Is Eating Behavior Manipulated by the Gastrointestinal Microbiota? Evolutionary Pressures and Potential Mechanisms," *BioEssays* 36, no. 10 (October 2014): 941, https://doi.org/10.1002/bies.201400071], "Microbial genes outnumber human genes by 100 to 1 in the intestinal microbiome, leading some to propose that it is a 'microbial organ' that performs important functions for the host, such as nutrient harvesting and immune development...lower diversity in gut microbiome should be associated with more unhealthy eating behavior and greater obesity (i.e., decreased host fitness)..."

INTERPERSONAL IDENTITY

Epigenetic information can be heritable, not just across generations, but from person to person. For example, the Demodex mites that live on all our faces do not necessarily get transferred from parent to child; children could easily receive their lifetime supply of face mites from a non-nuclear family member, the doctor that delivered them in the hospital, or even a stranger. The bacteria in our gut microbiome are a similar story—they do not necessarily come from an immediate family member. One fascinating example of this is a medical procedure known as a fecal transplantation, in which the transplantation of feces transfers gut bacteria from one person to another. Fecal transplantation is being researched as a cure for a variety of things, including recurrent infections due to antibiotic use, inflammatory bowel disease, and obesity.[270]

The transference of behavior is another clear example of interpersonal inheritance, much as the way that addiction and emotional states can travel through social networks as contagions (see Chapter 9). Though there are constant outcries to ban violent or "inappropriate" media for fear that consumers will copy the behaviors they see in video games or movies, the process of behavioral mimicry isn't often framed in terms of heritability or memetic replication. The concept of "offspring" is strongly ingrained in our minds to mean "organismal products of sexual reproduction." But reproduction and inheritance occur at many levels—even ideas and patterns of behavior have offspring.

Human brains are exquisitely tuned to mimic and interpret the body language and behavior of other humans and animals. This capacity to imitate allows us to replicate the actions and thoughts of other people with relatively high fidelity. When you watch someone else perform an action you create a template in your mind that helps you to perform the same action. This is an example of a process by which memes and behavior literally reproduce.

Humans have a powerful system of brain cells called "mirror neurons" that process information about how the actions and emotions of other

---

270 Eric G. Pamer, "Fecal Microbiota Transplantation: Effectiveness, Complexities, and Lingering Concerns," *Mucosal Immunology* 7, no. 2 (March 2014): 212, https://doi.org/10.1038/mi.2013.117.

organisms relate to our own actions and emotions. This capacity gives humans interpersonal powers that have been referred to as "mind-reading."[271] These neurons were discovered through experiments in which monkeys performed behavioral tasks while the electrical activity of their brain cells was recorded. In a somewhat serendipitous accident, scientists discovered that the same brain cells that fired when a monkey performed an action would also fire when the monkey simply *watched an experimenter* perform that same action.[272]

Scientists have used the existence of mirror neurons to explain how humans can be empathetic, since the ability to reflect behavior allows us to simulate and understand the minds of others.[273] Even though mirror neurons respond to physical actions and cannot literally read thoughts, they do allow a deep insight into the bodily perspectives of other individuals. This is because feelings, emotions, and thoughts cause us to perform physical movements, which any casual observer can mirror and interpret. This is more obvious than it sounds—consider that smiles are contagious, and everyone smiles when they are happy. Anyone can recognize a smile as happiness and a frown as sadness, regardless of cultural background or upbringing.[274]

But there are three aspects to this that may surprise you. The first is that all humans make subtle and universal *micro-expressions* in response to our

---

271 Vittorio Gallese, and Alvin Goldman, "Mirror Neurons and the Simulation Theory of Mind-Reading," *Trends in Cognitive Sciences* 2, no. 12 (December 1998): 493–501, https://doi.org/10.1016/S1364-6613(98)01262-5.

272 Giuseppe di Pellegrino et al., "Understanding Motor Events: A Neurophysiological Study," *Experimental Brain Research* 91, no. 1 (October 1992): 176, https://doi.org/10.1007/BF00230027.

273 Marco Iacoboni, "Imitation, Empathy, and Mirror Neurons," *Annual Review of Psychology* 60, no. 1 (January 2009): 653–70, https://doi.org/10.1146/annurev.psych.60.110707.163604.

274 Charles Darwin used his theory of evolution to extend the universality of emotional expression, not just across human cultures, but to other animals as well. As he says in [Charles Darwin, *Expression of the Emotions in Man and Animals* (London: John Murray, 1872), 12], "With mankind some expressions, such as the bristling of the hair under the influence of extreme terror, or the uncovering of the teeth under that of furious rage, can hardly be understood, except on the belief that man once existed in a much lower and animal-like condition...He who admits on general grounds that the structure and habits of all animals have been gradually evolved, will look at the whole subject of Expression in a new and interesting light."

emotions that are much quicker and far less conscious than a smile or a frown.[275] The second is that humans tend to unconsciously mimic people that we like and we like people that mimic us[276] (in other words, the adage is true: imitation really is the sincerest form of flattery). Third, and finally, our facial expressions impact our feelings just as much as our feelings impact our facial expressions.[277] Taken together, these three facts logically imply that humans cannot help but mimic each other's feelings and emotions. Not only are all humans mind-readers, but at some level we simply cannot stop ourselves from intruding into the thoughts of others—personal privacy is illusory.

In this way, emotional states can replicate themselves like a meme or a virus. Interpersonal inheritance also extends to many aspects of subjective experience, like how memories are (at least in part) the result of ancestral experiences (see Chapter 8). But ancestral experiences are only one part of the story. Humans are designed to believe that our memories are factual and precise. But, in all actuality, memories are highly inaccurate and unstable. This may be discomforting, but it is a necessary element of our being. The instability of memory allows us to mold our identities and shape our personal narratives in constructive and healthy ways.[278] Similarly, the flexibility of memories allows people to interpersonally synchronize experiences and collective agreements about what happened in the past and how we will respond to the events of the future enable us to create societies.[279]

Memory is inherently social in nature, which means that people have powerful control over the memories of their fellow humans. Just like

275 "The Definitive Guide to Reading Microexpressions," Science of People, Accessed September 29, 2018, https://www.scienceofpeople.com/microexpressions/.

276 Liam C. Kavanagh, and Piotr Winkielman, "The Functionality of Spontaneous Mimicry and Its Influences on Affiliation: An Implicit Socialization Account," *Frontiers in Psychology* 7 (March 2016): 2, https://doi.org/10.3389/fpsyg.2016.00458.

277 Michael. B. Lewis, "Exploring the Positive and Negative Implications of Facial Feedback," Emotion 12, no. 4 (August 2012): 852–859, http://dx.doi.org/10.1037/a0029275.

278 Anne E. Wilson, and Michael Ross, "From Chump to Champ: People's Appraisals of Their Earlier and Present Selves," *Journal of Personality and Social Psychology* 80, no. 4 (April 2001): 573–74, https://doi.org/10.1037/0022-3514.80.4.572.

279 Adam D. Brown, Nicole Kouri, and William Hirst, "Memory's Malleability: Its Role in Shaping Collective Memory and Social Identity," *Frontiers in Psychology* 3 (July 2012): 1–3, https://doi.org/10.3389/fpsyg.2012.00257.

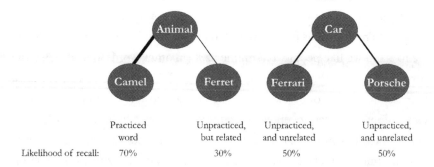

FIGURE 10.1 When you practice to remember a word (like "camel") you become less likely to remember unpracticed words that are related (like "ferret"), even though the likelihood of remembering unpracticed, unrelated words remains unchanged.

behaviors (smoking) and feelings (depression) can be transmitted from person to person, memory is contagious as well. Take for example a peculiar type of forgetting known as a "practice effect." This happens when you exert a lot of attention and effort to remember something, which causes you to forget something else. For example, when subjects are asked to focus on a specific word while they remember a list of words, they are more likely to forget words that are conceptually similar to the focus word (see figure 10.1). This practice effect can cause us to forget very specific things, and this forgetfulness can be transmitted from one person to another through conversation.[280] As of yet, no one has pinned down specific epigenetic mechanisms that explain these kinds of interpersonal connections, but a new field of science called social epigenetics has emerged to provide and test such theories.[281]

280 Alin Coman, and William Hirst, "Cognition through a Social Network: The Propagation of Induced Forgetting and Practice Effects," *Journal of Experimental Psychology: General* 141, no. 2 (September 2011): 321–36, https://doi.org/10.1037/a0025247.

281 Emma Chung et al., "Social Epigenetics: A Science of Social Science?" *The Sociological Review Monographs* 64, no. 1 (February 2017): 168–85, https://doi.org/10.1111/2059-7932.12019.

MEMETIC IDENTITY

Transgenerational heritability, the epigenetic nature of diseases, and interpersonal inheritance have powerful implications about the origins of our thoughts. The idea that our behaviors and perception are influenced by the experiences of our ancestors prompts some substantial questions about how much personal control we exert over our own behavior. Epigenetic mechanisms and the heritability of experience can call into question some key aspects of selfhood and identity. A strong recurring theme of this book is that humans are not indivisible—we are built from an unfathomable number of smaller lifeforms. Humans are also not disconnected or separated from our surroundings and other organisms. Cells, genes, DNA, RNA, and proteins are just a few of the features that humans share with every other biological life form on the planet. These connections become even more direct when heritability, epigenetics, and memetics are considered.

Memes are comparable to viruses as poorly defined units of evolving information (see Chapter 6). There is a clear parallel that is evidenced by the conception of "*viral* internet memes." Viruses have a negative connotation, but they are actually integral to our existence as a collection of microorganisms. Memes (replicating, evolving ideas like culture) *organ*ize us by providing rigid conceptual boundaries, and memetic *organ*izations like countries, local book clubs, and even terrorist groups, replicate using human brains, language, and behavior. For example, a member of the local PTA is going to have much different thoughts and actions than a member of ISIS. These extreme examples are meant to show that humans affiliate with particular groups because of how we already act, but the groups exert control over our behavior as well. Just like our cells behave based on the genes they express, humans behave based on the memes we express. The individuals within a social group are held together by memes that set "acceptable" homeostatic (see Chapter 9) limits for how to act within the group. There aren't going to be any beheadings at a PTA meeting and there won't be any discussion of how to make science education more rigorous at an ISIS meeting.

This memetic glue that holds people together is analogous to the mechanisms that prevent our individual cells from living independently of our body and our rhythms. It is possible, but unlikely, for one of our cells to exist in total isolation. When true separation occurs, most "normal" processes break down and it becomes difficult (if not impossible) to reintegrate back into the whole organism. This is true for both cells and humans. In horrible experiments in the 1950s, a doctor named Rene Spitz found that orphaned infants rapidly degenerated when deprived of emotional attention and attachment—nearly 40% of his test subjects died before they were two years old.[282] Social isolation has been repeatedly shown to be unhealthy, and even deadly, in adults as well.[283]

Memes are necessary to hold humans together as organisms within a society, through organizations like governments, schools, and social groups. But memes are not just a cultural adhesive—they have behavior and lives of their own. Memes are, by definition, subject to evolution by natural selection. Just like a living thing needs energy and shelter to sustain growth and function, ideas have survival requirements too. Memes need a physical body (like the hardware of the human brain) to replicate and survive. However, any space or process that can propagate information is a fertile breeding ground for memes. Despite the popular view of memes as purely human creations, the "physical body" of an idea does not need to be a living organism. After all, you're reading this book, which is inanimate but full of ideas.

---

282 byPepone, "Emotional Deprivation in Infancy: Study by Rene A. Spitz 1952," YouTube video, 7:18. April 22, 2010, https://www.youtube.com/watch?v=VvdOe10vrs4/.

283 Lisa F. Berkman, Linda Leo-Summers, and Ralph I. Horwitz, "Emotional Support and Survival after Myocardial Infarction: A Prospective, Population-Based Study of the Elderly," *Annals of Internal Medicine* 117, no. 12 (December 2012): 1003–9, https://doi.org/10.7326/0003-4819-117-12-1003; Eduardo A. Colón et al., "Depressed Mood and Other Variables Related to Bone Marrow Transplantation Survival in Acute Leukemia," *Psychosomatics* 32, no. 4 (November 1991): 420–425, https://doi.org/10.1016/S0033-3182(91)72045-8; Dean Ornish, *Love and Survival: The Scientific Basis for the Healing Power of Intimacy* (New York: HarperCollins Publishers, 1999), 12. "... [L]ove and intimacy are among the most powerful factors in health and illness...I am not aware of any other factor in medicine—not diet, not smoking, not exercise, not stress, not genetics, not drugs, not surgery—that has a greater impact on our quality of life, incidence of illness, and premature death from all causes."

Memes and Viruses

Many biologists consider viruses to be more like inanimate ideas than living things. Viruses are simple enough that they can be stored entirely as a piece of latent information in the "symbolic" dimension of evolution[284]—the same dimensional space that memes occupy. Symbols are marvelously abstract and somewhat independent from physical bodies, since symbolic information doesn't care where it is stored as long as it can be retrieved and replicated.

This means that symbolic information can be easily translated between systems and transported across dimensions (like from a book to your mind, or from your mind to another mind). As described in Chapter 2, the way in which bits and nucleotides store information is similar enough that genetic information can be stored in computers and vice versa. A biological virus can literally lay dormant in a word document as a string of As, Ts, Cs, and Gs, (see figure 10.2). But the virus is nothing more than an idea until it finds a host within which it can replicate itself. Despite the fervent cries of Neo-Darwinists,[285] viruses can and do exist independently of genetics, solely in the symbolic dimension of evolution. This is the equivalent of coding your entire being into a computer—you wouldn't be able to do much, but it would be a kind of survival beyond the need for your physical body.

In a sense, memetic replication and behavioral expression are comparable to the processes of transcription (DNA into RNA) and translation (RNA into protein) respectively. Memes can "transcribe" themselves into language to replicate into other brains. Every word and sentence that you've read in this book is another concept that has been replicated from my brain onto these pages, then retrieved, translated, and reproduced in yours. In this way memes can also "translate" themselves from words or thoughts into actions.

---

284 Jablonka, *Evolution in Four Dimensions*, 197–200.

285 Haig, "Epigenetics and the Lamarckian Temptation," 423. "Modern neo-Darwinists do not deny that epigenetic mechanisms play an important role during development nor do they deny that these mechanisms enable a variety of adaptive responses to the environment...However, most neo-Darwinists would claim that the ability to adaptively switch epigenetic state is a property of the DNA sequence...If I could choose, I would ban discussion of 'the inheritance of acquired characters'..."

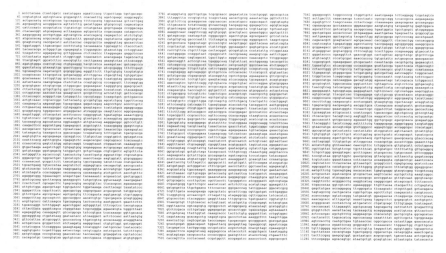

FIGURE 10.2 A complete transcript of a viral genome.

For example, you can deliberate about what to eat when you feel hungry, but eventually you will physically get yourself some food—a behavior dictated by the idea of hunger. This memetic concept of hunger can also make *other people* behave. If you transcribe your thoughts into words and simply ask someone to get you a sandwich, it is possible that your memetic transcript will be translated into a behavior that originates from *someone else's body*!

Interestingly, cells can do this too: one cell can transcribe a gene onto a piece of RNA and give it to a completely different cell through tiny, fat-based bubbles that move through cell membranes.[286] This allows cells to control each other's behavior by regulating gene expression with RNAi or by creating brand new proteins with mRNA. You can think of this in terms of creating blueprints of a shed for your neighbor—it was your idea, but it is up to them to turn the idea into something physical. Aside from RNA, there are small pieces of circular DNA called *plasmids* that can be transferred from bacteria to bacteria in a process known as *horizontal gene transfer* (HGT). This is an easy way for individual cells to share genes with each other, and it is well established that HGT plays a major role in the evolution of bacteria. For example, when one bacterium evolves an antibiotic-resistant gene, it can transcribe the gene

286 Hadi Valadi et al., "Exosome-mediated Transfer of mRNAs and microRNAs is a Novel Mechanism of Genetic Exchange Between Cells," *Nature Cell Biology* 9, no. 6 (June 2007): 654–59, http://doi.org/10.1038/ncb1596.

onto a plasmid and perform HGT to share the novel survival strategy with nearby bacteria.[287] It is called horizontal because the genes are transferred from one living individual to another, as opposed to a vertical transfer in which genes are shared from a parent to an unborn offspring. HGT is very similar to the interpersonal inheritance discussed in the last section, as it is like the bacteria have shared written instructions (a type of meme) with each other in the form of DNA.

There are endless possibilities that arise from cell-to-cell transfer of nucleotides and brain-to-brain transfer of memes. This book considers HGT and memetic replication to be types of inheritance. Even though neither process requires transfer of information from a parent to an offspring, both are technically unidirectional and create a new "generation" of the idea or genetic sequence. Ideas clearly spread back and forth in feedback loops (as in conversations) to create a continuous lineage of conceptual generations and it may soon be discovered that the same level of high-frequency feedback occurs in the transfer of DNA from cell to cell, or from species to species. Species-to-species HGT has been shown to occur from the parasite that causes Chagas disease, *T. cruzi*, to its human hosts.[288] In this instance of interspecies HGT, genes from the mitochondria of *T. cruzi* found their way into human gametes (see Chapter 4) and were then passed on to the descendants of the infected individuals.[289] Mitochondria can also use horizontal gene transfer to "talk" to their host cells[290]—a process that could be happening inside your body right now!

---

287 Christian J.H. von Wintersdorff et al., "Dissemination of Antimicrobial Resistance in Microbial Ecosystems through Horizontal Gene Transfer," *Frontiers in Microbiology* 7 (February 2016): 1–10, https://doi.org/10.3389/fmicb.2016.00173.

288 Mariana M. Hecht et al., "Inheritance of DNA Transferred from American Trypanosomes to Human Hosts," *PLoS ONE* 5, no. 2 (February 2010): E9181, https://doi.org/10.1371/journal.pone.0009181.

289 *Ibid*. The transfer of information from the mitochondria of one species through the lineage of another perfectly exemplifies why HGT is a type of inheritance. It is also a good example of why inheritance doesn't necessarily mean a transfer from parent to child, as one of the subjects of this study could literally say, "I inherited gene so-and-so from my grandmother, and she got it from a different species."

290 Julie C. Dunning Hotopp, "Horizontal Gene Transfer between Bacteria and Animals," *Trends in Genetics* 27, no. 4 (April 2011): 158, https://doi.org/10.1016/j.tig.2011.01.005.Horizontal.

There is evidence that HGT can happen from bacteria to animals as well,[291] and a fascinating example of this is the evolution of a particular kind of DNA methylation (see Chapter 7) in multicellular organisms. Most of the research on methylation in multicellular creatures has focused on the "C" (cytosine) nucleotide, while a great deal of research in bacteria and prokaryotes has focused on methylation of the "A" (adenine) nucleotide. Amazingly, many multicellular organisms have independently evolved systems to methylate their "A" nucleotides, and this has occurred through the transfer of genes from prokaryotes and viruses to multicellular organisms.[292] Although no gene transfer from bacteria to humans has been documented, the intricate connection between organisms in the web of evolution suggests that such a discovery is right around the corner. Since the human genome is filled with virus-like sequences (see Chapter 7), it seems likely that bacterial sequences are also hidden somewhere in our DNA.

THE ILLUSION OF IDENTITY

> "Metabolism means sharing one's own matter, and hence a part of one's own identity, with the world… An organism's constant intercourse with the universe builds it up through that which it is not, transforming it in the process."
>
> —ANDREAS WEBER, *The Biology of Wonder*

Humans have a strong desire to be individuals—singular units that are separate from other humans and organisms. Despite this, we are deeply connected to each other and to other organisms through a variety of mechanisms, memetic transfer and HGT being only two examples. Human identity is intricately wrapped up in memetic constructs, such as the way we were raised and the social environments in which we are inescapably embedded. Just like you

---

291 Filip Husnik, and John P. McCutcheon, "Functional Horizontal Gene Transfer from Bacteria to Eukaryotes," *Nature Reviews Microbiology* 16, no. 2 (February 2018): 67–79, https://doi.org/10.1038/nrmicro.2017.137.

292 Iyer, "Adenine Methylation in Eukaryotes," 34.

can't leave the universe, it is impossible to escape some form of social network. You could walk into the woods and live self-sustained for the rest of your life. But even if you never see your friends and loved ones again, they won't stop existing within your mind. You would also never stop existing within the minds of your friends and loved ones.

In some form, people exist in every other brain they've ever interacted with. Brains are incredible *organic* machines capable of internally representing, identifying, and responding to external (and internal) environments. Objects, organisms, and other people are a necessary part of the outer world and our brains do a marvelous job of representation when it comes to these things. This leads to a strange situation: our perceptions are simulations of an outer reality that is represented in a virtual, mental space. You can see, touch, smell, and taste an apple, but the apple itself is never really in your mind; you only ever have access to a representation of the sensations and concepts associated with the memetic construct ("apple").

In a more philosophical sense, it may not even be possible to interact with our external realities at all[293]—a "real" apple will only ever be a representative simulation, because that is simply how conscious perception seems to work. But this does not mean that you are trapped in a prison of your own mind; genes, memes, and behaviors are technically transferrable from one internal reality to another. Mammals are exquisitely tuned to simulate and represent ideas, behaviors, and other minds within our own minds. For example, you can certainly imagine the voices and faces of your relatives, loved ones, and even strangers. Beyond this, you can almost certainly imagine their plausible (but previously unobserved) behaviors and emotions, like how they would

---

293 The "Interface Theory of Perception" takes this philosophical claim to a scientific level to test whether or not evolution selects for veridical (accurate, truthful, objectively realistic) perceptions. In this theory, our conscious perception is compared to the interface of a computer, or, as it is explained in [Donald D. Hoffman, Manish Singh, and Chetan Prakash, "The Interface Theory of Perception," *Psychonomic Bulletin and Review* 22, no. 6 (December 2015): 1503]: "Knowing that the icon is in the center of the desktop does not entail that the file itself is in the center of the computer. Similarly, knowing where in space-time to rendezvous with you does not entail any knowledge of objective reality; indeed it does not even entail that space-time itself is an aspect of objective reality. An interface can be an accurate guide to behavior without being an accurate guide to the nature of objective reality."

respond and react to specific hypothetical situations (e.g., "my best friend would love this" or "I hope my mom doesn't find out").

The ability to ascribe beliefs, thoughts, and intentions to other people is referred to as *the intentional stance* by philosopher Daniel Dennett.[294] If you've ever said things like "the thermostat *wants* to keep the temperature at 70 degrees," you know it's quite easy to take the intentional stance with objects as well.[295] Human beings can take the intentional stance (see Chapter 10) for basically anything—even inanimate objects and seemingly motionless life like plants. We apply intentionality so readily that it can be hard for us to decipher what things do or don't have intentions and minds. For example, we can easily be misled into anthropomorphizing the intentional system in question—even if a thermostat does have goals and desires, they wouldn't be the same as a human's.

And indeed, Dennett argues that "smart" systems like "self-replicating macromolecules, thermostats, amoebas, plants, rats, bats, people, and chess-playing computers" are all most effectively considered from the intentional stance.[296] Intentional systems like thermostats and plants *do* have predictable goals and desires, even if only from a pragmatic point of view. As Dennett puts it, "Does the macromolecule *really* want to replicate itself? The intentional stance explains what is going on, regardless of how we answer that question... Seeking one's own good is a fundamental feature of any rational agent, but are these simple organisms seeking or just 'seeking?' We don't need to answer that question. The organism is a predictable intentional system in either case."[297]

Much smaller things (i.e., proteins, RNA, and single cells) and much larger things (i.e., social networks, countries, and planets) certainly have "motivations," "goals," and "desires" to maintain homeostasis, although

---

294 Daniel C. Dennett, *Kinds of Minds: Towards an Understanding of Consciousness* (New York: Basic Books, 1997), 27.

295 *Ibid*, 30–32. However, Dennett is careful to distinguish between *the intentional stance and the design stance*. For example, if you say, "the thermostat is *supposed* to keep the temperature at 70 degrees," that is the design stance. It is only when we ascribe beliefs, desires, and rational consideration to a thing ("the thermostat *wants*...") that we have taken the intentional stance.

296 *Ibid*, 34.

297 *Ibid*, 32.

these drives will look different for different *organisms*—biological, memetic, or otherwise. For example, corporations are "a number of persons united in one body for a purpose" and, legally now, they are just as much "persons" as you are.[298] The concepts of intentionality, mind, and the constitution of living organisms will return in Chapters 11 and 12.

For now, let us leave it at this: minds are nothing more or less than a collection of other minds—the emergent system that occurs from the summation of all the people and things you've ever simulated through interaction. The next chapter will explore how consciousness and mind can be described as feedback loops of simulations simulating other simulations simulating themselves.[299] So far, the concepts in this section have been relatively disconnected from molecular biology and epigenetics, so let's return there with some mechanistic explanation for all this.

MeCP2 is a protein that binds to methylated DNA to regulate gene expression (see Chapters 3 and 7). The function of this transcriptional repressor is an epigenetic example of the way that our physiology constantly and actively reconfigures itself to maintain *an updated representation of our experiences and the external world*. There is twice as much MeCP2 in neurons as there are nucleosomes, which makes it one of the most abundantly expressed proteins in these brain cells.[300] MeCP2 binds to methylated DNA in neurons and covers large swathes of the genome. When MeCP2 is bound to DNA it prevents the

---

298 Nina Totenberg, "When Did Companies Become People? Excavating the Legal Evolution," *NPR*, Morning Edition, July 28, 2014, https://www.npr.org/2014/07/28/335288388/when-did-companies-become-people-excavating-the-legal-evolution.

299 This quote from [John Michael, "The Intentional Stance and Cultural Learning: A Developmental Feedback Loop," in *Content and Consciousness Revisited* (Cham: Springer, 2015), 164] describes such a self-referential and recursive process in terms of the intentional stance: "...young children's use of the intentional stance during cognitive development enables them to learn from and thereby become more similar to the adults in their culture, whereby they themselves become increasingly predictable and intelligible for other people taking the intentional stance. Thus, the intentional stance and cultural learning constitute a feedback loop that (partially) explains the reliability of the intentional stance."

300 Peter J. Skene et al., "Neuronal MeCP2 Is Expressed at Near Histone-Octamer Levels and Globally Alters the Chromatin State," *Molecular Cell* 37, no. 4 (February 2010): 457, 465, https://doi.org/10.1016/j.molcel.2010.01.030.

transcription of methylated gene sequences, both through physical occlusion of RNA polymerases and through alteration of local chromatin states (see Chapter 7). However, MeCP2 does much more than inhibit gene expression—it also activates and regulates transcription in a way that is dependent on cellular activity levels. What this means is that MeCP2 unbinds from specific DNA sequences in response to electrical activity called *depolarization*,[301] which is the main form of neuronal communication (a process often described as the neuron "firing"). This is amazing, because everything you do, think, and experience makes your neurons depolarize. MeCP2 provides an epigenetic mechanism by which your day-to-day and moment-to-moment experiences can literally alter your gene expression and physiology, whether you are conscious of those experiences or not.

Chapter 3 compared the human body to the ship of Theseus, and this chapter has taken that idea one step further—our identities and "selves" are constantly shifting and far less stable than many of us would like to admit. Even if you could someday say that you have accurately identified yourself, the act of identification changes that very identity (see figure 11.2 in Chapter 11), a concept that will return in the next chapter. Chapter 11 will also return to the idea that it is impossible to disentangle individuals from each other—groups of humans are just as much "living *organisms*" as singular humans.

---

301 Maria Fasolino, and Zhaolan Zhou, "The Crucial Role of DNA Methylation and MeCP2 in Neuronal Function," *Genes* 8, no. 5 (May 2017): E141, https://doi.org/10.3390/genes8050141.

CHAPTER 11

Levels of Description

"...[E]verything we do could in principle be described in terms of cells... Most of us accept this in a rather matter-of-fact way...We read about DNA and 'genetic engineering' and sip our coffee. We seem to have reconciled these two inconceivably different pictures of ourselves simply by disconnecting them from each other... Seldom do we have to flip back and forth between these two concepts of ourselves, wondering 'How can these two totally different things be the same me?'"

—DOUGLAS HOFSTADTER, *Gödel, Escher, Bach*

This chapter will take the epigenetic and non-genetic inheritance systems discussed in previous chapters to suggest that Lamarckian theory was on to something—behavior does seem to influence the process of evolution by natural selection. Since behavior clearly influences survival, it is absurd to suggest that it is distinct from evolution. This behavioral influence on evolution extends into the process of speciation, which, at some level, can only be described as "Lamarckian." In other words, our choices as individuals are intricately linked to our evolution as a species. I will take this concept one step further and argue that behavior and consciousness are inseparable. Unfortunately, consciousness is the most slippery topic imaginable because it is an infinitely recursive and self-referential process of self-awareness. Strangely, any self-referential loop will have this same problem. A descriptive system will never be able to wholly describe itself, because as soon as a complete description is generated there is a new "whole" (the complete description) that needs a new description. Behavior and consciousness are connected by *emotion* and *feeling*, where emotion is a directed response to environmental change and a feeling is internal awareness that occurs in response to these responses. Human consciousness (as well as other forms of "higher" self-awareness) emerges from an infinite and recursive loop of feeling a feeling a feeling ad infinitum. Because of the descriptive slipperiness of this internalized dimension of feeling, I have created an acronym that reframes our descriptions of reality to become more manageable: the LoD, or the Level of Description. LoDs provide reference points for description by making a conceptual anchor out of the dimension or level of the thing that is being described. Even beyond humans, LoDs suggest there are many living things that have the necessary features of evolution and conscious awareness.

LAMARCKISM REVISITED

"Would a renewed attention to behavior as a factor in evolution deserve to be called 'Lamarckian'? Surely it would depend on how it was framed."

—RICHARD W. BRURKHARDT, JR.

By reading this far you have accrued the hefty dose of biological and philosophical background required to revisit Lamarckism with a new perspective. If you'll recall, Lamarck himself would likely have wanted to be remembered for the idea that "behavioral change was a leading factor in organismal change."[302] In spite of the complexity of Lamarck's theories, Lamarckism is often framed as nothing more than an inaccurate version of Darwin's theory of evolution by natural selection. We will soon see that this is simply not the case.

This book has touched on many examples of how natural selection is a substrate independent process, but substrate independence (see Chapter 1) does not mean that everything in the universe undergoes natural selection. Rather, it is *possible* that anything in the universe can be affected by natural selection. NASA, in fact, uses this distinction to specify that life is anything that undergoes natural selection, a definition we will come back to in Chapter 12.

---

302 Burkhardt, "Lamarck," 804.

Here is a formalized list of the four necessary conditions for evolution by natural selection to occur:[303]

1. Reproduction (replication)
2. Variation (imperfection of replication)
3. Heredity (replication of traits)
4. Competition (the possibility of replicative failure)

Evolution by natural selection is a near certainty when these four conditions are met. This does not say anything about what kind of life will evolve, the specifics of how that evolution will occur, or when any of this will happen; this list is simply a definition of the context in which natural selection will work its magic.

Like gravity, evolution by natural selection seems to be so fundamental and explanatory in our understanding of the world that it is tempting to label it a natural law rather than a scientific theory. In our observable corner of reality, both gravity and natural selection work in consistent ways, no matter what material is used as the underlying substrate: a steel beam falls just as fast as a feather (without air resistance) and a bacterium evolves through the same mechanisms as a human (in outwardly different, but surprisingly similar ways). Although it is perfectly plausible that natural selection does not work uniformly in every nook and cranny of the universe, it is very hard to imagine a scenario in which those four conditions are met but natural selection does not occur.

Many people take the substrate independence (or at least the massive flexibility) of natural selection for granted. This leads to some very unnecessary fights, like the debate between Neo-Darwinism and Lamarckism (see Chapter 1). It is undeniable that genes play a defining role in evolution. But hopefully the numerous examples provided so far have convinced you that epigenetic factors influence natural selection in important and measurable ways. Like the examples of heritable memories, fears, and addictions, the behavior of an organism is one of the epigenetic factors that can alter the course of evolution. Despite this evidence, anti-Lamarckian sentiment still runs rampant in the

---

303 Lewontin, "The Units of Selection," 1.

biological sciences. A popular YouTube intellectual, Michael Stevens (also known as Vsauce), provides an excellent example of this phenomenon. In one of his videos on the evolution of the human buttocks, he provides a wonderful and entertaining description of how human beings are designed by natural selection to run long distances. However, at the end of the video, he makes a startlingly inaccurate statement: "… running specialization was naturally selected because it helped our prehistoric ancestors survive. Actually, enjoying all of that running was not naturally selected—it was just a part of their daily lives."[304]

It is absurd to think that the enjoyment of running is somehow dissociable from running specialization. Feelings, thoughts, and behaviors are vitally important for heritability—in both direct and indirect ways—and running specialization is no exception. A runner's high, for example, is a natural form of reward that many people experience while running. This "high" is caused by endorphins, which are a type of opioid produced naturally in the brain and spinal cord and released under periods of exercise. Recent research happens to have shown that endocannabinoids (the bodily-produced versions of the chemicals in marijuana) are also involved in this process[305]—running and heavy exercise can *literally* get you high. Long-distance running is a very risky and injury-prone behavior, so a smart and self-preserving animal would not voluntarily take part in this activity. Therefore, it is theorized that pain-relieving neuromodulators (like opioids and cannabinoids) were—and still are—a motivating reward for long-distance running. This subjective motivation is a product of natural selection that decreases the perceived risk/reward ratio for a behavior that is prone to cause injuries.[306]

---

304 Vsauce, "Why is Your Bottom in the Middle?" YouTube video, 10:21, January 7, 2014, https://youtu.be/xKg9Vl_Wg5U/.

305 David A. Raichlen et al., "Wired to Run: Exercise-Induced Endocannabinoid Signaling in Humans and Cursorial Mammals with Implications for the 'Runner's High,'" *Journal of Experimental Biology* 215, no. 8 (March 2012): 1334–35, https://doi.org/10.1242/jeb.063677.

306 *Ibid*, 1331. "Goal-oriented behaviors that impose risks or high energy costs are often motivated by neurobiological rewards, which are thought to condition fitness-enhancing activities…A neurobiological reward to encourage exercise may be especially important because high levels of aerobic activity are more energetically costly than walking and have a higher potential for both traumatic and overuse injuries."

Extrapolating from just this one example, there seems to be more than enough evidence to indicate that behavior guides natural selection. It does not seem unreasonable to suggest that epigenetics—non-genetic influences on heritability, like behavior, et al.— provides a perfect and proper frame for a revival of Lamarckian concepts. And, whether or not the scientific paradigm is ready to admit it, consciousness is impossible to disentangle from behavior, which affects survival, and this intentional influence on the progression of life leads directly to natural selection.

SPECIATION

> "...evolutionary change is not so much to turn organisms into morphologically different ones, but to turn them more into 'themselves.'"[307]

Scientists treat creationism and intelligent design with a justifiable level of scorn and hostility, but many researchers treat the epigenetic revolution of evolution in a similar manner.[308] In a sense, the scientists who disapprove of epigenetic evolution operate with a similar emotional motivation as creationists who deny speciation (the emergence of new species through successive generations of evolution by natural selection). Both epigenetic evolution and speciation seem difficult to accept because they disrupt our commonly held notions of identity (see Chapter 10). Speciation connects humanity to all other organisms through common ancestry, but epigenetics goes even further in its

---

307 Stuart A. Newman, Gabor Forgacs, and Gerd B. Müller, "Before Programs: The Physical Origination of Multicellular Forms," *International Journal of Developmental Biology* 50, no. 2–3 (February 2006): 296, https://doi.org/10.1387/ijdb.052049sn.

308 Like this quote from [Kevin Laland et al., "Does Evolutionary Theory Need a Rethink?" *Nature* 514, no. 7521 (October 2014): 163-64, https://doi.org/10.1038/514161a]: "What [epigenetic advocates] term the standard evolutionary theory is a caricature that views the field as static and monolithic. They see today's evolutionary biologists as unwilling to consider ideas that challenge convention. We see a very different world...," or this quote from [Haig, "Epigenetics and the Lamarckian Temptation," 423]: "If I could choose, I would ban discussion of 'the inheritance of acquired characters'..."

contradiction of human exceptionalism (the notion that humanity occupies a privileged position in the hierarchy of earthly organisms and the hierarchy of the universe itself). This is because non-genetic influences on evolution remove the blinders from natural selection and provide all organisms (not just humans) with the power to influence their epigenetics through choice and experience. Epigenetic inheritance then provides a means for these choices and experiences to have an impact on evolution.

Epigenetics implies that developmental processes, the environment, and the experiences of our ancestors all exert an influence over our evolution that is inseparable from genetic processes. In addition, conscious thoughts, behaviors, and reactions to environments will induce epigenetic changes that alter phenotypes. Like the MeCP2 example in Chapter 10, our perceptions and decisions constantly change our bodies through epigenetic mechanisms.

Although the more extreme versions of this argument are debatable, epigenetics undeniably provides some direction (conscious or not) to genetic mutations. The most common DNA mutation turns a "C" into a "T," and the rate at which this mutation occurs is increased by DNA methylation[309]—a clear example how epigenetic mechanisms can influence evolutionary change.[310] Jablonka and Lamb have argued that environmental factors can induce specific, predictable, and heritable epigenetic variations, or *epimutations*.[311] These epimutations may in turn exert powerful effects over the process of speciation through reproductive isolation by preventing two populations from breeding with each other. This is a fascinating concept, because it implies that consciousness and directed behavior affect speciation and natural selection, and this is undeniably "Lamarckian."

Because of this (and for other reasons), epigenetics is suggested to be one of the main mechanisms that drives the process of speciation. For example,

---

309 Peter A. Jones et al., "Methylation, Mutation and Cancer," *BioEssays* 14, no. 1 (January 1992): 33, https://doi.org/10.1002/bies.950140107.

310 As mentioned in Chapter 10, methylation is somewhat controlled by diet, which provides a tantalizing (if indirect) link between conscious choices, directed mutations, and evolutionary change.

311 Eva Jablonka, and Marion J. Lamb, "The Inheritance of Acquired Epigenetic Variations," *International Journal of Epidemiology* 44, no. 4 (April 2015): 1096, https://doi.org/10.1093/ije/dyv020.

the speed of bone growth in finches has been shown to drastically increase in response to a mite infestation of their nest—a process that happens far too quickly to be controlled by genetic evolution alone. This rapid phenotypic change is mediated by a heritable epigenetic mechanism that is activated when a pregnant bird has chronically elevated levels of cortisol[312] (not really cortisol, but the avian version of the stress hormone). In other words, when periods of uncontrollable stress occur, non-genetic inheritance steps in to rapidly increase the pace of evolutionary change.

In this fascinating example, it is the *experience of stress* that induces changes in future offspring, rather than any specific "objective" stressor. This real-world example is very reminiscent of the proposed intergenerational heritability of the caricature of Lamarckian theory taught in schools (see Chapter 1)—the intergenerational heritability of increased neck length in giraffes. Another real-world example of Lamarckism comes from the differences between various types of finches on the Galapagos Islands, which have been tied to changes in epigenetic mechanisms.[313] This is a perfect combination of Lamarckian and Darwinian theory, since Darwin's study of the Galapagos finches is one of the most famous examples of speciation that he documented in his travels. Epigenetic examples of this sort provide a particularly observable aspect of the complex process of speciation. In these cases of non-genetic heredity, epigenetic mechanisms act as a short-term buffer of experience-induced phenotypic transformation that can drive evolutionary change in the long-term. In other words, epigenetic mechanisms can serve as a form

---

312 Alexander V Badyaev, "Epigenetic Resolution of the 'curse of Complexity' in Adaptive Evolution of Complex Traits," *Journal of Physiology* 592, no. 11 (April 2014): 2258, https://doi.org/10.1113/jphysiol.2014.272625. "Breeding females accumulate mites when collecting nest material and infect their future nest site. During a breeding attempt that coincides with the infestation period, nestlings have a distinct ontogeny, growing their long bones up to 50% faster and earlier than nestlings of the same breeding pair during other times of the year, which enable these nestlings to leave infested nests earlier and minimize their exposure to mites... Epigenetic effects in this case can recruit, expose, or integrate calcium biosynthesis from novel genetic pathways responding to corticosterone-mediated stress and enable faster 'emergency' growth."

313 Michael K. Skinner et al., "Epigenetics and the Evolution of Darwin's Finches," *Genome Biology and Evolution* 6, no. 8 (July 2014): 1987, https://doi.org/10.1093/gbe/evu158.

of short-term evolutionary memory so that future generations can have a historical record of things that happened too quickly for genes to react. Over time, this epigenetic record can be transcribed into the genetic record (this is technically a form of "reverse transcription"), which is more stable and transmissible through generations.

Epigenetic mechanisms provide several explanations for how phenotypic changes and environmental interactions (like those seen in finches when their nests are threatened by mite invasions) can lead to speciation. Evolutionary information is contained within the environment as much as it is within individual organisms or species. The way in which organisms modify their environments and habitats to provide safety and security for their children[314] is an aspect of natural selection that the gene-centric view cannot explain. Beaver dams, beehives, and human cities are excellent examples of the non-genetic inheritance of environmental changes that were induced by organismal behavior.

It has even been proposed that these kinds of epigenetic influences play a *more* important role in the process of speciation than genetic mechanisms.[315] Indeed, in the study of Galapagos finches mentioned above there were more epimutations than genetic mutations among the various species. And, unlike genetic mutations, the number of epimutations was linearly correlated with the level of phenotypic difference between species—in other words, the more epimutations these birds underwent, the more they physically changed from each other.[316] It is possible that epigenetic changes control genetic evolution. One example of this is the "control" that plants exert over human

---

314 Laland, "Does Evolutionary Theory Need a Rethink?" 164, "[Epigenetics] also encompasses those structures and altered conditions that organisms leave to their descendants through their niche construction—from beavers' dams to worm-processed soils."

315 Newman, "Physical Origination of Multicellular Forms," 290. "...[E]pigenetic mechanisms, rather than genetic changes, are the major sources of morphological novelty in evolution. In our usage 'epigenetic' refers to the context-dependence of developmental mechanisms, not to DNA-associated mechanisms of inheritance, such as methylation and chromatin assembly."

316 Skinner, "Darwin's Finches," 1987–1988. This is, however, just correlational data. As of now, there is not quite enough evidence to say with certainty that epimutations are the direct cause of these changes, even though a great deal of the available evidence suggests that this is the case.

behavior,[317] like how some species of plants domesticated humanity into agrarian societies that would eventually lead to the building of cities.[318] In this way, organisms like plants can create massive changes on a planetary scale (think globalization or climate change). For example, photosynthetic organisms (like plants) evolved to exist on dry land about 400 to 1200 million years ago.[319] These organisms used sunlight to process the carbon dioxide in the atmosphere into oxygen, and this would eventually allow animal life to evolve out of the oceans and flourish on land. Photosynthetic life seems to have had a directed influence over the development of the planet and the evolution of other species.

Despite this evolutionary influence, many philosophers and scientists are skeptical that plants have any sort of consciousness or perspective. And this leads us to a very important aspect of how Lamarckism relates to evolution: if the behavior of individuals affects the long-term outcomes of evolution, how does subjective experience come into play and what is the relationship between consciousness and behavior? And for that matter, what does it even mean to have a conscious perspective?

---

317 Michael Pollan, *The Botany of Desire: A Plant's-Eye View of the World* (New York: Random House, 2001), xvi. "We automatically think of domestication as something we do to other species, but it makes much just as much sense to think of it as something certain plants and animals have done to us, a clever evolutionary strategy for advancing their own interests. The species that have spent the last ten thousand years or so figuring out how to best feed, heal, clothe, intoxicate, and otherwise delight us have made themselves some of nature's greatest success stories."

318 *Ibid*, xvi-xx. "...[I]t makes just as much sense to think of agriculture as something the grasses did to people as a way to conquer the trees...edible grasses (such wheat and corn)...incited humans to cut down vast forests to make more room for them."

319 John A. Raven, and Dianne Edwards, "Roots: Evolutionary Origins and Biogeochemical Significance," *Journal of Experimental Botany* 52, Roots Special Issue (March 2001): 384, https://doi.org/10.1093/jexbot/52.suppl_1.381.

Consciousness

> "I seem, like everything else, to be a center, a sort of vortex, at which
> the whole energy of the universe realizes itself... A sort of aperture,
> through which the whole universe is conscious of itself."
>
> —ALAN WATTS

Traditionally, a conscious perspective is not just a metaphorical space of internalized experience, but a literal set of portals, such as eyes, ears, mouths, and noses. These sensory apertures transmit information from an external reality to an internal realm of being; they turn the objective into the subjective, translate analog information into digital sensation, and transfer external motion into internal emotion (e-motion?). This concept of conscious sensation as a portal from a "physical" dimension to a "mental" (or purely informational) dimension is so ephemeral that consciousness is considered to be one of the greatest mysteries of all time. Even many neuroscientists and philosophers of consciousness believe that there are some sort of "non-physical," logically indescribable aspects of subjectivity known as *qualia*. The broadest definition of qualia is not objectionable, as it refers to the phenomenal aspects of subjectivity. In other words, even if no two people see colors exactly the same, who can deny the existence of smells, tastes, and textures—and the effects they have on our behaviors? However, the idea of qualia quickly becomes distorted when philosophers argue that some organisms, like plants, experience no sensations because, "nothing that goes on inside them is poised to make a direct difference to what they believe or desire, since they have no beliefs or desires."[320]

Perhaps this is a simple quibble over interpretations of "beliefs" and "desires." But the definition of life outlined in chapter nine as "a *self*-sustaining process that *organ*izes disorder into order" suggests that all living beings have at least two "desires": survival and *organ*ization. By this definition, plants are certainly privy to qualia, because every process inside them occurs for the purposes of survival and the maintenance of homeostatic mechanisms

---

320 Michael Tye, "Qualia," Stanford Encyclopedia of Philosophy, last modified December 18, 2017, https://plato.stanford.edu/entries/qualia/.

(see Chapter 9). Plants even use many of the same proteins as humans do to process sensations[321] and to formulate complex behaviors in response to these sensations.[322] Plants almost certainly experience the world in a very different way than humans. We cannot directly experience the life of a plant, but it is unreasonable to assume that they have no subjective experiences at all. In the web of evolution, humans are related to plants just as we seem to be related to all living things.

It seems almost obvious that plants can react to their environments in meaningful and direct ways. For example, they can grow towards the sun, fend off predators, and sense the changing of the seasons. Plants perceive, process, and respond to their environments in such deeply complex ways that a new field of study known as "plant neurobiology" has begun to develop—a new framework that conceives of plants as intelligent and social organisms.[323] The question of what a plant feels (or if it even feels at all) is up for debate, but if we doubt their capacity to react and make choices, why not doubt this capacity in humans?

This kind of slippery reasoning about what we simply cannot observe (i.e., the internality of feelings) makes the discussion of human consciousness very tricky. The main difficulty of discussing consciousness is that it may be impossible for any logical system (including consciousness) to truly define itself.[324] In other words, there is always one thing that a descriptive system

---

321 Alexandra V. Andreeva, and Mikhail A. Kutuzov, "Do Plants Have Rhodopsin After All? A Mystery of Plant G Protein-Coupled Signalling," *Plant Physiology and Biochemistry* 39, no. 12 (December 2001): 1027–35, https://doi.org/10.1016/S0981-9428(01)01328-6; Ron Mittler, Andrija Finka, and Pierre Goloubinoff, "How Do Plants Feel the Heat?" *Trends in Biochemical Sciences* 37, no. 3 (March 2012): 118–25, https://doi.org/10.1016/j.tibs.2011.11.007.

322 Masatsugu Toyota et al., "Glutamate triggers long-distance, calcium-based plant defense signaling," *Science* 361, no. 6407 (September 2018): 1112–1115.

323 Eric D Brenner et al., "Plant Neurobiology: An Integrated View of Plant Signaling," *Trends in Plant Science* 11, no. 8 (July 2006): 413–14, https://doi.org/10.1016/j.tplants.2006.06.009.

324 See [Douglas Hofstadter, *I Am a Strange Loop* (New York: Basic Books, 2007)] for an extensive and compelling argument about the relationship between consciousness and the *incompleteness theorem*—a mathematical proof created by the mathematician Kurt Gödel that demonstrates that any sufficiently complex algorithmic system is necessarily incomplete by nature.

cannot describe: itself. This is easily demonstrable through paradoxical self-reference like, "this sentence is false." It is possible to construct these non-tautological statements (a contradiction; a statement that is true if false and false if true) in any symbolic system. Consciousness is just like any other self-referential system—it is necessarily incomplete, since it must continuously update to contain itself inside itself. As soon as you have a novel experience or learn something new you must integrate this into your identity. Then, this new identity needs to be integrated into a new identity, which needs to be integrated into a new identity, and this sequential process can go on and on forever. This infinitely recursive and self-referential logic is known as a "strange loop."[325] One easily demonstrable example of a strange loop is what happens when you point a video camera at its own output on a screen[326] (see figure 11.1). Any motion or change that the camera detects will ripple through the layered images as an infinitely regressive wave (a good example of the substrate independence of waves discussed in Chapter 1).

In a way, the essence of consciousness is that it cannot be defined because it is the absolute reference point for all possible definitions—it is the lynchpin that holds the self-referential system of words together. Some sects of Buddhism refer to this indefinable essence of consciousness as *Zen*. The brilliant philosopher Douglas Hofstadter tries to describe Zen like this: "...there is no way to characterize what Zen is. No matter what verbal space you try to enclose Zen in, it resists, and spills over...the Zen attitude is that words and truth are incompatible, or at least that no words can capture truth."[327] The ever-elusive concept of Zen—the indescribability of consciousness—has also been called *The Tao* in Chinese philosophy: the essence of experience, the thing (or no-thing) that has no opposite. Alan Watts, a philosopher of Zen Buddhism, says it like this: "The present moment is infinitely small; before we can measure it, it has gone, and yet it persists for ever. This movement

---

325 *Ibid*.

326 Technically, Hofstadter considers this an example of a simple feedback loop, *not* a strange loop. However, there is a strangeness injected into this scenario when you consider that a human being is involved in setting up the loop and perceiving the infinitely regressive feedback.

327 Douglas Hofstadter, *Gödel, Escher, Bach: An Eternal Golden Braid* (New York: Basic Books, 1979), 254.

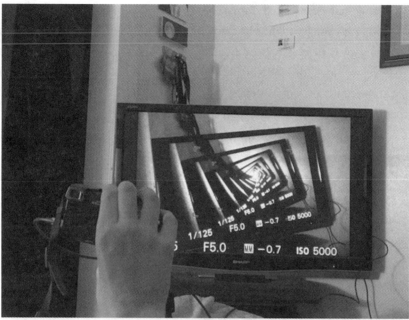

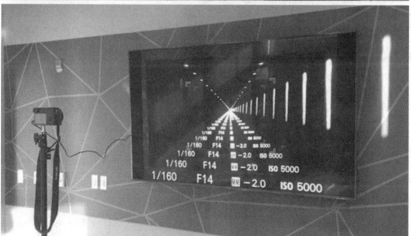

FIGURE 11.1 Two examples of what happens when a camera is pointed at its own output on a screen.

and change has been called Tao…The infinite Tao is something which you can neither escape by flight nor catch by pursuit; there is no coming toward it or going away from it; it is, and you are it."[328] Consciousness, Zen, the Tao. Whatever we call it, this indefinable and absolute reference point is like a black hole at the center of self-awareness that binds together an entire dimension of experience with its inescapable pull: "…it *is*, and you are it."

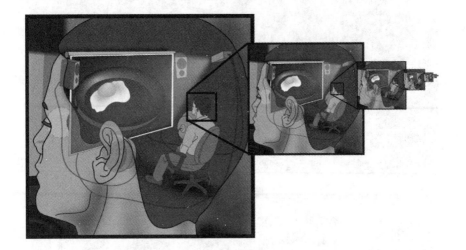

FIGURE 11.2 Subjective experience as consciousness simulating consciousness leads to an infinite regression of representations of representations of representations, etc., etc.

Consciousness, to be clear, does not refer to identity or memory—rather, humans are conscious of our memories and our identities in the same way that we can be conscious of a tap on the shoulder. Instead, consciousness refers to the deeply transcendental essence that rests at the heart of all experience: the feeling of *being* that sits behind all perspectives. Furthermore, besides the objects, people, and environments around it that consciousness constantly simulates, human consciousness also simulates itself. This self-conception is a holistic summation of 1) all other representations, 2) the representor themselves, and 3) the representation of the representation of the representation, *ad infinitum* (see figure 11.2).

---

328 Alan Watts, *Become What You Are* (Boston: Shambhala, 2003), 10–11.

Consciousness can be a deceptively difficult topic, despite it being the most universal feature of creatures that can communicate. Language is often considered to be integral to our conscious experience as human beings. But consciousness is a more fundamental aspect of being than the complexity of language. There are thousands of human languages that are composed of an uncountable number of unique words. Despite this, all words share one feature—they are self-referential. All words are defined by another word and every word defines itself by virtue of its definition. To put this another way, a word is only a word if it has meaning, which means that it refers to some "thing" or "concept" that exists in a non-linguistic realm. To visualize this, imagine that every word is connected to another word in a vast, two-dimensional web of definition. Every word in this web must also have a connection with something *outside* that two-dimensional web of words. The web only maintains its structure because it is anchored in an independent reality—a dimension that exists above and beyond the linguistic web.

Consciousness is often conflated with language, because it shares the self-referential features of words, but there are easily dissociable aspects of consciousness that are distinct from language. Humans share many of these aspects with animals, pre-linguistic infants, and other humans that speak different languages. The main example of these shared aspects of consciousness is emotion: the ability to prepare for and react to specific situations.[329]

By this definition, emotions are the capacity for directed and intentional physiological movement—the capability to change yourself in response to the environment. To use an example from before, a plant can sense the sunlight and grow towards it. As an example of emotion in terms of humans, when we are threatened our heart rate and breathing increase in preparation for a

---

329 Damasio, *The Feeling of What Happens*, 53–54. "The biological function of emotions is twofold. The first function is the production of a specific reaction to the inducing situation. In an animal, for instance, the reaction may be to run or to become immobile or to beat the hell out of the enemy...The second biological function of emotion is the regulation of the internal state of an organism such that it can be prepared for the specific reaction. For example, providing increased blood flow to arteries in the legs so that muscles receive extra oxygen and glucose, in the case of a flight reaction, or changing heart and breathing rhythms, in the case of freezing on the spot."

fight or flight reaction. These changes will happen whether we are consciously aware of a threat or not. Even if we are not aware of why particular emotions are happening or how to interpret them, we often *feel* these changes (*"Why are you crying?"* ... *"I don't know! I'm just really happy"*)—and this is an interesting dissociation to make between *emotions* and *feelings*. Emotions are bodily responses, but feelings are the subjective perception of those emotions and the reason why we can regulate our internal states. In this framework, feelings are just a type of emotion: an internal emotion in response to an external emotion—meta-emotions, as it were. Conscious awareness of emotions happens in the form of an associated feeling, like fear about a looming shadow behind you, anger because of the way that guy looked at you, or generalized anxiety for no discernable reason at all.

And this is where things get interesting. In and of itself, emotion is a form of self-awareness and a kind of self-reference, because an adaptive reaction to external change requires some functional distinction between the individual and its environment. This emotional capacity to react, adapt, and survive is one of the most integral components of the evolutionary process and, therefore, of life. Emotion is essentially synonymous with behavior—the way in which a living thing engages its body to react to the environment. In this way, emotions are required for life, and more complex emotions provide an expanded repertoire of reactions to possibly life-threatening changes in the environment.[330]

To follow this line of logic, the ultimate adaptive tool is the ability to respond to responses—*to feel*. This kind of infinitely recursive and self-referential reactionary capacity is exactly what seems to drive the exceptional progress of human intelligence. While emotion is a required component of even the most basic lifeforms, the complexity of feeling is what we often ascribe to "higher" consciousness, or self-recognition. Although any emotion is a form of self-awareness, human consciousness is a more explicit and expressible form of self-awareness that arises from the feeling of a feeling. The awareness of our own awareness allows us to metaphorically step aside as an "agent" of our own

---

330 *Ibid*, 54. "...[F]or certain classes of clearly dangerous or clearly valuable stimuli in the internal or external environment, evolution has assembled a matching answer in the form of emotion."

internal processes. In this way, consciousness is a looped chain of emotion: emotions in response to emotions in response to emotions. Consciousness is the process of feeling our own feelings from a different viewpoint, which creates a stream of experience—the transformation of external events into an internal dimension of emotions, feelings, and, eventually, consciousness awareness.

LEVELS OF DESCRIPTION (LoDs) AND SELF-REFERENTIALITY

> "…[T]he subjectivity of organisms is a physical factor—an objective reality in its own right."
>
> —ANDREAS WEBER, *The Biology of Wonder*

Dimensions have come up a few times in this book, but this usage of the word does not mean dimensions in the physical sense of length, width, height, depth, time, etc. In this book, dimension means a metaphorical space that is somewhat isolated due to boundaries that are strict or difficult to cross. In simulations of physical reality (like video games), people call these bounded spaces "levels," as in, "I can beat all the levels of Super Mario in five minutes" or "I got stuck on the last level of Guitar Hero." In some games, like Grand Theft Auto, the "levels" have achieved such stunning proportions that people literally refer to them as "open world" games.

In a more literal sense, the term "levels" commonly refers to a metaphorical description of a vertical distance between things, as in, "having a *higher* level of intelligence" or "my blood sugar is at *low* levels." These examples provide cues to the existence of a vital feature of levels: without a reference point, there is no orientation like "left," "right," or "time." Levels are self-referential systems just like words and consciousness. This means that a level needs to refer to other levels in order to make sense. For example, when you beat a level in a video game you usually unlock a new, successive level. In addition, to exist as self-referential systems, levels need to refer to a space outside of the game to exist—there is no way to play if you can't access a game. The levels and simulations held within a game are dormant and purely informational until they have some avenue of expression, like the viral genome in figure 10.2. While here I am describing the levels of a video game, keep in mind that levels exist in real life too.

In reality, a level that is inaccessible is "out of reach." It does seem that there are levels of "reality" that humans can never achieve, access, or comprehend, such as what lies beyond the edge of the universe, the speed of light, or the smallest particulate constituent of matter. There are certain things that are simply unreachable, which is a feature of any logical system that is sufficiently complex—paradoxical reference points seem to be required for a system to have descriptive power, otherwise everything can be defined and the system will become absolute, rigid, and inflexible. It is not that there are specific regions or dimensions of the universe that are totally off-limits, it is simply that all self-referential systems require reference points to maintain the coherence of meaning. Since reference points can only be defined in terms of other reference points, there isn't a way to tether the entirety of the system to anything stable (except another system). Logical, self-referential systems (strange loops) can maintain a "shape" and internal consistency, but they are impossible to define as holistic units of singularity.

The problem here (as outlined in the last section) is that it is impossible to utilize a self-referential system to create a truly accurate description of itself. But humans have no other choice than to exist and express from within our own consciousness. Therefore, I have coined the acronym LoD (levels of description) to talk about the different "levels" of human reality.[331] For example, there are distinct LoDs for atomic particles, molecules like RNA and proteins, cellular life, and planetary bodies. From our perspective as human beings, the observable LoDs of the universe seem to be nested within each other.[332] Organizations of atoms create molecules; groups of molecules create

---

331 The term "levels of description" is already used in information and complexity theories, specifically by [Hofstadter, *Gödel, Escher, Bach*, 291–315], but the acronym *LoDs* is my coinage.

332 See [Eames Office, "Powers of Ten™ (1977)," YouTube video, 9:00, August 26, 2010, https://youtu.be/0fKBhvDjuy0] and [Kees Boeke, *Cosmic View: The Universe in 40 Jumps* (New York: The John Day Company, 1957), retrieved October 1, 2018, http://www.vendian.org/mncharity/cosmicview/] for some explanatory visual comparisons of how various LoDs stack up to the scale of a single human being.

cells; conglomerations of cells create us; and the entirety of living *organ*isms creates The World. In other words, small things compose big things and big things are comprised of small things. The isolated nature of LoDs makes them seem totally disconnected from each other—the existence of atoms was theorized thousands of years ago,[333] but it is difficult for the average non-physicist to comprehend or directly observe how atoms affect our lives. Even the most brilliant of quantum mechanical scientists have yet to come up with a suitable explanation of how subatomic physics can co-exist with our subjective experience of reality.[334]

But by definition, symbolic and self-referencing systems (like levels, words, and consciousness) only exist because they indirectly refer to every other thing in existence. LoDs are embedded within each other, but they also interact with each other in an uncountable number of unpredictable ways. Individual living things are inseparable from other living things just like atoms are inseparable from planets and planets are inseparable from the universe. Like LoDs, biological organisms *in and of themselves* form a self-referential system. Thanks to Darwin and Lamarck, the theory of evolution is a mainstream scientific idea that connects any organism to all other organisms through common ancestry and speciation.

As we have discussed in this chapter, epigenetics plays a vitally important role in these processes. Many examples of epigenetic and non-genetic mechanisms of experiential memory and inheritance have been presented throughout the course of this book. When taken together, these examples suggest that choice and experience play powerful roles in the development of life, the planet, and possibly the universe as a whole.

---

333 Some of the ancient Greek philosophers who pondered the nature of atoms were amazingly accurate in their contemplations, as described in [Bernard Pullman, *The Atom in the History of Human Thought* (Oxford: Oxford University Press, 1998), 33], "Atoms undergo a continual and endless motion, random and not preordained, determined by mutual collisions. The many consequences resulting from this process are due to the various quantitative and mechanical characteristics of the atoms involved. For instance, upon colliding atoms can either recoil 'in the direction where fate throws them,' or 'coalesce according to the congruence of shapes, sizes, positions and arrangements, and remain bound, thereby causing the generation of aggregates,' according to Simplicius's account."

334 Steven Carlip, "Quantum Gravity: A Progress Report," *Reports on Progress in Physics* 64, no. 8 (July 2001): 886–7, https://doi.org/10.1088/0034-4885/64/8/301.

CHAPTER 12

Organa

"...our life is situated inside a nested hierarchy of self-organized systems...
Each of these levels are non-equilibrium systems that owe their existence
to processes of self-organization...Is there a sense in which the universe
as a whole could be a non-equilibrium, self-organized system?"

—LEE SMOLIN, *The Life of the Cosmos*

This chapter will revisit Neo-Darwinian theory in terms of Levels
of Description (LoDs) rather than evolutionary substrates. Within the
framework of LoDs it becomes more apparent why it is so absurd to
suggest that genes are the sole substrate of natural selection, because
the LoD of genetics is just one among a seemingly infinite number of
inseparable dimensions that are all interconnected and affected by the
processes of evolution and natural selection. The concept of LoDs and
the substrate independence of natural selection leads to some startling
implications. For example, this new perspective rewrites the history of
life and places epigenetics as the precursor to genetics. In addition, this
may mean that the stability of physical bodies emerged more recently in
the history of evolution than the self-replicative capacity of informational
templates. In other words, the *concept* of life existed before the physicality
of living things. The traditional definition of life as an organism (i.e.,
something affected by natural selection) simply isn't clear enough to truly
explore the depth of pre-genetic history and the implications of LoDs.
Therefore, I have co-opted an old medieval word, *organum*, to describe
a new view of life—not just as "things" affected by natural selection,
but as cooperative groups of self-directed, self-contained, and self-
referential replicators. In this way, the entire universe can be described as
infinitely embedded series of organa surviving, multiplying, changing,

and interacting. *Organumics*, a word I have coined to mean "the study of organa," aims to reframe the human perspective from the LoD of evolution. After all, "nothing in biology makes sense except in the light of evolution"—and we are nothing if not biology.

THE EVOLUTIONARY SUBSTRATES

> "…[T]he principles of natural selection…can be applied equally to genes, organisms, populations, species, and at opposite ends of the scale, prebiotic molecules and ecosystems…any entities in nature… may evolve."
>
> —RICHARD C. LEWONTIN

In this book I have tried to present a clear picture of evolutionary theory and how it relates to contemporary ideas about genetics. But there is a lot of confusion about both the individual concepts of natural selection and genetics and the ways they interrelate, even within the scientific community. One reason for this lack of clarity may simply be that genes have been the defining unit of selection for centuries. In other words, the Neo-Darwinian view of evolution frames the genetic LoD (Level of Description—the metaphorical dimension in which genes exist) as the only one that is shaped, molded, and modified by natural selection.

This quote by David Haig, a Harvard professor of evolutionary biology and genetics, is just one example of the prevailing murkiness between natural selection and genetics: "One can imagine a system that detects a blacksmith's arms… and… causes an epigenetic change that results in his sons possessing more muscular forearms. But, how could such a system evolve, if not by natural selection?"[335] This statement is part of a rebuttal to an epigenetically-based theory of evolution. But the creators of this theory do not deny that epigenetic inheritance operates through natural selection. Therefore, Haig's view seems to be a direct attack on Lamarckism, rather than a true criticism of epigenetic inheritance—an unfortunate, but predictable conditioned response

---

335 Haig, "Epigenetics and the Lamarckian Temptation," 427.

in the context of biological education (see Chapters 1 and 8). As a side note, it was recently discovered that there actually is an epigenetic mechanism of muscle memory that could be inherited[336]—blacksmiths may indeed pass on their muscular forearms to their sons.

Here is another passage that echoes an anti-Lamarckian sentiment: "... [Epigenetics] smells terribly of Lamarckism, but...evolutionary biologists should not fall into the trap of rejecting a priori the possibility of a broad expansion of our understanding of what counts as genetic."[337] This isn't just insulting to Lamarckism, it's also an absurd suggestion. Anything *can* be explained from the intentional stance of genes, but that doesn't mean that everything should be explained as genetics. In other words, we can see the world from the perspective of the gene if we so choose—an existence confined to the inside of a cell and the mechanisms of transcription and translation (DNA, RNA, and proteins). Technically, we can describe *anything and everything* in terms of how that gene might be causally responsible for a thing or event in question. Did a certain gene *cause* my eyes to be blue? If a tree falls in the forest, was it cut down *because* of a gene in the muscle of a woodcutter? This is a natural way to think about the world—in terms of a singly isolated level—because everything we can possibly know is in relation to our own personal LoD: "How does it affect *me*?" While this is a useful strategy for individual survival, it doesn't necessarily create an accurate or even explanatory description of the world.[338] But that is the way the Neo-Darwinian theory considers evolution, as if the LoD of genes is the only one that matters in the long run. Besides, Darwin had absolutely no way to know what the substrate of natural selection and inheritance might be. He would probably be appalled to hear the suggestion of modern biologists that evolution only has one mechanism to enforce the principles of natural selection. This is not even to mention the similarities between Lamarckian

---

336 Robert A. Seaborne et al., "Human Skeletal Muscle Possesses an Epigenetic Memory of Hypertrophy," *Scientific Reports* 8, article 1898 (January 2018): 12–15, https://doi.org/10.1038/s41598-018-20287-3.

337 Massimo Pigliucci, "Do We Need an Extended Evolutionary Synthesis?" *Evolution* 61, no. 12 (October 2007): 2747, https://doi.org/10.1111/j.1558-5646.2007.00246.x.

338 In fact, it has been suggested that evolution actually selects *against* veridical perception. See [Hoffman, "The Interface Theory of Perception," 1480–1506].

and Darwinian theories that were reviewed in Chapter 1.

My concept of LoDs allows us to talk about distinct but interconnected dimensions of natural selection, rather than substrates (like genes or memes). Jablonka and Lamb, the authors of *Evolution in Four Dimensions*, divide these dimensions into genetics, epigenetics, behavior, and symbols. But this book has covered at least two examples of heritable systems that do not fall neatly into any of these four categories: the inheritance of the bacterial microbiome and the intergenerational contagion of *Demodex* face mites (see Chapter 9). Both of these examples might be considered a form of "organismal inheritance," or what some have called *the hologenome theory of evolution*.[339] Due to the universal nature of symbiotic relationships between animals and microorganisms, the theory of hologenetics proposes a unit of selection known as a *holobiont*, or the *hologenome*.[340] The hologenome describes plants, animals, and their associated bacteria, fungi, and parasites as *superorganisms* that evolve together in a seemingly infinite web of interconnectivity. But this quickly becomes confusing, because there are a seemingly uncountable number of smaller organisms that live in and on our bodies in organized "societies," much like humans live on the planet Earth. It may be impossible to name them all, but many examples of the LoDs embedded within each human organism have popped up through the course of this book: molecules like proteins and RNA; individual cells like red blood cells and neurons; "communities" of organisms like the *Demodex* mites on our faces; and the various types of bacteria and fungi that coat our gut and skin.[341] There are also larger arrangements in which humans are embedded: ecological networks like our bodies and the food chain; memetic organizations like social identity and government; and astronomical systems like the planet and solar system. There may be more than the four outlined by Jablonka and Lamb, but the description of

---

339 Ilana Zilber-Rosenberg, and Eugene Rosenberg, "Role of Microorganisms in the Evolution of Animals and Plants: The Hologenome Theory of Evolution," *FEMS Microbiology Reviews* 32, no. 5 (June 2008): 723, https://doi.org/10.1111/j.1574-6976.2008.00123.x.

340 *Ibid.*

341 Keisha Findley et al., "Topographic Diversity of Fungal and Bacterial Communities in Human Skin," *Nature* 498, no. 7454 (June 2013): 367–70. https://doi.org/10.1038/nature12171.Human.

evolutionary dimensions is quite apt. This is because LoDs as dimensions are distinct, but mutually interdependent; LoDs have strict boundaries but are embedded within each other like humans are embedded within the universe or a single neuron is embedded within a brain.

The deeply interconnected nature of these hierarchically embedded systems makes it very difficult to categorize them as separate and unique. This results in a great deal of resistance that evolutionary biologists (and others) display towards epigenetic and non-genetic heritability. Scientists are slowly accepting that epigenetics does not supersede genetics. Instead, epigenetics provides additional means through which natural selection can modify organisms, heritability, and genes.[342] In addition, it can explain quite a few confusions that arise from a gene-centric view of evolution. For example, the origins of life itself. The view from an epigenetic LoD uncovers a subtle and powerful implication, that the evolution of the first biological lifeforms was accomplished through epigenetic (and not genetic) mechanisms of heredity and identity.[343]

Three premises reviewed in this book are required to produce this conclusion: 1) natural selection is substrate independent,[344] 2) genetics almost certainly came after other replicators,[345] and 3) life is "a self-sustaining chemical system capable of Darwinian evolution."[346] Together, these three facts indicate that the original "living system" was self-templating information. This sounds quite a bit like "replicating ideas," but it is not the same as saying

---

342 Skinner, "Epigenetics and a Unified Theory," 1296–1302; Ruth Flatscher et al., "Environmental Heterogeneity and Phenotypic Divergence: Can Heritable Epigenetic Variation Aid Speciation?" *Genetics Research International* 2012 (March 2012): 1–2, https://doi.org/10.1155/2012/698421.

343 This an extension of the argument in [Newman, "Physical Origination of Multicellular Forms," 296] that multi-cellular organisms arose in spite of genetic variation, not because of it: "...[T]he body plans of contemporary organisms, for all their variety, would be produced more or less with the same 'genetic toolkit.' Their morphological variety would, by our hypothesis, have originated by conditional physical determinants acting on viscoelastic, chemically excitable materials, not primarily by genetic evolution..."

344 Lewontin, "The Units of Selection," 1–2.

345 Guimarães, "The Protein-First Hypothesis," 193–99; Cech, "The RNA Worlds in Context," a006742.

346 NASA, "About Life Detection."

that "memetics" was the first replicative system. This is because, as they were originally defined by Dawkins, memes live and operate within brains.[347] Instead, the origins of life lie within the process of "template replication"—how spatiotemporal structure is copied and reconstructed.

We already discussed one example of this idea in prion replication—the way in which the shape of one protein can be transmitted to another (see Chapter 6). Another example of the epigenetic inheritance of 3-dimensional conformation is the way in which cellular membranes are reproduced. Every time a cell divides, all its membranes need to be recreated along with its DNA. The information needed to replicate a membrane is not stored within the genome but is contained inherently within the structure of the membranes themselves.[348]

Even though this idea is focused on physical bodies, it is not tied to a particular kind of body the way a meme is tied to a brain. It is possible to transfer a template independently from the specifics of a physical form (even though a bodily form and a template are deeply and inextricably interconnected[349]). For example, the information necessary to create a protein is held within a DNA sequence, which can be copied to an RNA molecule, and subsequently translated into a protein. Only one of these molecules is the actual protein, but the informational template for the protein exists in many

---

347 Dawkins, *The Selfish Gene*, 192.

348 Eva Jablonka, and Gal Raz, "Transgenerational Epigenetic Inheritance: Prevalence, Mechanisms, and Implications for the Study of Heredity and Evolution," *The Quarterly Review of Biology* 84, no. 2 (June 2009): 135, https://doi.org/10.1086/598822. "The reproduction of most membranes, including the plasma membrane, the endoplasmic reticulum, and the mitochondrial membrane, requires the presence and templating of pre-existing membrane structures...the information embedded in this 'membranome' is as essential for the construction of a cell as genomic information...crucial events in the evolution of cells and major groups were associated with heritable changes in membranomes."

349 According to [Newman, "Physical Origination of Multicellular Forms," 296], the relationship between form (physical properties of material structure) and template (abstract heritable potential) is what allowed multi-cellular genetic programs to exist in the first place. "...[M]ulticellular forms were originally based on the inherent physical properties of tissue masses...such forms...would have served as templates for the accumulation of stabilizing and reinforcing genetic circuitry." This book extends this argument further into the past to suggest that the first genetic organisms arose by a similar process of cooperation between self-replicating molecules like RNA and proteins (see Chapter 3).

forms spread across multiple "bodies" simultaneously.

REPLICATORS AND VEHICLES

"By enlarging our field of view, what is thought of as a whole becomes, in fact, nothing more than one part of a larger whole. Yet another whole encloses this whole in a concentric series that continues on to infinity."

—MASANOBU FUKUOKA

Richard Dawkins tried to differentiate between informational templates and physical bodies with the concepts of "replicators" and "vehicles"—a difference that he exemplified with genes and the organisms that they are encapsulated within.[350] He explained that replicators are "any entity in the universe of which copies are made,"[351] but he qualified this statement with an unfortunate attack on Lamarck: "...to treat an organism as a replicator in the same sense as a gene is tantamount to Lamarckism. If you change a replicator, the change will be passed on to its descendants. This is clearly true of genes and genomes. It is not true of organisms, since acquired characteristics are not inherited."[352] Many counterexamples to this claim have been presented over the course of this book and, given the available evidence, it is hard to disagree that acquired characteristics are in fact heritable in yeast, flies, mice, rats, plants, and probably humans as well. Dawkins's effort to separate our physical bodies from the genetic information carriers within us is an admirable attempt to simplify biology, but the new science of epigenetics just doesn't fit within this argument.

There is a conceptual distinction to be made between vehicles and replicators, but DNA is by no means the only biological replicator. In

---

350 Richard Dawkins, "Replicators and Vehicles," in *Current Problems in Sociobiology*, ed. by King's College Sociobiology Group (London: Cambridge University Press, 1982), 45–65.

351 *Ibid*, 46.

352 *Ibid*, 51.

addition, the two classifications are not mutually exclusive—a vehicle can be a replicator and vice versa; it is all a matter of LoD. In the framework presented in the next section, vehicles are always replicators and replicators are always vehicles. The terms are simply perceptual reference points that are necessary because there seem to be an infinite number of possible LoDs that can frame any given discussion. In other words, a cell is a vehicle from the perspective of a gene, but a replicator from the perspective of a human. Therefore, it is helpful to create artificial boundaries in the form of LoDs to keep track of conceptual orientations. Otherwise, it becomes too easy to fall into the traps of isolationism and exceptionalism, like the claims that genes are the sole carriers of heredity and the privileged units on which natural selection operates. One problem with creating conceptual boundaries like LoDs is that they are only that: conceptual. In reality, LoDs overlap with each other, because all LoDs are embedded within other LoDs—a cell is a vehicle to a gene, but the human body is a vehicle to both cells and genes.

Like Dawkins, Jablonka and Lamb make a functional distinction between replicators and their vehicles. They do this distinguishing between copying and reconstructing, where reconstructing is dependent on the meaning of the replicated content, while copying is not. According to them, DNA replication and photocopying are examples of copying processes while nursery rhymes and behavioral imitation are examples of reconstructing processes.[353] But this argument is dangerously reminiscent of "nature versus nurture," or the isolation of an organism from its surroundings. Just like an organism cannot exist without an environment, DNA replication and photocopying do not happen in isolation. Technically, any string of nucleotides can be replicated, but DNA replication does not occur in nature without a specific sequence of nucleotides called an "origin of replication."

Similarly, a photocopier can hypothetically replicate any piece of paper, but people tend to photocopy things with a consideration of the content—photocopies are made because the information is too important to lose, or because a picture of a butt looks funny on a piece of paper. On the flip side of this argument, nonsensical or "meaningless" behaviors and rhymes are perfectly fair game for imitation. For example, please follow these

---

353 Jablonka, *Evolution in Four Dimensions*, 206.

instructions: wiggle your index finger as you read this sentence, "Good blingle floppin dorp, bad gloogin orcin korp." This is a demonstration of a useless and meaningless process of behavioral imitation and memetic spread. The nonsensical sentence and finger-wiggling behavior are obviously capable of replication through reconstruction despite their lack of association with meaningful content. Although maybe you didn't perform this action, it is entirely possible that any number of other readers did.

Jablonka and Lamb further argue that memes are a poor concept because they lack discrete and unchanging boundaries from generation to generation. However, the same criticism can be used against genes: they do not have easily discernable boundaries or well-defined features.[354] While genes are replicated with relatively high fidelity, it is all a matter of LoD. From the human perspective, genes certainly seem to be replicated more accurately than memes. But neither genes nor memes would be affected by natural selection if they were replicated perfectly from generation to generation (see Chapter 11). Another way to think about this is in terms of organismal reproduction. From the LoD of a human, it is easy to see the differences between a parent and their children, but the differences between a bacterium and its daughter cells are irrelevant. Despite our inability to distinguish one from another, any two given bacteria are unique individuals.

Like memes and genes, organisms have very poorly defined boundaries and are inseparable from other organisms and their surroundings. A human cannot exist without a group of other humans and other organisms, much like one organ cannot exist without a body. This is partly because every organism depends on preceding generations to provide a variety of templates for its existence. For humans this means a physiological template from our parents in the form of sexual reproduction, a memetic template from other humans in the form of behaviors to be mimicked, a social template from tradition in the form of cultural fabric, etc., etc.

The vital importance of template replication requires a new fundamental

---

354 Helen Pearson, "Genetics: What Is a Gene?" *Nature* 441, no. 7092 (May 2006): 399, https://doi.org/10.1038/441398a. "Many scientists are now starting to think that the descriptions of proteins encoded in DNA know no borders—that each sequence reaches into the next and beyond...The more expert scientists become in molecular genetics, the less easy it is to be sure about what, if anything, a gene actually is."

unit of natural selection, so I have coined the term *organum*, or *organa* for a plurality. It is my intention that organa be a very fuzzy label which is highly dependent on both context and perspective—in other words, the LoD largely determines what is or isn't an organum.

Consider organa to be the original type of replicator that emerged even before RNA or proteins (although both RNA and proteins can be considered organa). Organa are also an extension of the NASA definition of life—an organum is any "thing" that is subject to natural selection. An organum is an entity that is bounded, singular, and self-directed. Although an organum is a singular entity, organa always seem to *organ*ize in groups because of their inherently replicative capacity. In a way, an organum is an expansion of Dawkins's definition of a vehicle, which he describes as "any unit discrete enough to seem worth naming."[355] Both vehicles and replicators (like genes and organisms) can be considered organa. The organum is a unit of organization; standing in contrast to disorder—it re-positions life as a homeostatic collection of replicators in cooperation to compose something ever-larger than individual lifeforms. While they may be comprised of many things, organa are single units of heredity, identity, and evolution.

ORGANA

> "Every component of the organism is as much of an organism as every other part."
>
> —BARBARA MCCLINTOCK

The epigenetic inheritance systems described in this book are not all identical, so the organum concept is an attempt to organize genes, behavior, epigenetics, memetics, organismal heritability (i.e., things like the transfer of microbiomes or *Demodex* mites between organisms), and organization itself into a universal framework of functional inheritance. Organa can be considered the basic building blocks of organisms and organizations, while also being organisms

---

355 Dawkins, *The Extended Phenotype*, 173.

or organizations themselves. For a long time, cells have been considered the basic building blocks of organisms and the most fundamental unit of life. Cells are so fundamental to the concept of life that even the whole universe has been theorized to be a cell.[356] However, in the framework of this book, cells are a subset of the most primal type of living replicators: organa. The category of organum expands the definition of life beyond cellular-based organisms and into the domain of self-organized replicators of all kinds. By this definition, both multicellular organisms (like humans) and acellular replicators (like viruses) are organa.

Mitochondria are another perfect example of a self-organized replicator that is undoubtedly an organum but is not considered an organism. They have their own cell membranes, genomes, and metabolisms, but they aren't considered independent organisms because they are permanently embedded as organelles within human cells. However, by this criterion humans aren't independent organisms either, as we are also permanently embedded within larger structures that are required for our survival. (These larger structures—like families, social networks, and culture— are all affected by natural selection, which makes them organa in their own right). Despite this conceptual similarity between humans and mitochondria, we consider ourselves to be individual organisms. Organa show that humans are like mitochondria in a paradoxical sense—we are independent individuals whose survival depends on being components of a collective. For example, a properly functioning cell requires thousands of freely moving mitochondria, and each mitochondrion requires a functioning cell to survive. Individuals will be born and die, but the overall structure and function of the cell will remain relatively the same (in the vast majority of cases). Similarly, an operational organization (like a company) needs many individual humans working in the same place (or at least towards the same goal), and each of these humans needs the income from their job to survive. Certainly, a person can maintain their survival independently of that company, for instance, by getting a different job. But it appears mitochondria can do this too. It has

---

356 Seyed H. Anjamrooz, Douglas J. Mcconnell, and Hassan Azari, "The Cellular Universe: A New Cosmological Model Based on the Holographic Principle," *International Journal of the Physical Sciences* 6, no. 9 (May 2011): 2176–79, https://doi.org/10.5897/IJPS10.461.

recently been shown that (at least in plants) mitochondria can move from cell-to-cell and even from species to species![357]

Perhaps it is not outlandish to suggest that organizations made up of living humans might be alive themselves. Beyond this, it does not seem absurd to consider that many living organizations composed of many humans might themselves compose an even bigger organum, like a living society or a living planet.[358] Similarly to a hologenome, an organum describes an organism that is a member of a nearly infinite number of larger superorganisms. Each individual organum is also composed of many smaller organa and is itself a superorganism in this regard. For example, one human is a part of a family, a society, and the planet as a whole. That same human is also composed of a series of embedded organa, like individual cells, which are further composed of mitochondria, which are further composed of RNA and proteins. These organa all interact with each other and can exist in overlapping subsets of superorganisms (like how you can move from one friend group to another, how a cell can be transferred from a pregnant mother to a developing fetus and vice versa,[359] and how a mitochondrion can move from cell-to-cell or even from species-to-species[360]).

The beauty of organa is that they always play multiple roles simultaneously

---

357 Csanad Gurdon et al., "Cell-to-Cell Movement of Mitochondria in Plants," *Proceedings of the National Academy of Sciences* 113, no. 12 (March 2016): 3397, https://doi.org/10.1073/pnas.1518644113.

358 Indeed, it has been hypothesized that the earth is a massive superorganism (known as Gaia) composed of all the lifeforms on the planet. See [Andrei G. Lapenis, "Directed Evolution of the Biosphere: Biogeochemical Selection or Gaia?" *Professional Geographer* 54, no. 3 (August 2002): 379–91, https://doi.org/10.1111/0033-0124.00337] for some of the historical context of this idea.

359 Kristina M. Adams, and J. Lee Nelson, "Microchimerism: An Investigative Frontier in Autoimmunity and Transplantation," *Journal of the American Medical Association* 291, no. 9 (March 2004): 1127–31, https://doi.org/10.1001/jama.291.9.1127. "Recent studies indicate cells transfer between fetus and mother during pregnancy and can persist in both decades later. The presence within one individual of a small population of cells from another genetically distinct individual is referred to as microchimerism... naturally acquired fetal and maternal microchimerism are common in healthy individuals...Some studies have provided support for the concept that naturally acquired microchimerism can contribute to autoimmune diseases but at the same time suggest microchimerism may have beneficial effects to the host."

360 Gurdon, "Cell-to-Cell Movement of Mitochondria," 3397.

and can be nested within one another to a seemingly infinite degree. Living organa can conglomerate to create conscious beings, or what Dawkins would call "vehicles." Confusingly, a conglomeration of organa is itself an organum. The consciousness of organa seems to arise because an organum is a self-referencing unit, like a gene, a word, or a level (see Chapter 11), and when two organa cooperate they become interdependent and start to reference each other in addition to themselves. This is analogous to the way several words can combine into a sentence. A new form emerges (the sentence) with a meaning that is not contained within either of the individuals (the words), but within their *interaction*—the way in which multiple organa combine is, in of itself, a new organum.

When two organa interact, they will maintain their individual capacities to respond to the environment (emotion). One organum will sense the behavior of another and respond, just like it might respond to any event in its environment. Each organum acts as a reflection of the other, which creates a feedback loop of responses responding to responses responding to responses etc., etc. This process is precisely the same as the emergence of human consciousness through our capacity to feel our emotions—the awareness of our own responses to the environment creates a recursive loop of self-reference. And we are only capable of such complex self-awareness due to our constant interactions with other humans. Consciousness occurs through reflection, and organa can provide each other with the necessary responsive feedback to start the loop of self-awareness.

If all organa are conscious, what's the point of ascribing a new definition to the word organum to better describe, better organize life? Isn't consciousness close enough? Not really, because it is easy to dissociate consciousness from life with some arbitrary cut-off point of "inanimate-ness" to deprive some living things of conscious awareness. For the strongly religious this comes in the form of denying animals a soul, while for the more science-minded this inclusivity arises by denying viruses the label of "living beings," or plants the attribute of "consciousness" or "qualia." But according to the implications of *organumics*, this dissociation between consciousness and life is all backwards when conscious awareness is built on the foundations of life. Instead, the first living replicators in evolutionary history that we could call organa must have emerged from a system that was conscious, but not alive. In other words, self-replication (one of the elements for natural selection to occur) requires a self—life is to consciousness as squares are to rectangles. *Organa* must have evolved from things that were capable of both dissociating themselves from their environment and responding to external events to maintain internal order. The act of self-replication was an extension of this attempt to survive— instead of continuously maintaining the same form as you grow and become more complicated over time, just distill down the essence of your self into a simplified code and recreate your form *de novo*. And thus, the first organum was born.

EPIGENETICS, PAST AND FUTURE

> "You are a function of what the whole universe is doing in the same way that a wave is a function of what the whole ocean is doing."
>
> —ALAN WATTS

> "You are not a drop in the ocean. You are the entire ocean, in a drop."
>
> –RUMI

This chapter has suggested a new word, organum, as a description of the simplest theoretical living thing. In terms of the way that NASA defines life,[361] organa can be thought of as the most basic units of natural selection—yes, in the same way that genes are regarded by the paradigm of the Modern Synthesis, otherwise known as Neo-Darwinism, or the gene-centric view of biology (see Chapter 1). However, the concept of organa expands the substrate of natural selection to encompass a broad definition of life in which viruses, ideas, proteins, and RNA are all conscious, living things (organa). The concept of organa overlaps nicely with the definition of consciousness as *the various homeostatic mechanisms* (see Chapter 9) *that change the individual "self" in response to changes in the environment* (see Chapter 11). If a thing undergoes

---

361 NASA, "About Life Detection."

natural selection it *absolutely must* be conscious by this definition, because evolution is nothing more than *the act of modifying yourself and your descendants in response to your surroundings.* This occurs both on an individual level as well as an interpersonal and transgenerational level.

Organa as units of natural selection, therefore, are necessarily conscious. At the very least, all living things are conscious of their "selves," or where the boundary of the individual ends and the environment begins. Although it is not a new idea, it is gaining some traction that the feeling of subjective consciousness is "the fundamental moving force in all life, from the cellular level up to the complexity of the human organism...survival is only possible for something that can feel."[362] In a sense, this is how Lamarck would want to be remembered, for the idea that conscious behavior and emotional affect can produce a strong influence on the evolution of life and the process of speciation. And in terms of *organumics*, a word I have created to describe the study of organum, the influence of conscious decision making on the direction of evolutionary progress cannot be understated.

In the organumic framework, life requires consciousness, but consciousness does not require life. In other words, all living things are conscious, but not all conscious things are living. With organa as a reference point for the theoretical division between animate and inanimate things it becomes possible to theorize about the origins of the first forms of life. Most theorists assume that replication occurred before there was life, but under the framework of organa it is possible to assume that the beginnings of self-replication *were* the beginnings of life. What came before the first organum can only be described as "conscious but non-living entities"—a form of self-sustained, self-contained homeostatic mechanisms that did not have the capacity to replicate. This can be a dangerous line of thought when applied practically—it is not meant to imply that an infertile human is not a living thing. It is a purely philosophical thought exercise that illuminates some of the confusion about the origins of life and consciousness and the utility of an organumic framework.

Natural selection seems to be universal, so anything could technically be considered alive or organumic under the right circumstances. This suggests that natural selection operates independently on different LoDs and that

---

362 Weber, *Biology of Wonder*, 2, 12.

they can compete against each other. For example, the organa within a single organism can fight for control like the distinct personalities in a person with multiple-personality disorder. This is observable in the antiquated description of genetic variations as "predispositions" toward a certain behavior. In other words, genes can "fight" our conscious attempts to control the behavior of our bodies.

Another example of this inter-LoD competition is the relationship between your diet and the bacteria that live in your gut (see Chapters 9 and 10): "Evolutionary conflict between the host and microbiota may lead to cravings and cognitive conflict with regard to food choice. Exerting self-control over eating choices may be partly a matter of suppressing microbial signals that originate in the gut."[363] Perhaps our existence as conscious beings is defined by the relationships (some competitive, some cooperative) among the organa that compose us.

It is difficult to separate our lives from the lives and influence of the other organisms around us. As organa, we are composed of a seemingly infinite number of smaller things and compose a seemingly infinite number of larger things. We are units of life with poorly defined boundaries that replicate imperfectly with heredity and variation—stable superorganisms that live, grow, and undergo natural selection on many levels, from the mitochondria in our cells to the memes in our brains. Given all the available evidence, the word epigenetics seems practically silly in the context of organa and evolution, since genes are such a small piece of what makes a living organism. Perhaps the meaning of epigenetics should be restricted to what happens "on top of" genes, like chromatin modifications and DNA methylation, rather than some broad description of non-genetic memory systems "in addition to" or "above" genes. Truly, it is organumics that refers to the myriad ways in which heredity, identity, and consciousness interact with evolution.

In this book I sought to use epigenetics to describe the amazing variation in what can be considered an "organum," or a unit of natural selection. Organa are drastically diverse, because they are unique in the degrees and ways that the four necessary components of natural selection (see Chapter 11) operate on them. Despite this diversity, the conceptual unit "organa" is meant

---

363 Alcock, "Is Eating Behavior Manipulated by the Gastrointestinal Microbiota?" 946.

to consolidate genetic, epigenetic, memetic, and other types of inheritance into a unit of functional description analogous to a gene or a meme. A single organum is the sum total of the "reliably transferred developmental resources needed to reconstruct, express and modify... a lineage."[364] Given the vast array of diverse resources that are required to reconstruct, express, and modify a lineage, a single organum may never have truly defined boundaries. However, organumics would have utility as a multidisciplinary field that aims to explain reality in terms of evolution. If, as Theodosius Dobzhansky once wrote, "nothing in biology makes sense except in the light of evolution,"[365] perhaps nothing in the universe makes sense unless it is framed from an evolutionary LoD. After all, everything that humans have ever thought or perceived has been sculpted by natural selection.[366] Our genes, ideas, bodies, and even our "artificial" creations are subject to natural selection and the other forces of evolution.[367] Everything that exists and everything that humans have ever known can be considered organumic. Natural selection has the *capacity* to affect everything in existence, but only things that imperfectly replicate, inherit traits from their ancestors, and participate in a competition for survival can be considered organa, be they viruses, cells, humans, memes, or societies.

The variety of observable LoDs that contain organum (replicating, self-contained, conscious life forms) suggest that choice and free will exist, but boundaries and restrictions prevent the organum in any one LoD from exerting

---

364 Badyaev, "Epigenetic Resolution of the 'Curse of Complexity,'" 2253.

365 Dobzhansky, "Nothing in Biology Makes Sense except in the Light of Evolution," title.

366 Newman, "Evolution Is More Than Natural Selection."

367 Yes, there are other forces that drive evolution—natural selection is not the only mechanism by which living things evolve. See [Stuart Aa Newman, "Evolution Is More Than Natural Selection," *Huffington Post*, February 10, 2013, https://www.huffingtonpost.com/stuart-a-newman/evolution-is-more-than-natural-selection_b_2274252.html] for a description of one example of this: adaptation. Adaptation is a concept that emerged coincidentally with Darwin's theory of evolution by natural selection and refers to developmental modifications that occur without necessarily being affected by natural selection. If such an adaptive modification promotes survival and is heritable, it becomes a naturally selected trait. But, if it has no long-term effects on the evolution of the species, it is simply an evolutionary adaptation that exists transiently and independently from natural selection. Consider that such adaptations can exert influence over naturally selected processes without being subject to natural selection in and of themselves.

too much influence on the system as a whole—there is no omnipotence in such a democratic system. All life is an inseparable, holistic unit that has no choice but to reside amongst the other forms of life within the universe. But organa do seem to have a choice in how our futures will unfold. Conscious control over evolution provides us with the capacity to take responsibility for ourselves, our environments, and the future of humanity and the world.

Epilogue

"Our powers of representation permit us, for instance, to represent…
our own prehistory and discover the unrepresented reasons
everywhere in the tree of life."

—DANIEL C. DENNETT

ORGANA, EPIGENETICS, AND QUANTA

"The recognition that life shapes environment which then shapes
life which then shapes environment destroys the foundation of the
neo-Darwinian system. It begins to destroy the whole concept of
cause-and-effect. Evolution begins to take on quantum characteristics;
linear thinking is no longer foundational."

—STEPHEN HARROD BUHNER, *Plant Intelligence and the Imaginal Realm*

Organa embedded within each other are the essence of life as defined by
NASA, and likely represent the first type of *organic* life. In this book I have
given a name, organumics, to the study of organa. Organumics is more of a
perceptual framework than a field of study, more speculation than theory, and
more paradigm shift than scientific hypothesis. I intend for the organumic
framework to reorient and recategorize all of human knowledge and perception
from an evolutionary LoD—to describe reality in terms of biology. As of
now, existential frameworks that aim to explain the universe frame reality
from the LoD of physics. From this LoD our world is a mechanical object
that can be poked, prodded, and studied into submission. Unfortunately,
this approach simply cannot explain the internal dimension of subjectivity.

Identity, consciousness, and the human experience are discounted from the equation, as if psychic space is a dimension separate from the physical, as if human experience is somehow outside the reality of the universe.

The advent of quantum mechanics (the physics of the tiniest imaginable objects) nearly broke the dogma of scientific materialism. In this branch of physics, there is none of the predictability or familiarity of the human LoD— at very small scales the universe does not act how we expect it to and our everyday experience fails us. Even the most brilliant of human minds cannot fathom the paradoxical nature of our relationship with the quantum world. As the popular theoretical physicist Richard Feynman said, "I think I can safely say that nobody understands quantum mechanics."[368] Perhaps because of this confusion, or because of some deeper transcendental truth in the science, pseudoscientific spiritualists like Deepak Chopra have coopted the term "quantum physics" to connect consciousness to the reality of physical existence.

Epigenetics has befallen a very similar fate, with a growing following of holistic medical practitioners using the term to describe an unrestricted form of Lamarckism—a way for choice, experience, and the subjective dimension to influence the direction of evolution. Over the course of this book I have built a very similar argument, but hopefully with a more restrained and reasoned conclusion. I truly believe that just as quantum mechanics overcame the physical determinism of Newtonian physics, epigenetics threatens to topple the genetic determinism of the Central Dogma of molecular biology. Bruce Lipton, a popular scientist with an approach comparable to Deepak Chopra's, says it like this, "…epigenetics reveals a completely different truth. Genes do not control life. It is the environment, and more specifically, our perception of the environment that controls gene activity. In the end, it comes down to a simple case of 'mind over matter' in controlling the fate of our lives."[369] Indeed, epigenetics shows that organa are inseparable from the environment, and it is the interaction between LoDs that truly molds speciation and evolution.

---

368 Richard Feynman, *The Character of Physical Law* (Cambridge: MIT Press, 1985), 129.

369 Bruce Lipton, "Insights into the Convergence of Science and Spirituality," accessed October 1, 2018, https://www.personalgrowthcourses.net/stories/00a.lipton_biology.htm/.

Along with their overall thematic similarities and adoption by pseudoscientists, quantum mechanics and epigenetics share some strikingly similar details. For example, it is possible to represent the "fitness" of a genome in a 3-dimensional graphical space. This creates what is known as a "fitness landscape, in which the peaks of each hill represent an "optimal" genotype and the valleys represent low levels of fitness given specific environmental survival pressures, which can technically be anything. One example is shown in the figure below, where the peaks represent a genotype in bacteria that provides antibiotic resistance to a specific drug (see figure E.1). The figure depicts that resistance to drug B is a low level of fitness when drug A is present in the environment, while resistance to drug A is low fitness when drug B is in the environment. This makes sense, because an individual population of bacteria will die in the presence of drug A, even if they are resistant to drug B and vice versa. Similarly, there are two paths that lead from resistance to the wrong drug to resistance to the right drug: the bacteria can either become resistant to both or lose their current resistance to become resistant to the more immediate threat.

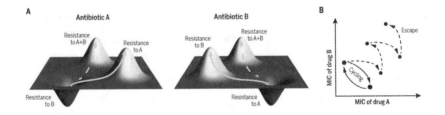

FIGURE E.1 An example of a fitness landscape. In this graphic the peaks represent two ways for a bacterium to be resistant to an antibiotic that is present in the environment, while the valley represents resistance to a drug that isn't in the environment and a lack of resistance to an antibiotic that is present.

Like most computer models, this one is overly simplified, but it is an effective means of describing how populations of organisms undergo natural selection in relation to a specific fitness variable. These fitness landscapes are used to model antibiotic resistance and create more effective drugs to overcome bacterial evolutionary strategies.[370]

As an aside, these landscapes can be used to model anything, including systems and processes that we wouldn't normally consider as evolutionary. For example, there is a mathematical problem known as a Hamiltonian path problem (one type of which is known as the traveling salesman problem) that attempts to determine the most efficient path to take if you want to visit each place on a map exactly one time. A practical and simple-sounding task. But, as the number of points on the map increase, this problem gets so complicated that there is no way to tell if a computer can calculate the answer in a finite amount of time. As of October 1, 2018, the Clay Mathematics Institute's website claims that they will give you a one-million-dollar prize if you can prove that these problems are solvable!

There is a very interesting phenomenon that can be observed in fitness landscapes called "peak shift." This describes a jump that occurs when a population is at a local peak, but ends up at an even higher adjacent peak, as is represented by the dotted line in figure E.2. This is an interesting and paradoxical occurrence, because natural selection cannot select for decreased fitness—by definition, only increased levels of fitness lead to survival. If a trait or genotype helps a population survive it is necessarily considered as an increase in fitness. But to go from one peak to a higher peak the population needs to traverse a valley, which means a decrease in its level of fitness. Despite the fact that this happens in reality, it is impossible by definition. This impossible event is a phenomenon known as "peak shift." Peak shift has been compared to "quantum tunneling," which is when a subatomic particle physically moves through a barrier in a way that seems to break the classical laws of physics.[371] Quantum tunneling is teleportation through a solid wall, while peak shift is a jump over an impassable valley.

---

370 Michael Baym, Laura K. Stone, and Roy Kishony, "Multidrug Evolutionary Strategies to Reverse Antibiotic Resistance," *Science* 351, no. 6268 (January 2016): aad3292, https://doi.org/10.1126/science.aad3292.

371 Wolfgang Banzhaf, and Frank H. Eckman, eds. *Evolution and Biocomputation: Computational Models of Evolution*. (New York: Springer-Verlag Berlin Heidelberg, 1995), 185.

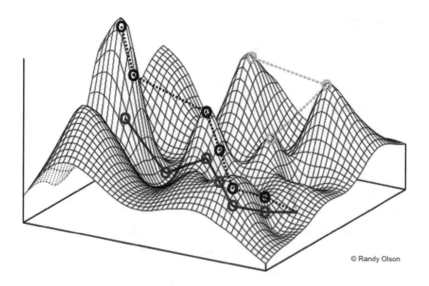

© Randy Olson

FIGURE E.2 A fitness landscape that exhibits evolutionary motion from one local peak of fitness to another—a paradoxical concept known as peak shift.

There is some debate about whether peak shift contradicts the modern synthesis of biology,[372] but it is certainly evidence for the existence of extra-dimensional processes. In this case, "extra-dimensional" does not literally refer to dimensions like some explanations of quantum processes do (e.g., string theory). Instead, these extra dimensions are unseen LoDs—perspectives that seem impossible and paradoxical from the traditional explanation. Since fitness landscapes are often made to model genomic fitness, it makes sense that the 3-dimensional rules of the model could be broken by the existence of non-genetic heritability and adaptation—the LoD of epigenetics. As this book has discussed, epigenetics provides a means for the inheritance of non-genetic information, like memories, fears, traumas, behaviors, and even identity itself. In the same way that quantum mechanics is used to argue for the power of consciousness and free will, the possibilities of epigenetics imply some interesting and unbelievable things about our mortality as organumic beings.

372 Pigliucci, "Do We Need an Extended Evolutionary Synthesis?" 2747–48.

THE IMMORTALITY OF ORGANA

Organa, speciation, and common ancestry lead to a deep and unavoidable interconnectedness of all life. In conflict with this, human beings strive to be different from other species and individual humans strive to be distinct from other human beings. It does make sense that we would fight for uniqueness—variation is required for natural selection and is therefore rewarded by evolution. Despite our concerns, no two things *are* the same no matter how similar they may seem. There are drastic differences between individuals within the same species, and even within the same individual viewed over time. You are not your parents and they are not your grandparents. And yet, every living organism is based on a template that was provided by the previous generation.

Every living organism competes for survival with whatever skills and strategies they inherit, stumble upon, or both. After all, everything that humans have "stumbled upon" has been provided directly by nature. No matter how effective our ancestors were or how well they fought for their lives, they had to return to the unity of nature. No matter how effective our technology and medicine become, every living organism will die. But do the details of epigenetics and non-genetic inheritance really support this intuitive claim of universal mortality? Just as Deepak Chopra sees epigenetics as the doorway to "…unlimited influence on our fate,"[373] Bruce Lipton sees it as evidence that death may not be as final as we think. In his words, "[Epigenetics] convinced me that we are immortal, spiritual beings who exist separately from our bodies. I had heard an undeniable inner voice informing me that I was leading a life based not only on the false premise that genes control biology, but also on the false premise that we end when our physical bodies die."[374]

Even before epigenetics was a popular topic, the concept of heritable identity had led some people to claim that immortality is not only achievable, but already exists. Chess master and professor Andrzej Szyszko-Bohusz devised a theory which he called "The Theory of Genetic Immortality."[375]

---

373 Chopra, "You Can Transform Your Own Biology."

374 Lipton, "Convergence of Science and Spirituality."

375 Andrzej Szyszko-Bohusz, "Hypothesis of Genetic Immortality," accessed October 1, 2018, http://members.upcpoczta.pl/z.ryznar3/haplife/life-against-death/bohusz.htm/.

Despite the name, his ideas are not solely based on genetic heritability, they are just derived strongly from genetic evidence. Professor Szyszko-Bohusz believes that heritable identity is itself a form of immortality. He says, "the notion of 'heredity' can be understood as continuity of the parents' life [and consciousness] in children...the chain of life has not been destroyed from the immemorial time, when the primordial cell appeared."[376]

This idea is reminiscent of the concept of the protoplasm theories discussed in Chapter 2—that the essence of life is an unbroken chain of cytoplasmic transfer from cell to cell at each generational division.[377] This may be an attractive theory, but it is unlikely. To see why, recall the mythological Ship of Theseus from Chapter 3, the idea that the body of an individual organism is almost entirely recycled in one lifetime. If this is the case, how could a piece of the original lifeform still be within our bodies? If an organism can't maintain parts of its original form for a few decades, how could a lineage keep individual pieces for billions of years? This question isn't a problem for an organum. Even if there is no physical substance left over from our ancient origins, the template of replicative ability has been a part of all organa from the very beginnings of life.

Beyond pure theory, there is even some semi-legitimate science attempting to uncover the mechanisms of aging to achieve immortality. Aubrey de Grey has been spearheading this effort to halt the aging process and create undying humans. This is a valiant attempt, but his work is largely based on genetics with very little mention of epigenetics.[378] Although the basics of his theory are epigenetic in essence, he does not frame it this way. He proposes that immortality is achievable through series of regenerative medicine techniques called SENS (Strategies for Engineered Negligible Senescence) that are meant

---

376 *Ibid.*

377 Weismann, *Essays Upon Heredity*, 104.

378 And when de Grey does mention "epigenetics" it is only so that he can functionally define it as synonymous with genetics. As he says in [Aubrey de Grey, and Michael Rae, *Ending Aging: The Rejuvenation Breakthroughs That Could Reverse Human Aging in Our Lifetime* (New York: St. Martin's Griffin, 2008), 276], "...changes in the epigenetic scaffolding of a cell's DNA ultimately have the same range of *functional* effects on the cell as changes to the genes themselves... I'll mostly be using 'mutations' to refer to *both* kinds of genetic damage—true mutations and epimutations."

to halt the aging process.

Senescence (aging) is a process that can likely be overcome, since there are many species that do not ever seem to succumb to the health problems associated with aging. For example, lobsters will continue to grow until they receive a mortal injury or die from very rare cancers unrelated to age[379] (several lobsters have been caught that were well over 100 years old). Despite the amazing immunity to aging that lobsters display, it is extraordinarily unlikely that immortality will ever be achievable without some form of replication. This is because replication seems to be a universally selected feature of all life and an essential aspect of evolution.

But even if a true evasion of death is implausible, replication is in and of itself a form of immortality. After all, replicating yourself is quite literally making more of "you." A theory called the Algorithmic Reincarnation Hypothesis seeks to address the idea of replicative immortality through the study of near-death experiences.[380] The theory has a relatively simple premise: near-death experiences have a form of universal grammar, a structured sequence of subjective experiences that are universal across cultures. Todd Murphy, the originator of the theory, takes this to mean that natural selection operates on the subjective experience of death. In principle, this could not happen unless some form of reincarnation occurs to pass on the information contained within the death experience. He does not focus on the mechanism by which this could occur, but Mr. Murphy believes that this "algorithmic reincarnation" is mediated epigenetically.[381]

Even if Mr. Murphy's theory does not stand up to rigorous scrutiny, a form of organumic reincarnation is clearly observable through template replication. In other words, each generation of life bears an undeniable resemblance to the generation that came before it. But offspring are not identical to their parents, they are modified and adapted versions of previous generations—this is an

---

379 C. Stephen Downes, "What the Books Say: Senescence and the Genome or, Change and Decay in All Except Lobsters I See," *BioEssays* 15, no. 5 (May 1993): 359, https://doi.org/https://doi.org/10.1002/bies.950150512.

380 Todd Murphy, "The Structure and Function of Near-Death Experiences: An Algorithmic Reincarnation Hypothesis," *Journal of Near-Death Studies* 20, no. 2 (December 2001): 101–18.

381 Personal e-mail correspondence with Todd Murphy, April 2018.

essential ingredient in the process of natural selection and the existence of organa. Each successive wave of reproduction contains the most updated forms of life in the gradual procession that is evolution.

While this is an idea attributed solely to Darwin, Lamarck also promoted "the successive production of all living forms from the simplest to the most complex"[382] (see Chapter 1). As we've seen over the course of this book, Lamarckian theory deserves at least a fraction of the positive attention that Darwin's have received. Epigenetics provides all the evidence necessary to integrate these two great evolutionary theorists into a single organumic framework: an LoD in which we are connected to the entirety of life; an existence in which consciousness plays a key role in the progression of biological change; a reality in which the intentionality of evolution is an essential part of the universe. And I think that Darwin, in all his brilliance, would wholeheartedly agree. At the very least, he laid the foundation for an organumic framework as an extension of his evolutionary theory. In his words: "We cannot fathom the marvelous complexity of an organic being... a little universe, formed of a host of self-propagating organisms, inconceivably minute and as numerous as the stars in heaven."[383]

---

382 Burkhardt, "Lamarck," 804.

383 Charles Darwin, *The Variation of Animals and Plants Under Domestication, Volume 2* (London: John Murray, 1868), 404.

Afterword

"...I would advise any young scientist looking for a new and fresh topic to research to seek the flaw in anything claimed by the orthodox to be certain."

—JAMES LOVELOCK, *Homage to Gaia*

This book has been in my mind for a while now, but this is the perfect time to spread these ideas and use them to discuss some extremely important topics. At this moment in history there seems to be a strong tension between logic and emotion—political, moral, and scientific debates have literally become divided between "facts" and "alternative facts." But to invoke a quote from philosopher Daniel Dennett: "when a long-standing controversy seems to be getting nowhere, with both 'sides' stubbornly insisting they are right, as often as not the trouble is that there is something they both agree on that is just not so."[384]

Perhaps the misconception in this particular fight is the existence of "facts" at all. Even many scientists hold philosophical opinions about the "truth values" of scientific statements, as science does not produce truth, it only falsifies. Another great philosopher, Karl Popper, once said: "In so far as a scientific statement speaks about reality, it must be falsifiable; and in so far as it is not falsifiable, it does not speak about reality."[385] In other words, science cannot falsify its way into creating factual knowledge.

---

384 Daniel C. Dennett, *Intuition Pumps and Other Tools for Thinking* (New York and London: W.W. Norton & Company, 2013), 46.

385 Karl R. Popper, *The Logic of Scientific Discovery* (London and New York: Routledge Classics, 2004), 316.

Scientific "facts" like gravity, electricity, and a globular Earth are actually not facts as we conventionally understand that them, but confident beliefs that arise from *consilience*, or the convergence of evidence from many different perspectives. In other words, when a bunch of people see the same result happen a bunch of times in repeated, rigorously controlled conditions. It is easy to forget about the "repeated, rigorously controlled" part of this equation, but it is vitally important because of the malleability of memory discussed in Chapter 8—humans are very easy to persuade and witness testimony is notoriously unreliable. Independent verification without proper controls is often used to justify religious beliefs: if a majority of the people on Earth believe it, mustn't it be true? Unfortunately, our intuitions almost always seem to lead us astray: the sun and stars don't rotate around the earth, heavier objects do not in fact fall faster than lighter objects, and physical matter is not as solid as we perceive it to be. Perception and belief just aren't effective tools for discerning the true nature of reality. Even rigorous experiments can lead us horribly astray when designed poorly.

This is not to say that religious beliefs are useless or unconscionable like some of my favorite authors think (i.e., Richard Dawkins or Daniel Dennett). It can certainly seem like a belief in god or a disagreement with macro-evolution are nonveridical, or an inaccurate depiction of reality. But veridicality is strongly selected against in models of evolution, meaning that our perceptions are unlikely to provide us with truthful, accurate simulations of our universe.[386] This is okay though, because the scientific method clearly provides a way to functionally improve our lives, even if it doesn't embody the spirit of unknowable truth like "God" or "spirituality." A big part of the current confusion (and basically all conflict) is that we erect boundaries to separate ourselves from others. We divide ourselves by means of our memories, beliefs, and identities. In philosophy, this is known as *reductionism*—an attempt to explain the whole by explaining each of the pieces. Reductionism is opposed to holistic philosophies, which accept the interconnectedness of all things. Szyszko-Bohusz and his theory of genetic immortality (see Chapter 12) are a perfect example of a holistic attitude. He makes the argument that science

---

386 Hoffman, "The Interface Theory of Perception," 1480–1506.

should be the subject of religious and metaphysical scrutiny,[387] and I agree. When scientific theory becomes detached from its intuitive, creative roots it can try to overcompensate—an interesting example of an organum restoring homeostasis. This book has presented several examples of this, like the central dogma, the gene-centric view of natural selection, and the resistance to epigenetic influences on evolution. Evolution itself is even frequently referred to as a "secular religion."[388]

The animosity between religion and science is unfortunate and unnecessary. But it is a symptom of a larger problem within the scientific and medical communities: a complete lack of patience for anything emotional or purely holistic. As Kevin Laland says about the resistance to the inclusion of epigenetic mechanisms in evolutionary theory, "...the mere mention of the EES [extended evolutionary systems] often evokes an emotional, even hostile, reaction among evolutionary biologists. Perhaps haunted by the specter of intelligent design, evolutionary biologists wish to show a united front to those hostile to science."[389] Even though many religious leaders (e.g., the pope) accept the power and progress of scientific theory, the average person can have a difficult time reconciling their beliefs with a scientifically-based reality. It can be upsetting for an outside force to try and convince you that your perspective is inaccurate, or unjustifiable. And there is no doubt that everyone has their own unique, subjective perspectives. The existence and individuality of each conscious experience is arguably the only thing that can be considered "Truth."

Consilience provides an amazingly powerful means of getting a functional advantage on the world, while religious doctrines are very effective at organizing humans into like-minded groups by providing a wholesome explanation for the foundations of reality. Dangerous fanaticism arises from one of two imbalances between these forces: 1) when reverence for the unknown is not informed by what we know, and 2) when what we know is not kept in check by the realization that we cannot know everything (or even anything at all). The wisest of all people embrace the paradoxical nature of

---

387 Szyszko-Bohusz, "Genetic Immortality."

388 Ruse, "Is Evolution a Secular Religion?" 1523–24.

389 Laland, "Does Evolutionary Theory Need a Rethink?" 162.

Zen/The Tao/conscious existence (see Chapter 11)—they only know that they know nothing. Or, at the very least, they attempt to achieve balance between what can and cannot be known.

Most of the monumental thinkers of the world engaged in some aspect of mysticism that informed their science or philosophy. This quote about the history of mathematical evolution shows the power of mystical thinking, "The founders of calculus often grasped at concepts that they could not fully understand. The field relied on infinitesimals, which had a metaphysical aura so controversial that they were in part responsible for getting Galileo Galilei in hot water with the Catholic Church."[390] There is a strong religious power that nature can exert over our conscious minds which simply cannot be explained by science—in Einstein's words: "... a conflict between [science and religion] appears impossible. For science can only ascertain what is, but not what should be..."[391]

Despite the reverence for the unknown reflected in the enduring wisdom of illustrious minds, modern-day scientists often have no such respect for the unknowable holism of our universe. Many scientists seem to be positively frightened by the mystical and spiritual, but surely the concept of mysticism is not such a threat to scientific theory. Perhaps these anti-paranormal sentiments are a result of the modern scientific culture trending towards zealotry of religious proportions. It is my hope that epigenetics and organa can help to prevent the stagnation of scientific thought—we are only beginning to understand our biological origins and where we might be headed as a species. Hopefully this book has provided a doorway into a small aspect of the infinitude of scientific unknowns. There is so much to be learned about evolution, epigenetics, and life.

---

390 Davide Castelvecchi, "A Mathematical Revolutionary," *Nature* 528 (December 2015): 190, https://doi.org/10.1038/528190a.

391 Albert Einstein, "Religion and Science," *New York Times Magazine*, November 9, 1930, https://documents.epfl.ch/groups/l/la/lastro-unit/www/AstroI/2011-2012/albert_einstein_science_and_religion.pdf/.

Illustration Credits

2.1. Courtesy OpenStax College.

2.2. From Wikimedia Commons, by Andreas-horn-Hornig.

2.3. From Wikimedia Commons, derivative work by Radio89.

3.1. From Wikimedia Commons, by Sakurambo.

4.1. From Wikimedia Commons, by Волков Владислав Петрович.

4.2. Courtesy inviTRA.

4.3. From Wikimedia Commons, by Vladimir V. Medeyko.

4.4. Courtesy CNX OpenStax.

5.1. From Wikimedia Commons, by Ntyrrell.

6.1. From Wikimedia Commons, by AFADadcADSasd.

7.1. Courtesy the National Human Genome Research Institute.

7.2. From Wikimedia Commons, by Chris Woodcock.

7.3. From Wikimedia Commons, by Richard Wheeler.

7.4. Courtesy StemBook.

7.5. From Wikimedia Commons, by Emw.

8.1. From Wikimedia Commons, by Joseph C Boone and Phil from Sydney, Australia.

8.2. Original work by author.

9.1. Courtesy the National Institute on Drug Abuse.

9.2. From Wikimedia Commons, by Kuebi.

10.1. Original work by author.

10.2. Original work by author.

11.1. Original work by author.

11.2. From Wikimedia Commons, by Jennifer Garcia.

E.1. From [Baym, Michael, Laura K. Stone, and Roy Kishony "Multidrug evolutionary strategies to reverse antibiotic resistance." *Science* 351 no. 6268 (January 2016): aad3292]. Reprinted with permission from AAAS.

E.2. From Wikimedia Commons, by Randy Olson.

Bibliography

Abcam. "Histone Modifications: A Guide." Epigenetics. Accessed September 23, 2018. https://www.abcam.com/epigenetics/histone-modifications-a-guide/.

Adams, Kristina M., and J. Lee Nelson. "Microchimerism: An Investigative Frontier in Autoimmunity and Transplantation." *Journal of the American Medical Association* 291, no. 9 (March 2004): 1127–31. https://doi.org/10.1001/jama.291.9.1127.

Alcock, Joe, Carlo C. Maley, and C. Athena Aktipis. "Is Eating Behavior Manipulated by the Gastrointestinal Microbiota? Evolutionary Pressures and Potential Mechanisms." *BioEssays* 36, no. 10 (October 2014): 940–49. https://doi.org/10.1002/bies.201400071.

Alvarado-Esquivel, Cosme, Luis Francisco Sánchez-Anguiano, Jesús Hernández-Tinoco, Luis Omar Berumen-Segovia, Yazmin Elizabeth Torres-Prieto, Sergio Estrada-Martínez, Alma Rosa Pérez-Álamos, et al. "*Toxoplasma Gondii* Infection and Depression: A Case—Control Seroprevalence Study." *European Journal of Microbiology and Immunology* 6, no. 2 (April 2016): 85–89. https://doi.org/10.1556/1886.2016.00010.

American Heart Association. "Is Broken Heart Syndrome Real?" Accessed September 25, 2018. http://www.heart.org/HEARTORG/Conditions/More/Cardiomyopathy/Is-Broken-Heart-Syndrome-Real_UCM_448547_Article.jsp.

Andersen, Barbara L., Hae-Chung Yang, William B. Farrar, Deanna M. Golden-Kreutz, Charles F. Emery, Lisa M. Thornton, Donn C. Young, and William E. Carson. "Psychologic Intervention Improves Survival for Breast Cancer Patients." *Cancer* 113, no. 12 (December 2008): 3450–58. https://doi.org/10.1002/cncr.23969.

Andreeva, Alexandra V., and Mikhail A. Kutuzov. "Do Plants Have Rhodopsin After All? A Mystery of Plant G Protein-Coupled Signaling." *Plant Physiology and Biochemistry* 39, no. 12 (December 2001): 1027–35. https://doi.org/10.1016/S0981-9428(01)01328-6.

Anjamrooz, Seyed H., Douglas J. Mcconnell, and Hassan Azari. "The Cellular Universe: A New Cosmological Model Based on the Holographic Principle." *International Journal of the Physical Sciences* 6, no. 9 (May 2011): 2175–83. https://doi.org/10.5897/IJPS10.461.

Arumugam, Manimozhiyan, Jeroen Raes, Eric Pelletier, Denis Le Paslier, Jean-michel Batto, Marcelo Bertalan, Natalia Borruel, and Francesc Casellas. "Enterotypes of the Human Gut Microbiome." *Nature* 473, no. 7346 (May 2011): 174–80. https://doi.org/10.1038/nature09944.Enterotypes.

Aton, Sara J., and Erik D. Herzog. "Come Together, Right…Now: Synchronization of Rhythms in a Mammalian Circadian Clock." *Neuron* 48, no. 4 (November 2005): 531–34. https://doi.org/10.1016/j.neuron.2005.11.001.

Ayala, Francisco J. "Design without Designer: Darwin's Greatest Discovery." *Proceedings of the National Academy of Sciences* 104, suppl. 1 (May 2007): 8567–8573. https://doi.org/10.1017/CBO9780511804823.005.

Babenko, Olena, Igor Kovalchuk, and Gerlinde A. S. Metz. "Stress-Induced Perinatal and Transgenerational Epigenetic Programming of Brain Development and Mental Health." *Neuroscience and Biobehavioral Reviews* 48: 70–91. https://doi.org/10.1016/j. neubiorev.2014.11.013.

Bachmann, Anthony W., Teresa L. Sedgley, Richard V. Jackson, John N. Gibson, Ross McD Young, and David J. Torpy. "Glucocorticoid Receptor Polymorphisms and Post-Traumatic Stress Disorder." *Psychoneuroendocrinology* 30, no. 3 (April 2005): 297–306. https://doi.org/10.1016/j.psyneuen.2004.08.006.

Badyaev, Alexander V. "Epigenetic Resolution of the 'Curse of Complexity' in Adaptive Evolution of Complex Traits." *Journal of Physiology* 592, no. 11 (April 2014): 2251–60. https://doi.org/10.1113/jphysiol.2014.272625.

Baldwin, David, and Shauna Rudge. "The Role of Serotonin in Depression and Anxiety." *International Clinical Psychopharmacology* 9 Suppl. 4 (January 1995): 41–45. https://doi. org/10.1097/00004850-199501004-00006.

Banzhaf, Wolfgang, and Frank H. Eckman, eds. *Evolution and Biocomputation: Computational Models of Evolution.* New York: Springer-Verlag Berlin Heidelberg, 1995.

Baym, Michael, Laura K. Stone, and Roy Kishony. "Multidrug Evolutionary Strategies to Reverse Antibiotic Resistance." *Science* 351, no. 6268 (January 2016): aad3292. https://doi.org/10.1126/science.aad3292.

Beale, Andrew David, David Whitmore, and Damian Moran. "Life in a Dark Biosphere: A Review of Circadian Physiology in 'Arrhythmic' Environments." *Journal of Comparative Physiology B: Biochemical, Systemic, and Environmental Physiology* 186, no. 8 (June 2016): 947–68. https://doi.org/10.1007/s00360-016-1000-6.

Belkaid, Yasmine, and Timothy W. Hand. "Role of the Microbiota in Immunity and Inflammation." *Cell* 157, no. 1 (March 2014): 121–41. https://doi.org/10.1016/j. cell.2014.03.011.

Benner, Steven A., Alonso Ricardo, and Matthew A. Carrigan. "Is There a Common Chemical Model for Life in the Universe?" *Current Opinion in Chemical Biology* 8, no. 6 (October 2004): 672–89. https://doi.org/10.1016/j.cbpa.2004.10.003.

Benyamin, Ramsin, Andrea M. Trescot, Sukdeb Datta, Ricardo Buenaventura, Rajive Adlaka, Nalini Sehgal, Scott E. Glaser, and Ricardo Vallejo. "Opioid Complications and Side Effects." *Pain Physician* 11 (2008): S105–S120. https://doi.org/11:S105-S120.

Berg, Jeremy M., John L. Tymoczko, and Lubert Stryer. "DNA Polymerases Require a Template and a Primer." In *Biochemistry 5th Edition,* chapter 27.2. New York: W.H. Freeman, 2002.

Berkman, Lisa F., Linda Leo-Summers, and Ralph I. Horwitz. "Emotional Support and Survival after Myocardial Infarction: A Prospective, Population-Based Study of the Elderly." *Annals of Internal Medicine* 117, no. 12 (December 1992): 1003–9. https://doi. org/10.7326/0003-4819-117-12-1003.

Bianconi, Eva, Allison Piovesan, Federica Facchin, Alina Beraudi, Raffaella Casadei, Flavia Frabetti, Lorenza Vitale, et al. "An Estimation of the Number of Cells in the Human Body." *Annals of Human Biology* 40, no. 6 (November 2013): 463–71. https:// doi.org/10.3109/03014460.2013.807878.

Bird, Adrian. "Perceptions of Epigenetics." *Nature* 447, no. 7143 (May 2007): 396–98. https://doi.org/10.1038/nature05913.

Blok, David J., Sake J. de Vlas, Pepijn van Empelen, and Frank J. van Lenthe. "The Role of Smoking in Social Networks on Smoking Cessation and Relapse among Adults: A Longitudinal Study." *Preventive Medicine* 99 (February 2017): 105–10. https://doi.org/10.1016/j.ypmed.2017.02.012.

Boeke, Kees. *Cosmic View: The Universe in 40 Jumps*. New York: The John Day Company, 1957. Accessed October 1, 2018. http://www.vendian.org/mncharity/cosmicview/.

Bonduriansky, Russell. "Rethinking Heredity, Again." *Trends in Ecology and Evolution* 27, no. 6 (June 2012): 330–36. https://doi.org/10.1016/j.tree.2012.02.003.

Bonduriansky, Russell, Angela J. Crean, and Troy Day. "The Implications of Nongenetic Inheritance for Evolution in Changing Environments." *Evolutionary Applications* 5, no. 2 (November 2011): 192–201. https://doi.org/10.1111/j.1752-4571.2011.00213.x.

Brenner, Eric D., Rainer Stahlberg, Stefano Mancuso, Jorge Vivanco, František Baluška, and Elizabeth Van Volkenburgh. "Plant Neurobiology: An Integrated View of Plant Signaling." *Trends in Plant Science* 11, no. 8 (July 2006): 413–19. https://doi.org/10.1016/j.tplants.2006.06.009.

Brown, Adam D., Nicole Kouri, and William Hirst. "Memory's Malleability: Its Role in Shaping Collective Memory and Social Identity." *Frontiers in Psychology* 3 (July 2012): 1–3. https://doi.org/10.3389/fpsyg.2012.00257.

Brown, Steven A. "Circadian Clock-Mediated Control of Stem Cell Division and Differentiation: Beyond Night and Day." *Development* 141, no. 16 (August 2014): 3105–11. https://doi.org/10.1242/dev.104851.

Browne, Hannah, Gerald Mason, and Thomas Tang. "Retinoids and Pregnancy: An Update." *The Obstetrician & Gynaecologist* 16, no. 1 (2014): 7–11. https://doi.org/10.1111/tog.12075.

Bull, Eleanor, ed. *A Simple Guide to Asthma*. Oxfordshire: CSF Medical Communications Ltd., 2005.

Burkhardt, Richard W. "Lamarck, Evolution, and the Inheritance of Acquired Characters." *Genetics* 194, no. 4 (August 2013): 793–805. https://doi.org/10.1534/genetics.113.151852.

byPepone. "Emotional Deprivation in Infancy: Study by Rene A. Spitz 1952." YouTube Video, 7:18. April 22, 2010. https://youtu.be/VvdOe10vrs4.

Caballero, Lorena, Bob Hodge, and Sergio Hernandez. "Conway's 'Game of Life' and the Epigenetic Principle." *Frontiers in Cellular and Infection Microbiology* 6, article 57 (June 2016): 1–8. https://doi.org/10.3389/fcimb.2016.00057.

Callif, Ben L., Brian Maunze, Nick L. Krueger, Matthew T. Simpson, and Murray G. Blackmore. "The Application of CRISPR Technology to High Content Screening in Primary Neurons." *Molecular and Cellular Neurosciences* 80, no. 1 (April 2017): 170–79. https://doi.org/10.1016/j.mcn.2017.01.003.

Carlip, Steven. "Quantum Gravity: A Progress Report." *Reports on Progress in Physics* 64, no. 8 (July 2001): 885–942. https://doi.org/10.1088/0034-4885/64/8/301.

Carr, Suzanne. "Exquisitely Simple or Incredibly Complex: The Theory of Entoptic Phenomena." MA diss., University of Newcastle upon Tyne, 1995. http://www. oubliette.org.uk/.

Castelvecchi, Davide. "A Mathematical Revolutionary." *Nature* 528 (December 2015): 190–91. https://doi.org/10.1038/528190a.

Castro-Vale, Ivone, Elisabeth FC van Rossum, José Carlos Machado, Rui Mota-Cardoso, and Davide Carvalho. "Genetics of Glucocorticoid Regulation and Posttraumatic Stress Disorder—What Do We Know?" *Neuroscience and Biobehavioral Reviews* 63, (April 2016): 143–157. https://doi.org/10.1016/j.neubiorev.2016.02.005

Cech, Thomas R. "A Model for the RNA-Catalyzed Replication of RNA." *Proceedings of the National Academy of Sciences* 83, no. 12 (June 1986): 4360–63. https://doi. org/10.1073/pnas.83.12.4360.

Cech, Thomas R. "The RNA World in Context." *Cold Spring Harbor Perspectives in Biology* 4, no. 7 (2012): a006742. https://doi.org/10.1101/cshperspect.a006742.

Cedar, Howard, and Yehudit Bergman. "Programming of DNA Methylation Patterns." *Annual Review of Biochemistry* 81 (February 2012): 97–117. https://doi.org/10.1146/ annurev-biochem-052610.

Champagne, Frances, and Michael J. Meaney. "Chapter 21 Like Mother, Like Daughter: Evidence for Non-Genomic Transmission of Parental Behavior and Stress Responsivity." *Progress in Brain Research* 133 (January 2001): 287–302. https://doi. org/10.1016/S0079-6123(01)33022-4.

Chen, Angus. "Watch: Bacteria Invade Antibiotics and Transform into Superbugs." *Shots: Health News Ffrom NPR*, September 8, 2016. www.npr.org/sections/health-shots/2016/09/08/492965889/watch-bacteria-invade-antibiotics-and-transform-into-superbugs.

Chen, George L., and Josef T. Prchal. "X-Linked Clonality Testing: Interpretation and Limitations." *Blood* 110, no. 5 (September 2007): 1411–19. https://doi.org/10.1182/ blood-2006-09-018655.

Chen, Steven. "Length of a Human DNA Molecule." *The Physics Factbook*. Accessed September 20, 2018. https://hypertextbook.com/facts/1998/StevenChen.shtml/.

Chhabra, Lovely, Narender Goel, Laxman Prajapat, David H Spodick, and Sanjeev Goyal. "Mouse Heart Rate in a Human: Diagnostic Mystery of an Extreme Tachyarrhythmia." *Indian Pacing and Electrophysiology Journal* 12, no. 1 (January 2012): 32–35. https://doi.org/10.1016/S0972-6292(16)30463-6.

Cho, Jun Ho, and Samuel Y Paik. "Association between Electronic Cigarette Use and Asthma among High School Students in South Korea." *PLoS ONE* 11, no. 3 (March 2016): 1–13. https://doi.org/10.1371/journal.pone.0151022.

Chopra, Deepak, and Rudolph Tanzi. "You Can Transform Your Own Biology." *The Chopra Center*. Accessed September 16, 2018. https://chopra.com/articles/you-can-transform-your-own-biology/.

Christakis, Nicholas A., and James H. Fowler. "The Spread of Obesity in a Large Social Network Over 32 Years." *New England Journal of Medicine* 357, no. 4 (July 2007): 370–79. https://doi.org/10.1056/NEJMsa066082.

Chung, Emma, John Cromby, Dimitris Papadopoulos, and Cristina Tufarelli. "Social Epigenetics: A Science of Social Science?" *The Sociological Review Monographs* 64, no. 1 (February 2017): 168–85. https://doi.org/10.1111/2059-7932.12019.

Coffey, J. Calvin, and D. Peter O'Leary. "The Mesentery: Structure, Function, and Role in Disease." *The Lancet Gastroenterology and Hepatology* 1, no. 3 (November 2016): 238–47. https://doi.org/10.1016/S2468-1253(16)30026-7.

Colón, Eduardo A., Allan L. Callies, Michael K. Popkin, and Philip B. McGlave. "Depressed Mood and Other Variables Related to Bone Marrow Transplantation Survival in Acute Leukemia." *Psychosomatics* 32, no. 4 (November 1991): 420–425. https://doi.org/10.1016/S0033-3182(91)72045-8.

Coman, Alin, and William Hirst. "Cognition through a Social Network: The Propagation of Induced Forgetting and Practice Effects." *Journal of Experimental Psychology: General* 141, no. 2 (September 2011): 321–36. https://doi.org/10.1037/a0025247.

Crick, Francis H. C. "Central Dogma of Molecular Biology." *Nature* 227, no. 5258 (August 1970): 561–63. https://doi.org/10.1038/227561a0.

Culotta, Elizabeth, and Elizabeth Pennisi. "Breakthrough of the Year: Evolution in Action." *Science* 310, no. 5756 (December 2005): 1878–79. https://doi.org/10.1126/science.310.5756.1878.

Damasio, Antonio R. *The Feeling of What Happens: Body and Emotion in the Making of Consciousness.* Wilmington: Mariner Books, 2000.

Darwin, Charles. *Expression of the Emotions in Man and Animals.* London: John Murray, 1872.

Darwin, Charles. *On the Origin of Species by Means of Natural Selection, or the Preservation of Favoured Races in the Struggle for Life.* London: John Murray, 1859.

Darwin, Charles. *The Variation of Animals and Plants Under Domestication, Volume 2.* London: John Murray, 1868.

Darwin, Charles, and Nora Barlow. *The Autobiography of Charles Darwin: 1809–1882.* New York: W.W. Norton & Company, 1993.

Darwin, Francis, and John van Wyhe. "The Life and Letters of Charles Darwin, Including an Autobiographical Chapter. London: John Murray. Volume 1." *The Complete Work of Charles Darwin Online.* Accessed September 2018. http://darwin-online.org.uk/.

Dawkins, Richard. *The Blind Watchmaker: Why the Evidence of Evolution Reveals a Universe Without Design.* New York: W. W. Norton & Company, 1986.

Dawkins, Richard. "Replicators and Vehicles." In *Current Problems in Sociobiology*, edited by King's College Sociobiology Group, 45–65. London: Cambridge University Press, 1982.

Dawkins, Richard. *The Selfish Gene.* Oxford: Oxford University Press, 1976.

De Grey, Aubrey, and Michael Rae. *Ending Aging: The Rejuvenation Breakthroughs That Could Reverse Human Aging in Our Lifetime.* New York: St. Martin's Griffin, 2008.

De Robertis, Edward M. "Spemann's Organizer and the Self-Regulation of Embryonic Fields." *Mechanisms of Development* 126, no 11–12 (July 2009): 925–41. https://doi.org/10.1016/j.mod.2009.08.004.

De Visser, J. Arjan G. M., Joachim Hermisson, Günter P. Wagner, Lauren Ancel Meyers, Homayoun Bagheri-Chaichian, Jeffrey L. Blanchard, Lin Chao, et al. "Perspective: Evolution and Detection of Genetic Robustness." *Evolution* 57, no. 9 (September 2003): 1959–72. https://doi.org/10.1111/j.0014-3820.2003.tb00377.x.

Deans, Emily. "Sunlight, Sugar, and Serotonin." *Psychology Today,* May 9, 2011. https://www.psychologytoday.com/us/blog/evolutionary-psychiatry/201105/sunlight-sugar-and-serotonin/.

Dellapolla, Adriano, Ian Kloehn, Harshida Pancholi, Ben Callif, David Wertz, Kayla E. Rohr, Matthew M. Hurley, et al. "Long Days Enhance Recognition Memory and Increase Insulin-like Growth Factor 2 in the Hippocampus." *Scientific Reports* 7, no. 1 (June 2017). https://doi.org/10.1038/s41598-017-03896-2.

Dennett, Daniel C. *Darwin's Dangerous Idea: Evolution and the Meanings of Life.* London: Penguin Books, 1995.

Dennett, Daniel C. "Darwin's 'Strange Inversion of Reasoning.'" *Proceedings of the National Academy of Sciences* 106, suppl. 1 (June 2009): 10061–65. https://doi.org/10.1073/pnas.0904433106.

Dennett, Daniel C. *Intuition Pumps and Other Tools for Thinking.* London and New York: W.W. Norton & Company, 2013.

Dennett, Daniel C. *Kinds of Minds: Towards an Understanding of Consciousness.* New York: Basic Books, 1997.

Dewane, Claudia J. "The Legacy of Addictions: A Form of Complex PTSD?" *Social Work Today* 10, no. 6 (December 2010): 16.

Dias, Brian G, and Kerry J Ressler. "Parental Olfactory Experience Influences Behavior and Neural Structure in Subsequent Generations." *Nature Neuroscience* 17, no. 1 (December 2013): 89–96. https://doi.org/10.1038/nn.3594.

Di Pellegrino, Giuseppe, Luciano Fadiga, Leonardo Fogassi, Vittorio Gallese, and Giacomo Rizzolatti. "Understanding Motor Events: A Neurophysiological Study." *Experimental Brain Research* 91, no. 1 (October 1992): 176–80. https://doi.org/10.1007/BF00230027.

Dobzhansky, Theodosius. "Nothing in Biology Makes Sense Except in the Light of Evolution." *The American Biology Teacher* 35, no. 3 (March 1973): 125–29.

Downes, C. Stephen. "What the Books Say: Senescence and the Genome or, Change and Decay in All Except Lobsters I See." *BioEssays* 15, no. 5 (May 1993): 359–62. https://doi.org/https://doi.org/10.1002/bies.950150512.

Dunning Hotopp, Julie C. "Horizontal Gene Transfer between Bacteria and Animals." *Trends in Genetics* 27, no. 4 (April 2011): 157–63. https://doi.org/10.1016/j.tig.2011.01.005.Horizontal.

Eager, Diane. "Homologous Structures? Vertebrate Limbs Have the Same Bone Structure. Is This Evidence for Evolution?" *Ask John Mackay: The Creation Guy,* May 24, 2016. http://askjohnmackay.com/homologous-structures-vertebrate-limbs-have-the-same-bone-structure-is-this-evidence-for-evolution/.

Eames Office. "Powers of Ten™ (1977)." YouTube Video, 9:00. August 26, 2010. https://youtu.be/0fKBhvDjuy0.

Edwards, John R, Olya Yarychkivska, Mathieu Boulard, and Timothy H Bestor. "DNA Methylation and DNA Methyltransferases." *Epigenetics & Chromatin* 10, no. 1 (May 2017): 23. https://doi.org/10.1186/s13072-017-0130-8.

Einstein, Albert. "Religion and Science." *New York Times Magazine,* November 9, 1930. https://documents.epfl.ch/groups/l/la/lastro-unit/www/AstroI/2011-2012/albert_einstein_science_and_religion.pdf

Ekwall, Karl, Tim Olsson, Bryan M Turner, Gwen Cranston, and Robin C Allshire. "Transient Inhibition of Histone Deacetylation Alters the Structural and Functional Imprint at Fission Yeast Centromeres." *Cell* 91, no. 7 (December 1997): 1021–32. https://doi.org/10.1016/S0092-8674(00)80492-4.

El Hady, Ahmed, and Benjamin B. Machta. "Mechanical Surface Waves Accompany Action Potential Propagation." *Nature Communications* 6, no. 6697 (October 2014): 1–7. https://doi.org/10.1038/ncomms7697.

Engelking, Carl. "The Mesentary Isn't the Organ You Think It Is." *Discover: The Crux,* January 6, 2017. http://blogs.discovermagazine.com/crux/2017/01/06/got-mesentery-news-wrong/#.W6Q-J3tKi6J.

Epel, Elissa S., Elizabeth H. Blackburn, Jue Lin, Firdaus S. Dhabhar, Nancy E. Adler, Jason D. Morrow, and Richard M. Cawthon. "Accelerated Telomere Shortening in Response to Life Stress." *Proceedings of the National Academy of Sciences* 101, no. 49 (September 2004): 17312–15. https://doi.org/10.1073/pnas.0407162101.

Erlich, Yaniv, and Dina Zielinski. "DNA Fountain Enables a Robust and Efficient Storage Architecture." *Science* 355, no. 6328 (March 2017): 950–54. https://doi.org/10.1126/science.aaj2038.

Everitt, Barry J, and Trevor W Robbins. "Neural Systems of Reinforcement for Drug Addiction: From Actions to Habits to Compulsion." *Nature Neuroscience* 8, no. 11 (November 2005): 1481–89. https://doi.org/10.1038/nn1579.

Fasolino, Maria, and Zhaolan Zhou. "The Crucial Role of DNA Methylation and MeCP2 in Neuronal Function." *Genes* 8, no. 5 (May 2017): E141. https://doi.org/10.3390/genes8050141.

Fedoroff, Nina V. "The Suppressor-Mutator Element and the Evolutionary Riddle of Transposons." *Genes to Cells* 4, no. 1 (January 1999): 11–19. https://doi.org/10.1046/j.1365-2443.1999.00233.x.

Fedoroff, Nina V. "Transposable Elements, Epigenetics, and Genome Evolution." *Science* 338, no. 6108 (November 2012): 758–67. https://doi.org/10.1126/science.338.6108.758.

Felitti, Vincent J., Robert F. Anda, Dale Nordenberg, David F. Williamson, Alison M. Spitz, Valerie Edwards, Mary P. Koss, and James S. Marks. "Household Dysfunction to Many of the Leading Causes of Death in Adults: The Adverse Childhood Experiences Study." *American Journal of Preventive Medicine* 14, no. 4 (May 1998): 245–58.

Feynman, Richard. *The Character of Physical Law*. Cambridge: MIT Press, 1985.

Findley, Keisha, Julia Oh, Joy Yang, Sean Conlan, Clayton Deming, Jennifer A Meyer, Deborah Schoenfeld, et al. "Topographic Diversity of Fungal and Bacterial Communities in Human Skin." *Nature* 498, no. 7454 (June 2013): 367–70. https://doi.org/10.1038/nature12171.Human.

Flatscher, Ruth, Božo Frajman, Peter Schönswetter, and Ovidiu Paun. "Environmental Heterogeneity and Phenotypic Divergence: Can Heritable Epigenetic Variation Aid Speciation?" *Genetics Research International* 2012 (March 2012): 1–9. https://doi.org/10.1155/2012/698421.

Franklin, Tamara B., Holger Russig, Isabelle C Weiss, Johannes Grff, Natacha Linder, Aubin Michalon, Sandor Vizi, and Isabelle M Mansuy. "Epigenetic Transmission of the Impact of Early Stress across Generations." *Biological Psychiatry* 68, no. 5 (September 2010): 408–15. https://doi.org/10.1016/j.biopsych.2010.05.036.

Frey, Teryl. "RNA Viruses." Accessed September 17, 2018. http://www2.gsu.edu/~biotkf/bio475/475lecture6.htm/.

Furusawa, Chikara, and Kunihiko Kaneko. "Epigenetic Feedback Regulation Accelerates Adaptation and Evolution." *PLoS ONE* 8, no. 5 (May 2013): 1–6. https://doi.org/10.1371/journal.pone.0061251.

Gallese, Vittorio, and Alvin Goldman. "Mirror Neurons and the Simulation Theory of Mind-Reading." *Trends in Cognitive Sciences* 2, no. 12 (December 1998): 493–501. https://doi.org/10.1016/S1364-6613(98)01262-5.

Gilmartin, Marieke R., Hiroyuki Miyawaki, Fred. J. Helmstetter, and Kamran Diba. "Prefrontal Activity Links Nonoverlapping Events in Memory." *Journal of Neuroscience* 33, no. 26 (June 2013): 10910–14. https://doi.org/10.1523/JNEUROSCI.0144-13.2013.

Goldstein, Gary W. "Lead Poisoning and Brain Cell Function." *Environmental Health Perspectives* 89 (November 1990): 91–94. https://doi.org/10.1289/ehp.908991.

Gorski, David. "Epigenetics: It Doesn't Mean What Quacks Think It Means." *Science-Based Medicine*, February 4, 2013. https://sciencebasedmedicine.org/epigenetics-it-doesnt-mean-what-quacks-think-it-means/.

Gould, Stephen J. *Leonardo's Mountain of Clams and the Diet of Worms: Essays on Natural History*. New York: Harmony Books, 1998.

Gradus, Jamie L. "Epidemiology of PTSD." National Center for Post-Traumatic Stress Disorder, Department of Veterans Affairs. Last modified March 30, 2017. https://www.ptsd.va.gov/professional/PTSD-overview/epidemiological-facts-ptsd.asp.

Greer, Eric L., Mario Andres Blanco, Lei Gu, Erdem Sendinc, Jianzhao Liu, David Aristizábal-Corrales, Chih Hung Hsu, L. Aravind, Chuan He, and Yang Shi. "DNA Methylation on N6-Adenine in C. Elegans." *Cell* 161, no. 4 (April 2015): 868–78. https://doi.org/10.1016/j.cell.2015.04.005.

Greer, Eric L., Travis J. Maures, Duygu Ucar, Anna G. Hauswirth, Elena Mancini, Jana P. Lim, Bérénice A. Benayoun, Yang Shi, and Anne Brunet. "Transgenerational Epigenetic Inheritance of Longevity in Caenorhabditis Elegans." *Nature* 479, no. 7373 (November 2011): 365–71. https://doi.org/10.1038/nature10572.

Gregoire, Carolyn. "Scientists Have Discovered A New Organ in The Digestive System." *Huffington Post*, January 4, 2017. https://www.huffingtonpost.com/entry/scientists-discover-new-organ-mesentery_us_586cfb55e4b0eb58648b3f76/.

Grice, Elizabeth A., Heidi H. Kong, Sean Conlan, Clayton B. Deming, Joie Davis, Alice C. Young, Gerard G. Bouffard, et al. "Topographical and Temporal Diversity of the Human Skin Microbiome." *Science* 324, no. 5931 (May 2009): 1190–92. https://doi.org/10.1126/science.1171700.

Guimarães, Romeu Cardoso. "Linguistics of Biomolecules and the Protein-First Hypothesis for the Origins of Cells." *Journal of Biological Physics* 20 (February 1994): 193–99. https://doi.org/10.1007/BF00700436.

Gurdon, Csanad, Zora Svab, Yaping Feng, Dibyendu Kumar, and Pal Maliga. "Cell-to-Cell Movement of Mitochondria in Plants." *Proceedings of the National Academy of Sciences* 113, no. 12 (March 2016): 3395–3400. https://doi.org/10.1073/pnas.1518644113.

Haig, David. "Retroviruses and the Placenta." *Current Biology* 22, no. 15 (August 2012): R609–13. https://doi.org/10.1016/j.cub.2012.06.002.

Haig, David. "Weismann Rules! OK? Epigenetics and the Lamarckian Temptation." *Biology and Philosophy* 22, no. 3 (June 2007): 415–28. https://doi.org/10.1007/s10539-006-9033-y.

Haque, F. Nipa, Irving I. Gottesman, and Albert H C Wong. "Not Really Identical: Epigenetic Differences in Monozygotic Twins and Implications for Twin Studies in Psychiatry." *American Journal of Medical Genetics, Part C: Seminars in Medical Genetics* 151, no. 2 (May 2009): 136–41. https://doi.org/10.1002/ajmg.c.30206.

Harris, Rachel. *Listening to Ayahuasca: New Hope for Depression, Addiction, PTSD, and Anxiety*. Novato, CA: New World Library, 2017.

Hecht, Mariana M., Nadjar Nitz, Perla F. Araujo, Alessandro O. Sousa, Ana De Cássia Rosa, Dawidson A. Gomes, Eduardo Leonardecz, and Antonio R L Teixeira. "Inheritance of DNA Transferred from American Trypanosomes to Human Hosts." *PLoS ONE* 5, no. 2 (February 2010): E9181. https://doi.org/10.1371/journal.pone.0009181.

Hill, Edward M., Frances E. Griffiths, and Thomas House. "Spreading of Healthy Mood in Adolescent Social Networks." *Royal Society Open Science* 4, no. 9 (August 2015): 1-6. https://doi.org/10.1098/rspb.2015.1180.

Hoffman, Donald D., Manish Singh, and Chetan Prakash. "The Interface Theory of Perception." *Psychonomic Bulletin and Review* 22, no. 6 (December 2015): 1480–1506.

Hofstadter, Douglas. *Gödel, Escher, Bach: An Eternal Golden Braid.* New York: Basic Books, 1979.

Hofstadter, Douglas. *I Am a Strange Loop.* New York: Basic Books, 2007.

Holmes, Bob. "First Glimpse at the Viral Birth of DNA." *New Scientist*, April 18, 2012. https://doi.org/https://doi.org/10.1016/S0262-4079(12)60990-7.

Holoch, Daniel, and Danesh Moazed. "RNA-Mediated Epigenetic Regulation of Gene Expression." *Nature Reviews Genetics* 16, no. 2 (January 2015): 71–84. https://doi.org/10.1038/nrg3863.

Huangfu, Danwei, Kenji Osafune, René Maehr, Wenjun Guo, Astrid Eijkelenboom, Shuibing Chen, Whitney Muhlestein, and Douglas A. Melton. "Induction of Pluripotent Stem Cells from Primary Human Fibroblasts with Only Oct4 and Sox2." *Nature Biotechnology* 26, no. 11 (November 2008): 1269–75. https://doi.org/10.1038/nbt.1502.

Huettel, Bruno, Tatsuo Kanno, Lucia Daxinger, Etienne Bucher, Johannes van der Winden, Antonius J.M. Matzke, and Marjori Matzke. "RNA-Directed DNA Methylation Mediated by DRD1 and Pol IVb: A Versatile Pathway for Transcriptional Gene Silencing in Plants." *Biochimica et Biophysica Acta - Gene Structure and Expression* 1769, no. 5–6 (March 2007): 358–74. https://doi.org/10.1016/j.bbaexp.2007.03.001.

Husnik, Filip, and John P. McCutcheon. "Functional Horizontal Gene Transfer from Bacteria to Eukaryotes." *Nature Reviews Microbiology* 16, no. 2 (February 2018): 67–79. https://doi.org/10.1038/nrmicro.2017.137.

Iacoboni, Marco. "Imitation, Empathy, and Mirror Neurons." *Annual Review of Psychology* 60, no. 1 (January 2009): 653–70. https://doi.org/10.1146/annurev.psych.60.110707.163604.

Isbell, Lynne A. *The Snake, the Tree, and the Serpent.* Cambridge and London: Harvard University Press, 2009.

Iyer, Lakshminarayan M., Dapeng Zhang, and L. Aravind. "Adenine Methylation in Eukaryotes: Apprehending the Complex Evolutionary History and Functional Potential of an Epigenetic Modification." *BioEssays* 38, no. 1 (December 2015): 27–40. https://doi.org/10.1002/bies.201500104.

Jablonka, Eva, and Marion J. Lamb. *Evolution in Four Dimensions: Genetic, Epigenetic, Behavioral, and Symbolic Variation in the History of Life.* Cambridge: The MIT Press, 2006.

Jablonka, Eva, and Marion J. Lamb. "The Inheritance of Acquired Epigenetic Variations." *International Journal of Epidemiology* 44, no. 4 (April 2015): 1094–1103. https://doi.org/10.1093/ije/dyv020.

Jablonka, Eva, and Gal Raz. "Transgenerational Epigenetic Inheritance: Prevalence, Mechanisms, and Implications for the Study of Heredity and Evolution." *The Quarterly Review of Biology* 84, no. 2 (June 2009): 131–76. https://doi.org/10.1086/598822.

Janowitz Koch, Ilana, Michelle M. Clark, Michael J. Thompson, Kerry A. Deere-Machemer, Jun Wang, Lionel Duarte, Gitanjali E. Gnanadesikan, et al. "The Concerted Impact of Domestication and Transposon Insertions on Methylation Patterns between Dogs and Grey Wolves." *Molecular Ecology* 25, no. 8 (April 2016): 1838–55. https://doi.org/10.1111/mec.13480.

Jarmuda, Stanislaw, Niamh O'Reilly, Ryszard Zaba, Oliwia Jakubowicz, Andrzej Szkaradkiewicz, and Kevin Kavanagh. "Potential Role of Demodex Mites and Bacteria in the Induction of Rosacea." *Journal of Medical Microbiology* 61, part 11 (November 2012): 1504–10. https://doi.org/10.1099/jmm.0.048090-0.

Jeyaraj, Darwin, Saptarsi M. Haldar, Xiaoping Wan, Mark D. McCauley, Jürgen A. Ripperger, Kun Hu, Yuan Lu, et al. "Circadian Rhythms Govern Cardiac Repolarization and Arrhythmogenesis." *Nature* 483, 7387 (March 2012): 96–101. https://doi.org/10.1038/nature10852.

Jian, Bo, Jie Xu, Jeanne Connolly, Rashmin Cc Savani, Navneet Narula, Bruce Liang, and Robert J. Levy. "Serotonin Mechanisms in Heart Valve Disease I: Serotonin-Induced Up-Regulation of Transforming Growth Factor-Beta1 via G-Protein Signal Transduction in Aortic Valve Interstitial Cells." *The American Journal of Pathology* 161, no. 6 (January 2003): 2111–21. https://doi.org/http://dx.doi.org/10.1016/S0002-9440(10)64489-6.

Johnson, Nicole L., Lindsay Carini, Marian E. Schenk, Michelle Stewart, and Elizabeth M. Byrnes. "Adolescent Opiate Exposure in the Female Rat Induces Subtle Alterations in Maternal Care and Transgenerational Effects on Play Behavior." *Frontiers in Psychiatry* 2, (June 2011): 1–10. https://doi.org/10.3389/fpsyt.2011.00029.

Jones, Peter A. "Functions of DNA Methylation: Islands, Start Sites, Gene Bodies and Beyond." *Nature Reviews Genetics* 13, no. 7 (July 2012): 484–92. https://doi.org/10.1038/nrg3230.

Jones, Peter A., William M. Rideout, Jiang-Cheng -C Shen, Charles H. Spruck, and Yvonne C. Tsai. "Methylation, Mutation and Cancer." *BioEssays* 14, no. 1 (January 1992): 33–36. https://doi.org/10.1002/bies.950140107.

Jorgensen, Richard A. "Epigenetics: Biology's Quantum Mechanics." *Frontiers in Plant Science* 2, (April 2011): 1–4. https://doi.org/10.3389/fpls.2011.00010.

Jorgensen, Richard. A. "Restructuring the Genome in Response to Adaptive Challenge: McClintock's Bold Conjecture Revisited." *Cold Spring Harbor Symposia on Quantitative Biology* 69 (2004): 349–54. https://doi.org/10.1101/sqb.2004.69.349.

Kalinka, Alex T., and Pavel Tomancak. "The Evolution of Early Animal Embryos: Conservation or Divergence?" *Trends in Ecology and Evolution* 27, 7 (April 2012): 385–93. https://doi.org/10.1016/j.tree.2012.03.007.

Kavanagh, Liam C., and Piotr Winkielman. "The Functionality of Spontaneous Mimicry and Its Influences on Affiliation: An Implicit Socialization Account." *Frontiers in Psychology* 7 (March 2016): 1–6. https://doi.org/10.3389/fpsyg.2016.00458.

Keller, Laurent. *Levels of Selection in Evolution.* Princeton: Princeton University Press, 1999.

Kellermann, Natan P.F. "Epigenetic Transmission of Holocaust Trauma: Can Nightmares Be Inherited?" *Israel Journal of Psychiatry and Related Sciences* 50, no. 1 (January 2013): 33–39.

Killian, J. Keith, Sven Bilke, Sean Davis, Robert L. Walker, Erich Jaeger, M. Scott Killian, Joshua J. Waterfall, et al. "A Methyl-Deviator Epigenotype of Estrogen Receptor-Positive Breast Carcinoma Is Associated with Malignant Biology." *American Journal of Pathology* 179, no. 1 (July 2011): 55–65. https://doi.org/10.1016/j.ajpath.2011.03.022.

Kim, Doe-Young, and Michael Camilleri. "Serotonin: A Mediator of the Brain-Gut Connection." *The American Journal of Gastroenterology* 95, no. 10 (October 2000): 2698–2709. https://doi.org/10.1111/j.1572-0241.2000.03177.x.

Kim, Jonghwan, and Stuart H. Orkin. "Embryonic Stem Cell-Specific Signatures in Cancer: Insights into Genomic Regulatory Networks and Implications for Medicine." *Genome Medicine* 3, no. 75 (November 2011). http://doi.org/10.1186/gm291.

Knecht, Leslie D., Gregory O'Connor, Rahul Mittal, Xue Z. Liu, Pirouz Daftarian, Sapna K. Deo, and Sylvia Daunert. "Serotonin Activates Bacterial Quorum Sensing and Enhances the Virulence of Pseudomonas Aeruginosa in the Host." *EBioMedicine* 9 (May 2016): 161–69. https://doi.org/10.1016/j.ebiom.2016.05.037.

Knoepfler, Paul, "Why Literally Everyone Has Cancer and What This Means for You," *Science 2.0*, August 23, 2011, https://www.science20.com/confessions_stem_cell_scientist/why_literally_everyone_has_cancer_and_what_means_you-81937.

Kong, Augustine, Gudmar Thorleifsson, Michael L. Frigge, Bjarni J. Vilhjalmsson, Alexander I. Young, Thorgeir E. Thorgeirsson, Stefania Benonisdottir, et al. "The Nature of Nurture: Effects of Parental Genotypes." *Science* 359, no. 6374 (January 2018): 424–28. https://doi.org/10.1126/science.aan6877.

Kim, Han Na, Yeojun Yun, Seungho Ryu, Yoosoo Chang, Min Jung Kwon, Juhee Cho, Hocheol Shin, and Hyung Lae Kim. "Correlation between Gut Microbiota and Personality in Adults: A Cross-Sectional Study." *Brain, Behavior, and Immunity* 69 (March 2018): 374–85. https://doi.org/10.1016/j.bbi.2017.12.012.

Koonin, Eugene V. "Archaeal Ancestors of Eukaryotes: Not so Elusive Any More." *BMC Biology* 13, no. 1 (2015): 1–7. https://doi.org/10.1186/s12915-015-0194-5.

Krulwich, Robert. "Which Is Greater, The Number of Sand Grains on Earth or Stars in the Sky?" *NPR: Krulwich Wonders*. September 17, 2012. https://www.npr.org/sections/krulwich/2012/09/17/161096233/which-is-greater-the-number-of-sand-grains-on-earth-or-stars-in-the-sky.

Kumar, Vivek, Bogi Andersen, and Joseph S Takahashi. "Epidermal Stem Cells Ride the Circadian Wave." *Genome Biology* 14, no. 11 (November 2013): 140. https://doi.org/10.1186/gb4142.

LaFreniere, Gabriel. "Matter Is Made of Waves." *Rhythmodynamics*. Last modified, June 19. 2011. http://www.rhythmodynamics.com/Gabriel_LaFreniere/matter.htm/.

Laland, Kevin N. *Darwin's Unfinished Symphony: How Culture Made the Human Mind.* Princeton: Princeton University Press, 2017.

Laland, Kevin, Tobias Uller, Marc Feldman, Kim Sterelny, Gerd B. Müller, Armin
Moczek, Eva Jablonka, et al. "Does Evolutionary Theory Need a Rethink?" *Nature*
514, no. 7521 (October 2014): 161–64. https://doi.org/10.1038/514161a.

Lanie, Angela D., Toby Epstein Jayaratne, Jane P. Sheldon, Sharon L. R. Kardia,
Elizabeth S. Anderson, Merle Feldbaum, and Elizabeth M. Petty. "Exploring the
Public Understanding of Basic Genetic Concepts." *Journal of Genetic Counseling* 13, no.
4 (August 2004): 305–20. https://doi.org/10.1023/B:JOGC.0000035524.66944.6d.

Lanius, Ruth A., Eric Vermetten, and Clare Pain. *The Impact of Early Life Trauma on Health
and Disease: The Hidden Epidemic.* Cambridge: Cambridge University Press, 2010.

Lapenis, Andrei G. "Directed Evolution of the Biosphere: Biogeochemical Selection
or Gaia?" *Professional Geographer* 54, no. 3 (August 2002): 379–91. https://doi.
org/10.1111/0033-0124.00337.

Lax, Alistair J., and Warren Thomas. "How Bacteria Could Cause Cancer: One Step at a
Time." *Trends in Microbiology* 10, no. 6 (June 2002): 293–99. https://doi.org/10.1016/
S0966-842X(02)02360-0.

Leavitt, Sarah. "Deciphering the genetic code: Marshall Nirenberg." *Office of NIH History.*
Accessed September 20, 2018. https://history.nih.gov/exhibits/nirenberg/glossary.
htm.

Ledford, Heidi. "Cancer Treatment: The Killer Within." *Nature* 508, no. 1 (April 2014):
24–26. https://doi.org/10.1038/508024a.

LeDoux, Joseph E. "The Amygdala." *Current Biology* 17, no. 20 (October 2007): PR868–
R874. https://doi.org/10.1016/j.cub.2007.08.005.

LeDoux, Joseph E. "The Amygdala Is Not the Brain's Fear Center." *Psychology Today,*
August 10, 2015. https://www.psychologytoday.com/us/blog/i-got-mind-tell-
you/201508/the-amygdala-is-not-the-brains-fear-center/.

Lee, David H., Juan R. Granja, Jose A. Martinez, Kay Severin, and M. Reza Ghadiri.
"A Self-Replicating Peptide." *Nature* 382, (August 1996): 525–8. https://doi.
org/10.1038/382525a0.

Leonard, Brian E. "The Concept of Depression as a Dysfunction of the Immune
System." *Current Immunology Reviews* 6, no. 3 (August 2010): 205–212. http://doi.
org/10.2174/157339510791823835.

Lewis, Michael. B. "Exploring the Positive and Negative Implications of Facial
Feedback." Emotion 12, no. 4 (August 2012): 852–859. http://dx.doi.org/10.1037/
a0029275.

Lewis, Thomas, Fari Amini, and Richard Lannon. *A General Theory of Love.* New York:
Knopf Doubleday Publishing, 2000.

Lewontin, Richard C. "The Units of Selection." *Annual Review of Ecology and Systematics* 1,
no. 1 (November 1970): 1–18. https://doi.org/10.1146/annurev.es.01.110170.000245.

Liao, Guoning, Lisa Mingle, Livingston Van De Water, and Gang Liu. "Control of Cell
Migration Through Mrna Localization and Local Translation." *Wiley Interdisciplinary
Reviews: RNA* 6, no. 1 (January 2015): 1–15. https://doi.org/10.1002/wrna.1265.

Ling, Gilbert. "Nano-Protoplasm: The Ultimate Unit of Life." *Physiological Chemistry and Physics and Medical NMR* 39, no. 2 (2007): 111–234.

Lipton, Bruce. "Insights into the Convergence of Science and Spirituality." Accessed October 1, 2018. https://www.personalgrowthcourses.net/stories/00a.lipton_biology.htm/.

LoBue, Vanessa, David H Rakison, and Judy S. DeLoache. "Threat Perception Across the Life Span: Evidence for Multiple Converging Pathways." *Current Directions in Psychological Science* 19, no. 6 (December 2010): 375–79. https://doi.org/10.1177/0963721410388801.

Lönnig, Wolf-Ekkehard. "The Laryngeal Nerve of the Giraffe: Does It Prove Evolution?" Last modified October 19, 2010. http://www.weloennig.de/LaryngealNerve.pdf/.

Lyko, Frank, Bernard H. Ramsahoye, and Rudolf Jaenisch. "Development: DNA methylation in Drosophila melanogaster." *Nature* 408, no. 6812 (November 2000): 538–40. http://doi.org/10.1038/35046205.

Lyons, Michael J., Jack Goldberg, Seth A. Eisen, William True, Ming T. Tsuang, Joanne M. Meyer, and William G. Henderson. "Do Genes Influence Exposure to Trauma? A Twin Study of Combat." *American Journal of Medical Genetics* 48, no. 1 (May 1993): 22–27. https://doi.org/10.1002/ajmg.1320480107.

McClintock, Barbara. "Topographical Relations Between Elements of Control Systems in Maize." *Carnegie Institution of Washington Year Book* 61 (1962): 448–461.

McGowan, Patrick O., Aya Sasaki, Ana C. D'Alessio, Sergiy Dymov, Benoit Labonté, Moshe Szyf, Gustavo Turecki, and Michael J. Meaney. "Epigenetic Regulation of the Glucocorticoid Receptor in Human Brain Associates with Childhood Abuse." *Nature Neuroscience* 12, no. 3 (February 2009): 342–48. https://doi.org/10.1038/nn.2270.

Mennella, Julie A., Coren P. Jagnow, and Gary K. Beauchamp. "Prenatal and Postnatal Flavor Learning by Human Infants." *Pediatrics* 107, no. 6 (June 2001): E88. https://doi.org/10.1016/j.pestbp.2011.02.012.Investigations.

Merikangas, Kathleen R., Marilyn Stolar, Denise E. Stevens, Joseph Goulet, Martin A. Preisig, Brenda Fenton, Heping Zhang, Stephanie S. O'Malley, and Bruce J. Rounsaville. "Familial Transmission of Substance Use Disorders." *Archives of General Psychiatry* 55 (1998): 973–79.

Michael, John. "The Intentional Stance and Cultural Learning: A Developmental Feedback Loop." In *Content and Consciousness Revisited*, 163–183. Cham: Springer, 2015.

Miller, Brooke H., Erin L. McDearmon, Satchidananda Panda, Kevin R. Hayes, Jie Zhang, Jessica L. Andrews, Marina P. Antoch, et al. "Circadian and CLOCK-Controlled Regulation of the Mouse Transcriptome and Cell Proliferation." *Proceedings of the National Academy of Sciences* 104, no. 9 (February 2007): 3342–47. https://doi.org/10.1073/pnas.0611724104.

Mittler, Ron, Andrija Finka, and Pierre Goloubinoff. "How Do Plants Feel the Heat?" *Trends in Biochemical Sciences* 37, no. 3 (March 2012): 118–25. https://doi.org/10.1016/j.tibs.2011.11.007.

"Molecular Facts and Figures." Coralville: *Integrated DNA Technologies,* 2005 & 2011. http://sfvideo.blob.core.windows.net/sitefinity/docs/default-source/biotech-basics/molecular-facts-and-figures.pdf/.

Morris, Kevin V. "Lamarck and the Missing Lnc." *The Scientist,* October 1, 2012. https://www.the-scientist.com/features/lamarck-and-the-missing-lnc-40429.

Murgia, Claudio, Jonathan K. Pritchard, Su Yeon Kim, Ariberto Fassati, and Robin A. Weiss. "Clonal Origin and Evolution of a Transmissible Cancer." *Cell* 126, no. 3 (August 2006): 477–87. https://doi.org/10.1016/j.cell.2006.05.051.

Murphy, Todd. "The Structure and Function of Near-Death Experiences: An Algorithmic Reincarnation Hypothesis." *Journal of Near-Death Studies* 20, no. 2 (December 2001): 101–18.

Nagano, Takashi, Yaniv Lubling, Tim J. Stevens, Stefan Schoenfelder, Eitan Yaffe, Wendy Dean, Ernest D. Laue, Amos Tanay, and Peter Fraser. "Single-Cell Hi-C Reveals Cell-to-Cell Variability in Chromosome Structure." *Nature* 502, no. 7469 (October 2013): 59–64. https://doi.org/10.1038/nature12593.

NASA. "About Life Detection." Astrobiology at NASA: Life in the Universe. Accessed September 22, 2018. https://astrobiology.nasa.gov/research/life-detection/about/.

Nelson, Paul N., P. Hooley, D. Roden, H. Davari Ejtehadi, P. Rylance, P. Warren, J. Martin, and P. G. Murray. 2004. "Human Endogenous Retroviruses: Transposable Elements with Potential?" *Clinical and Experimental Immunology* 138, no. 1 (August 2004): 1–9. https://doi.org/10.1111/j.1365-2249.2004.02592.x.

Neu, Josef, and Jona Rushing. "Cesarean Versus Vaginal Delivery: Long Term Infant Outcomes and the Hygiene Hypothesis." *Clinical Perinatology* 38, no. 2 (June 2011): 321–31. https://doi.org/10.1016/j.clp.2011.03.008.Cesarean.

Newman, Stuart A. "Evolution is More Than Natural Selection." *Huffington Post,* February 10, 2013. https://www.huffingtonpost.com/stuart-a-newman/evolution-is-more-than-natural-selection_b_2274252.html/.

Newman, Stuart A., Gabor Forgacs, and Gerd B. Müller. "Before Programs: The Physical Origination of Multicellular Forms." *International Journal of Developmental Biology* 50, no. 2–3 (February 2006): 289–99. https://doi.org/10.1387/ijdb.052049sn.

Nielsen, Rasmus. "Teaching Evolution in the Middle East." *Nielsen Lab,* February 25, 2016. www.nielsenlab.org/2016/02/teaching-evolution-in-the-middle-east/.

NIH: U.S. National Library of Medicine. "What Are Single Nucleotide Polymorphisms (SNPs)?" Genetics Home Reference, Last modified September 18, 2018. https://ghr.nlm.nih.gov/primer/genomicresearch/snp/.

Nilsson, Roland. "How Many Proteins Do All Human Ribosomes Together Produce Per Hour?" *Biology Stack Exchange.* November 28, 2016. https://biology.stackexchange.com/questions/53428/how-many-proteins-do-all-human-ribosomes-together-produce-per-hour/.

Nukazuka, Akira, Hajime Fujisawa, Toshifumi Inada, Yoichi Oda, and Shin Takagi. "Semaphorin Controls Epidermal Morphogenesis by Stimulating MRNA Translation via EIF2α in Caenorhabditis Elegans." *Genes and Development* 22, no. 8 (February 2008): 1025–36. https://doi.org/10.1101/gad.1644008.

Ocklenburg, Sebastian, Judith Schmitz, Zahra Moinfar, Dirk Moser, Rena Klose, Stephanie Lor, Georg Kunz, et al. "Epigenetic Regulation of Lateralized Fetal Spinal Gene Expression Underlies Hemispheric Asymmetries." *eLife* 6 (February 2017): 1–19. https://doi.org/10.7554/eLife.22784.

O'Leary, Dane. "Why Imprisonment Is More Harm Than Help to Addicted Offenders." Skywood Recovery. Accessed September 25, 2018. https://skywoodrecovery.com/why-imprisonment-is-more-harm-than-help-to-addicted-offenders/.

O'Neill, John S., and Akhilesh B. Reddy. "Circadian Clocks in Human Red Blood Cells." *Nature* 469, no. 7331 (January 2011): 498–504. https://doi.org/10.1038/nature09702.

Ornish, Dean. *Love and Survival: The Scientific Basis for the Healing Power of Intimacy.* New York: HarperCollins Publishers, 1999.

Ostashevsky, Luba. "Top 10 Anti-Slavery Quotes from Charles Darwin." *The Evolution Institute,* February 9, 2015. https://evolution-institute.org/top-10-anti-slavery-quotes-from-charles-darwin/.

Pamer, Eric G. "Fecal Microbiota Transplantation: Effectiveness, Complexities, and Lingering Concerns." *Mucosal Immunology* 7, no. 2 (March 2014): 210–14. https://doi.org/10.1038/mi.2013.117.

Pearce, Brad D., Deanna Kruszon-Moran, and Jeffrey L. Jones. "The Relationship Between *Toxoplasma Gondii* Infection and Mood Disorders in the National Health and Nutrition Survey." *Biological Psychiatry* 72, no. 4 (August 2012): 290-95. https://doi.org/10.1016/j.biopsych.2012.01.003.

Pearson, Helen. "Genetics: What Is a Gene?" *Nature* 441, no. 7092 (May 2006): 398–401. https://doi.org/10.1038/441398a.

Pedersen, Marianne G., Preben Bo Mortensen, Bent Norgaard-Pedersen, and Teodor T. Postolache. "*Toxoplasma Gondii* Infection and Self-Directed Violence in Mothers." *Archives of General Psychiatry* 69, no. 11 (July 2012): 1123–30. https://doi.org/10.1001/archgenpsychiatry.2012.668.

Pigliucci, Massimo. "Do We Need an Extended Evolutionary Synthesis?" *Evolution* 61, no. 12 (October 2007): 2743–49. https://doi.org/10.1111/j.1558-5646.2007.00246.x.

Pollan, Michael. *The Botany of Desire: A Plant's-Eye View of the World.* New York: Random House, 2001.

Popper, Karl R. *The Logic of Scientific Discovery.* London and New York: Routledge Classics, 2004.

Pratt, Ashley J., and Ian J. MacRae. "The RNA-Induced Silencing Complex: A Versatile Gene-Silencing Machine." *Journal of Biological Chemistry* 284, no. 27 (July 2009): 17897–901. https://doi.org/10.1074/jbc.R900012200.

Ptashne, Mark. "Epigenetics: Core Misconcept." *Proceedings of the National Academy of Sciences* 110, no. 18 (April 2013): 7101–3. https://doi.org/10.1073/pnas.1305399110.

Pullman, Bernard. *The Atom in the History of Human Thought.* Oxford: Oxford University Press, 1998.

Pye, Ruth J., David Pemberton, Cesar Tovar, Jose M. C. Tubio, Karen A. Dun, Samantha Fox, Jocelyn Darby, et al. "A Second Transmissible Cancer in Tasmanian Devils." *Proceedings of the National Academy of Sciences* 113, no. 2 (January 2016): 374–79. https://doi.org/10.1073/pnas.1519691113.

Raichlen, David A., Adam D. Foster, Gregory L. Gerdeman, Alexandre Seillier, and Andrea Giuffrida. "Wired to Run: Exercise-Induced Endocannabinoid Signaling in Humans and Cursorial Mammals with Implications for the 'Runner's High.'" *Journal of Experimental Biology* 215, no. 8 (March 2012): 1331–36. https://doi.org/10.1242/jeb.063677.

Rakison, David H., and Jaime Derringer. "Do Infants Possess an Evolved Spider-Detection Mechanism?" *Cognition* 107, no. 1 (April 2008): 381–93. https://doi.org/10.1016/j.cognition.2007.07.022.

Raven, John A., and Dianne Edwards. "Roots: Evolutionary Origins and Biogeochemical Significance." *Journal of Experimental Botany* 52, Roots Special Issue (March 2001): 381–401. https://doi.org/10.1093/jexbot/52.suppl_1.381.

Rebollo, Rita, Mark T. Romanish, and Dixie L. Mager. "Transposable Elements: An Abundant and Natural Source of Regulatory Sequences for Host Genes." *Annual Review of Genetics* 46, no. 1 (August 2012): 21–42. https://doi.org/10.1146/annurev-genet-110711-155621.

Rehan, Virender K., Jie Liu, Reiko Sakurai, and John S. Torday. "Perinatal Nicotine-Induced Transgenerational Asthma." *American Journal of Physiology Lung Cellular and Molecular Physiology* 305, no. 7 (October 2013): L501–7. https://doi.org/10.1152/ajplung.00078.2013.

Richards, Paul I. "Shock Waves on the Highway." *Operations Research* 4, no. 1 (February 1956): 1–137. https://doi.org/10.1287/opre.4.1.42

Rigal, Mélanie, and Olivier Mathieu. "A 'Mille-Feuille' of Silencing: Epigenetic Control of Transposable Elements." *Biochimica et Biophysica Acta - Gene Regulatory Mechanisms* 1809, no. 8 (April 2011): 452–458. https://doi.org/10.1016/j.bbagrm.2011.04.001.

Rogier, Eric. W., Aubrey. L. Frantz, Maria. E. C. Bruno, Leia Wedlund, Donald A. Cohen, Arnold J. Stromberg, and Charlotte S. Kaetzel. "Secretory Antibodies in Breast Milk Promote Long-Term Intestinal Homeostasis by Regulating the Gut Microbiota and Host Gene Expression." *Proceedings of the National Academy of Sciences* 111, no. 8 (February 2014): 3074–79. https://doi.org/10.1073/pnas.1315792111.

Rosenquist, J. Niels, James H. Fowler, and Nicholas A. Christakis. "Social Network Determinants of Depression." *Molecular Psychiatry* 16, no. 3 (March 2010): 273–81. https://doi.org/10.1038/mp.2010.13.

Rosenquist, J. Niels, Joanne Murabito, James H. Fowler, and Nicholas A. Christakis. "The Spread of Alcohol Consumption Behavior in a Large Social Network." *Annals of Internal Medicine* 152, no. 7 (April 2010): 426–33. https://doi.org/10.7326/0003-4819-152-7-201004060-00007.

Rupke, Nicolaas A. *Richard Owen: Biology Without Darwin, a Revised Edition*. Chicago and London: The University of Chicago Press, 2009.

Ruse, Michael. "Is Evolution a Secular Religion?" *Science* 299, no. 5612 (March 2003): 1523–1524.

Rutherford, Adam. "Beware the Pseudo Gene Genies." *The Guardian*, July 19, 2015. www.theguardian.com/science/2015/jul/19/epigenetics-dna--darwin-adam-rutherford/.

Santavirta, Torsten, Nina Santavirta, and Stephen E. Gilman. "Association of the World War II Finnish Evacuation of Children with Psychiatric Hospitalization in the next Generation." *JAMA Psychiatry* 75, no. 1 (November 2017): 21–27. https://doi.org/10.1001/jamapsychiatry.2017.3511.

Schippers, Klaske J., and Scott A. Nichols. "Deep, Dark Secrets of Melatonin in Animal Evolution." *Cell* 159, no. 1 (September 2014): 9–10. https://doi.org/10.1016/j.cell.2014.09.004.

Science of People. "The Definitive Guide to Reading Microexpressions." Accessed September 29, 2018. https://www.scienceofpeople.com/microexpressions/.

Seaborne, Robert A., Juliette Strauss, Matthew Cocks, Sam Shepherd, Thomas D. O'Brien, Ken A. Van Someren, Phillip G. Bell, et al. "Human Skeletal Muscle Possesses an Epigenetic Memory of Hypertrophy." *Scientific Reports* 8, article 1898 (January 2018): 1-17. https://doi.org/10.1038/s41598-018-20287-3.

Sender, Ron, Shai Fuchs, and Ron Milo. "Revised Estimates for the Number of Human and Bacteria Cells in the Body." *PLoS Biology* 14, no. 8 (August 2016): 1–14. https://doi.org/10.1371/journal.pbio.1002533.

Seymour, Tracy, Alecia Jane Twigger, and Foteini Kakulas. "Pluripotency Genes and Their Functions in the Normal and Aberrant Breast and Brain." *International Journal of Molecular Sciences* 16, no. 11 (November 2015): 27288–301. https://doi.org/10.3390/ijms161126024.

Shaheen, Kareem, and Gözde Hatunoğlu. "Turkish schools to stop teaching evolution, official says." *The Guardian*, June 23, 2017. www.theguardian.com/world/2017/jun/23/turkish-schools-to-stop-teaching-evolution-official-says.

Shorter, James, and Susan Lindquist. "Prions as Adaptive Conduits of Memory and Inheritance." *Nature Reviews Genetics* 6, no. 6 (June 2005): 435–50. https://doi.org/10.1038/nrg1616.

Shreiner, Andrew B., John Y. Kao, and Vincent B. Young. "The Gut Microbiome in Health and in Disease." *Current Opinion in Gastroenterology* 31, no. 1 (January 2015): 69–75. https://doi.org/10.1097/MOG.0000000000000139.The.

Skene, Peter J., Robert S. Illingworth, Shaun Webb, Alastair R.W. Kerr, Keith D. James, Daniel J. Turner, Rob Andrews, and Adrian P. Bird. "Neuronal MeCP2 Is Expressed at Near Histone-Octamer Levels and Globally Alters the Chromatin State." *Molecular Cell* 37, no. 4 (February 2010): 457–68. https://doi.org/10.1016/j.molcel.2010.01.030.

Skinner, Michael K. "Environmental Epigenetics and a Unified Theory of the Molecular Aspects of Evolution: A Neo-Lamarckian Concept That Facilitates Neo-Darwinian Evolution." *Genome Biology and Evolution* 7, no. 5 (April 2015): 1296–1302. https://doi.org/10.1093/gbe/evv073.

Skinner, Michael K., Carlos Gurerrero-Bosagna, M. Muksitul Haque, Eric E. Nilsson, Jennifer A.H. Koop, Sarah A. Knutie, and Dale H. Clayton. "Epigenetics and the Evolution of Darwin's Finches." *Genome Biology and Evolution* 6, no. 8 (July 2014): 1972–89. https://doi.org/10.1093/gbe/evu158.

Stearns, Beverly P. and Stephen C. Stearns. *Watching, From the Edge of Extinction*. New Haven: Yale University Press, 2000.

Stelling, Jörg, Uwe Sauer, Zoltan Szallasi, Francis J. Doyle, and John Doyle. "Robustness of Cellular Functions." *Cell* 118, no. 6 (September 2004): 675–85. https://doi.org/10.1016/j.cell.2004.09.008.

Stewart, Sherry H., Robert O. Pihl, Patricia J. Conrad, and Maurice Dongier. "Functional Associations Among Trauma, PTSD, and Substance-Related Disorders." *Addictive Behaviors* 23, no. 6 (December 1998): 797–812. https://doi.org/10.1016/S0306-4603(98)00070-7.

Sugden, Karen, Terrie E. Moffitt, Lauriane Pinto, Richie Poulton, Benjamin S. Williams, and Avshalom Caspi. "Is *Toxoplasma Gondii* Infection Related to Brain and Behavior Impairments in Humans? Evidence from a Population-Representative Birth Cohort." *PLoS ONE* 11, no. 2 (February 2016): 1–14. https://doi.org/10.1371/journal.pone.0148435.

Szyszko-Bohusz, Andrzej. "Hypothesis of Genetic Immortality." Accessed October 1, 2018. http://members.upcpoczta.pl/z.ryznar3/haplife/life-against-death/bohusz.htm/.

Taki, Faten A., Xiaoping Pan, Myon Hee Lee, and Baohong Zhang. "Nicotine Exposure and Transgenerational Impact: A Prospective Study on Small Regulatory MicroRNAs." *Scientific Reports* 4, no. 2713 (December 2014): 1–15. https://doi.org/10.1038/srep07513.

Thoemmes, Megan S., Daniel J. Fergus, Julie Urban, Michelle Trautwein, and Robert R. Dunn. "Ubiquity and Diversity of Human-Associated Demodex Mites." *PLoS ONE* 9, no. 8 (August 2014): 1–8. https://doi.org/10.1371/journal.pone.0106265.

Totenberg, Nina. "When Did Companies Become People? Excavating the Legal Evolution." *NPR, Morning Edition*, July 28, 2014. https://www.npr.org/2014/07/28/335288388/when-did-companies-become-people-excavating-the-legal-evolution.

Toth, Miklos. "Mechanisms of Non-Genetic Inheritance and Psychiatric Disorders." *Neuropsychopharmacology* 40, no. 1 (2015): 129–40. https://doi.org/10.1038/npp.2014.127.

Toyota, Masatsugu, Dirk Spencer, Satoe Sawai-Toyota, Wang Jiaqi, Tong Zhang, Abraham J. Koo, Gregg A. Howe, and Simon Gilroy. "Glutamate Triggers Long-Distance, Calcium-Based Plant Defense signaling." *Science* 361, no. 6407 (September 2018): 1112–1115.

Tye, Michael. "Qualia." Stanford Encyclopedia of Philosophy. Last modified December 18, 2017. https://plato.stanford.edu/entries/qualia/.

Valadi, Hadi, Karin Ekström, Apostolos Bossios, Margareta Sjöstrand, James J. Lee, and Jan O. Lötvall. "Exosome-mediated Transfer of mRNAs and microRNAs is a Novel Mechanism of Genetic Exchange Between Cells." *Nature Cell Biology* 9, no. 6 (June 2007): 654–59. http://doi.org/10.1038/ncb1596.

Van der Kolk, Bessel A. *The Body Keeps the Score: Brain, Mind, and Body in the Healing of Trauma.* New York: The Penguin Group, 2014.

Van Wyhe, John. "Darwin vs God: Did the 'Origin of Species' Cause a Clash Between Church and Science?" *History Extra,* November 24, 2016. www.historyextra.com/period/victorian/darwin-vs-god-did-the-origin-of-species-cause-a-clash-between-church-and-science/.

Van Wyhe, John. "Extracts from Letters Addressed to Professor Henslow." *The Complete Work of Charles Darwin Online.* Accessed September 2018. http://darwin-online.org.uk/content/frameset?itemID=F1&viewtype=text&pageseq=1.

Van Wyhe, John. "Journal of Researches." *The Complete Work of Charles Darwin Online.* Accessed September 2018. http://darwin-online.org.uk/EditorialIntroductions/Freeman_JournalofResearches.html.

Vassoler, Fair M., Samantha L. White, Heath D. Schmidt, Ghazaleh Sadri-Vakili, and R. Christopher Pierce. "Epigenetic Inheritance of a Cocaine-Resistance Phenotype." *Nature Neuroscience* 16, no. 1 (January 2013): 42–47. https://doi.org/10.1038/nn.3280.

Vassoler, Fair M., Siobhan J. Wright, and Elizabeth M. Byrnes. "Exposure to Opiates in Female Adolescents Alters Mu Opiate Receptor Expression and Increases the Rewarding Effects of Morphine in Future Offspring." *Neuropharmacology* 103, (April 2016): 112–121. https://doi.org 10.1016/j.neuropharm.2015.11.026.

Veenendaal, Marjolein. "The Fetal Origins of Adult Disease, the Evidence and Mechanisms." PhD diss., University of Amsterdam, 2012.

Villarreal, Luis P. "Viruses and the Placenta: The Essential Virus First View." *Acta Pathologica, Microbiologica et Immunologica Scandanavica.* 124, no. 1–2 (January 2016): 20–30. https://doi.org/10.1111/apm.12485.

Villota-Salazar, Andrea N., Artemio Mendoza-Mendoza, and Juan M. González-Prieto. "Epigenetics: From the Past to the Present." *Frontiers in Life Science* 9, no. 4 (July 2016): 347–70. https://doi.org/10.1080/21553769.2016.1249033.

Von Sydow, Momme. *From Darwinian Metaphysics towards Understanding the Evolution of Evolutionary Mechanisms: A Historical and Philosophical Analysis of Gene-Darwinism and Universal Darwinism.* Göttingen: Göttingen University Press, 2012.

Von Wintersdorff, Christian J.H., John Penders, Julius M. Van Niekerk, Nathan D. Mills, Snehali Majumder, Lieke B. Van Alphen, Paul H.M. Savelkoul, and Petra F.G. Wolffs. "Dissemination of Antimicrobial Resistance in Microbial Ecosystems through Horizontal Gene Transfer." *Frontiers in Microbiology* 7 (February 2016): 1–10. https://doi.org/10.3389/fmicb.2016.00173.

Vsauce. "Why is Your Bottom in the Middle?" YouTube Video, 10:21. January 7, 2014. https://youtu.be/xKg9Vl_Wg5U/.

Waddington, Conrad H. "The Epigenotype." *International Journal of Epidemiology* 1, no. 1 (February 2012): 10–13. https://doi.org/10.1093/ije/dyr184.

Walker, Larry C., and Harry LeVine. "Proteopathy: The Next Therapeutic Frontier?" *Current Opinion in Investigational Drugs* 3, no. 5 (June 2002): 782–7.

Watts, Alan. *Become What You Are*. Boston: Shambhala, 2003.

Weaver, Ian C. G., Nadia Cervoni, Frances A. Champagne, Ana C. D'Alessio, Shakti Sharma, Jonathan R. Seckl, Sergiy Dymov, Moshe Szyf, and Michael J. Meaney. "Epigenetic Programming by Maternal Behavior." *Nature Neuroscience* 7, no. 8 (August 2004): 847–54. https://doi.org/10.1038/nn1276.

Weaver, Ian C. G., Frances A. Champagne, Shelley E. Brown, Sergiy Dymov, Shakti Sharma, Michael J. Meany, and Moshe Szyf. "Reversal of Maternal Programming of Stress Responses in Adult Offspring through Methyl Supplementation: Altering Epigenetic Marking Later in Life." *Journal of Neuroscience* 25, no. 47 (November 2005): 11045–54. https://doi.org/10.1523/JNEUROSCI.3652-05.2005.

Weber, Andreas. *The Biology of Wonder: Aliveness, Feeling, and the Metamorphosis of Science*. Gabriola Island, B.C.: New Society Press. 2016.

Weismann, August. *Essays Upon Heredity and Kindred Biological Problems: Authorised Translation*. Oxford: Clarendon Press, 1889.

Williams, Sarah C. P. "Epigenetics." *Proceedings of the National Academy of Sciences* 110, no. 9 (February 2013): 3209. https://doi.org/10.1073/pnas.1302488110.

Wilson, Anne E., and Michael Ross. "From Chump to Champ: People's Appraisals of Their Earlier and Present Selves." *Journal of Personality and Social Psychology* 80, no. 4 (April 2001): 572–84. https://doi.org/10.1037/0022-3514.80.4.572.

Wolf, George. "The Discovery of the Visual Function of Vitamin A." *The Journal of Nutrition* 131, no. 6 (June 2001): 1647–50. https://doi.org/10.1093/jn/131.6.1647.

Wood, Jason G., and Stephen L. Helfand. "Chromatin Structure and Transposable Elements in Organismal Aging." *Frontiers in Genetics* 4 (December 2013): 1–12. https://doi.org/10.3389/fgene.2013.00274.

World Record Academy. "Slowest Heart Rate: Daniel Green Breaks Guinness World Records Record." Accessed September 22, 2018. http://www.worldrecordacademy.com/medical/slowest_heart_rate_Daniel_Green_breaks_Guinness_World_Records_record_214157.html.

Wulff, Katharina, Silvia Gatti, Joseph G. Wettstein, and Russell G. Foster. "Sleep and Circadian Rhythm Disruption in Psychiatric and Neurodegenerative Disease." *Nature Reviews Neuroscience* 11, no. 8 (August 2010): 589–99. https://doi.org/10.1038/nrn2868.

Yamaguchi, Shun, Hiromi Isejima, Takuya Matsuo, Ryusuke Okura, Kazuhiro Yagita, Masaki Kobayashi, and Hitoshi Okamura. "Synchronization of Cellular Clocks in the Suprachiasmatic Nucleus." *Science* 302, no. 5649 (November 2003): 1408–12. https://doi.org/10.1126/science.1089287.

Yano, Jessica M., Kristie Yu, Gregory P. Donaldson, Gauri G. Shastri, Phoebe Ann, Liang Ma, Cathryn R. Nagler, Rustem F. Ismagilov, Sarkis K. Mazmanian, and Elaine Y. Hsiao. "Indigenous Bacteria from the Gut Microbiota Regulate Host Serotonin Biosynthesis." *Cell* 161, no. 2 (April 2015): 264–76. https://doi.org/10.1016/j.cell.2015.02.047.

Yehuda, Rachel, Nikolaos P. Daskalakis, Amy Lehrner, Frank Desarnaud, Heather N. Bader, Iouri Makotkine, Janine D. Flory, Linda M. Bierer, and Michael J. Meaney. "Influences of Maternal and Paternal PTSD on Epigenetic Regulation of the Glucocorticoid Receptor Gene in Holocaust Survivor Offspring." *American Journal of Psychiatry* 171, no. 8 (August 2014): 872–80. https://doi.org/10.1176/appi.ajp.2014.13121571.

Zannas, Anthony S., Janine Arloth, Tania Carrillo-Roa, Stella Iurato, Simone Röh, Kerry J. Ressler, Charles B. Nemeroff, et al. "Correction: Lifetime Stress Accelerates Epigenetic Aging in an Urban, African American Cohort: Relevance of Glucocorticoid Signaling." *Genome Biology* 16, 1 (December 2015): 266. https://doi.org/10.1186/S13059-015-0828-5.

Zhou, Feng C. "DNA Methylation Program During Development." *Frontiers in Biology (Beijing)* 7, no. 6 (December 2012): 485-494. https://doi.org/10.1007/s11515-012-9246-1.

Zhu, Jinmin, Kevin P. Lee, Thomas J. Spencer, Joseph Biederman, and Pradeep G. Bhide. "Transgenerational Transmission of Hyperactivity in a Mouse Model of ADHD." *Journal of Neuroscience* 34, no. 8 (February 2014): 2768–73. https://doi.org/10.1523/JNEUROSCI.4402-13.2014.

Zilber-Rosenberg, Ilana, and Eugene Rosenberg. "Role of Microorganisms in the Evolution of Animals and Plants: The Hologenome Theory of Evolution." *FEMS Microbiology Reviews* 32, no. 5 (June 2008): 723–35. https://doi.org/10.1111/j.1574-6976.2008.00123.x.

Acknowledgments

This book practically wrote itself—the words flowed easily and each one seemed to know its place before I even wrote anything. But it wouldn't have been nearly that easy without years of preparation and brainstorming with Matthew Waas.

Waas, I've never met someone so in tune with my ideas. Your brilliance and vision seem to be boundless. I wanted so badly for your name to be on the cover of this book, but your dissertation work is far more important. I doubt that your life will slow down, as you will likely be burdened by the curse of competence forever. But I hope that our original plan of a four-part masterpiece will still come to fruition. I look forward to watching the emergence of our ideas as they spread.

Once this manuscript was fully written, things got a bit harder—I honestly didn't know if it would ever become a real book. But thanks to a friendly recommendation from the talented photographer and filmmaker Dick Blau, I found a publisher who made the process so much easier than it could have been.

Thank you, Sharon, for the time, energy, and interest that you've dedicated to this project. As I've told you before, your enthusiasm for my work has kept me motivated to see this through to the final product.

Thanks to all who read early drafts of this book and to those who helped me work through my ideas conversationally. Every quizzical look I got in response to the word "epigenetics" cultivated my desire to publish this book. Perhaps you didn't even know what you were helping to build, but that seems to be the way in which organa operate.

Thank you to everyone who has supported me throughout my life. The list is far too long for this page. But I hope you all know what a difference you've made.

Index

Page numbers followed by *f* indicate *figures*; *n* indicates *notes*.

About the Author

Credit – Mark Avery Photography

Ben Callif is a Milwaukee-based philosopher, scientist, YouTube educator at The Paradox Perspective, and owner of *eightstep me* coaching and consulting. His efforts seek to align a scientific paradigm that is cold, calculating, and logically coherent, with a sense of purpose that is visceral, mysterious, and emotionally fulfilling. His published research covers rhythmic memory in circadian biology and genetic engineering to enhance nerve regeneration. *Organumics* is his first book. He next plans to write about the interface between individual and group identity and how this interaction relates to the emergence of consciousness and responsibility.

Callif has been spellbound by the paradoxes of consciousness for as long as he can remember. His overactive intellect was occupied through his formative years by questions like "Why am I me and not you?" and "What makes a person do what they do?" He spent his school days chasing these lines of inquiry rather than participating in class. He spent his nights in the library reading about topics like quantum physics and ethics instead of doing his homework. By the time he was in high school his grades were suffering; he was a classic example of "failure through boredom."

Thanks to the compassion of his parents and a few supportive teachers, he dropped out of high school to homeschool himself. He used his academic freedom to dive into the depths of philosophy and psychology and achieved his first Bachelor of Science degree at 18 years old. After a brief stint in a Clinical Psychology graduate program, he realized that he was too introverted to deal with people all day, and he decided to approach the problem of consciousness from a more scientific angle. He went back and got another Bachelor of Science degree in Cellular and Molecular Biology, then got accepted into a Neuroscience PhD program.

Halfway through his PhD, Callif's grandmother fell ill with the rare and incurable Creutzfeldt-Jakob Disease. Her death changed everything for him—it was like he had opened his eyes for the first time. In life, she was everything that he wasn't, and he was suddenly aware of how incomplete he had been up to that point. He left his PhD program with a Master of Science degree and over the course of six months gave over 1,000 Lyft rides while he built a neuroholistic life coaching business. He honed his interpersonal skills, practiced his intuition, and balanced his overly developed intellect with empathy. For the first time, he saw the paradox of consciousness as an opportunity rather than a problem. *Organumics* is his way of integrating years of philosophical and scientific exploration with his recent personal experience.

Follow him on Facebook, Quora, and YouTube (The Paradox Perspective).